PRAISE FOR
SING BACKWARDS AND WEEP

"The artist's journey to find one's true voice can travel some very dark roads; addiction, violence, poverty, and soul-crushing alienation have taken the last breath of many I have called friend. Mark Lanegan dragged his scuffed boots down all of those bleak byways for years, managed to survive, and in the process created an astonishing body of work. *Sing Backwards and Weep* exquisitely details that harrowing trip into the heart of his particular darkness. Brutally honest, yet written without a molecule of self-pity, Lanegan paints an introspective picture of genius birthing itself on the razor's edge between beauty and annihilation. Like a Monet stabbed with a rusty switchblade, *Sing Backwards and Weep* is breathtaking to behold but hurts to see. I could not put this book down."

—D. RANDALL BLYTHE, author of *Dark Days*
and lead vocalist of Lamb of God

"If you ever wondered how Mark Lanegan's music came to blossom, here's a taste of the dark dirt that fertilized it. But saying that, or something like it, feels irresponsible, almost like saying, 'If you want to make great, soul-shattering art, traumatize yourself to the limit and beyond' . . . *Sing Backwards and Weep* is gnarly, naked, and true."

—MICHAEL C. HALL of *Dexter* and *Six Feet Under*

"A no-holds-barred memoir of uncompromising honesty. All of the usual suspects are here—sex, drugs, rock and roll—and if that were all, it would be compelling enough on the strength of Lanegan's writing and the setting of '80s and '90s Seattle, a near mythical time and place in music history. But what elevates *Sing Backwards and Weep* above the pack is the window into Lanegan's development as an artist, from his first musical influences to the singular singer and songwriter we see today. He seamlessly weaves that story line into the more conventional rock memoir fabric, and the results are outstanding."

—TOM HANSEN, author of *American Junkie*
and *This Is What We Do*

"Harrowing, edgy, tense, and hypnotic. A very truthful, sobering account of what it's like in the throes of addiction, with shades of Bukowski, Burroughs, and Hunter S. Thompson."

—GERARD JOHNSON, director and writer
of *Tony*, *Hyena*, and *Muscle*

"Some books amuse you, some intrigue you, and some—they don't come along often—like Mark Lanegan's *Sing Backwards and Weep*, squeeze you by the throat and drag you down the back stairs of the author's soul and blast you till you see what he's seen and feel what he's felt. Mark Lanegan spares no detail of the toxic and maniacal things he's done and had done to him, nor of the glorious, weird beauty he walked out with on the other side. You can't look, and you can't look away. This is my kind of book. Fucked-up, full of heart, and as hardcore as a shot of battery acid in the eye."

—JERRY STAHL, author of *Permanent Midnight*;
I, Fatty; and *Happy Mutant Baby Pills*

"*Sing Backwards and Weep* is powerfully written and brutally, frighteningly honest. First thought that came to my mind was, *Mark Lanegan gives the term* bad boy *a whole new meaning*. These are gritty, wild tales of hardcore drugs, sex, and grunge. But this is also the story of a soulful artist who refused the darkness when it tried to swallow him whole. And who found redemption through grace and the power of his unique and brilliant music. Finally, the song becomes truth. And the truth becomes song."

—LUCINDA WILLIAMS

SING BACKWARDS
AND WEEP

ALSO BY MARK LANEGAN

I Am the Wolf: Lyrics and Writings

SING BACKWARDS AND WEEP

a memoir

MARK LANEGAN

edited by

MISHKA SHUBALY

WHITE RABBIT

First published in the United States of America by Hachette Books, an imprint of Perseus Books, LLC, a subsidiary of Hachette Book Group, Inc.

This edition published in Great Britain by White Rabbit, an imprint of The Orion Publishing Group Ltd, Carmelite House, 50 Victoria Embankment, London EC4Y 0DZ

An Hachette UK Company

10 9 8 7 6 5 4

Cover design by Alex Camlin
Cover photograph by Anna Hrnjak
Print book interior design by Jeff Williams

A CIP catalogue record for this book is available from the British Library.

ISBN (Hardback) 978 1 4746 1548 8
ISBN (Export Trade Paperback) 978 1 4746 1549 5
ISBN (eBook) 978 1 4746 1551 8

Printed and bound in Great Britain by Clays Ltd, Elcograf S.p.A.

www.orionbooks.co.uk
www.whiterabbitbooks.co.uk

For Tony
And all my other absent friends

Fix
It's true
It keeps raining baby
So crystalline in my head
Gonna watch from the balcony
Sing backwards and weep

———————————————

CONTENTS

Contents

Contents

SING BACKWARDS
AND WEEP

PROLOGUE

"POLICE."

At first his warning didn't register, my mind fixated on the pinprick ending of the morning's routine, the relief from what at this point was only a dull, aching pain.

"Police," the African cab driver whispered again in a thick accent while motioning with a roll of the eyes and quick hunch of his shoulders to look in the rearview mirror where, sure enough, the three young guys following in the van behind looked like undercover cops, eager to beat someone's ass. Maybe mine.

My six-foot-four cross-dressing drug buddy St. Louis Simon and I had just scored a bag of dope and a bag of coke, both of which I had thrown somewhat carelessly in my unbuttoned shirt pocket. I had a sack of new rigs stuffed in the front pocket of my tight pants as I hadn't expected to encounter the authorities today. Now I felt totally exposed.

Another ten blocks across Seattle's Capitol Hill and it was obvious we were indeed being followed. As the car pulled up just down the street from my building I hopped out and started walking up the sidewalk, trying my best to act naturally. Simon got out the other side and, wearing a trailer-park-style denim skirt and wedge shoes that made him even taller, started to cut across the gravel lot between buildings where out the corner of my eye I saw two guys tackle him to the ground . . . not good. I was almost to the corner when a short, young cop in jeans and muscle shirt suddenly jumped around in front of me, held a badge in my face, and said, "Hold on a second, buddy! Where ya off to so fast, buddy?"

Hands raised automatically, I did my best full-of-shit, bewildered, what's-this-all-about look.

"I'm just going home." I pointed dumbly to my apartment building.

"What's this?" he asked, reaching out to squeeze the drugs through the thin cloth of my shirt.

"What the fuck, man? I *live* here! What do you want?" I yelled while pulling away from him with phony indignation. In my head, I quickly calculated how sick I'd be in jail before making bail since I hadn't done a shot yet that morning. Down the street, I could see both Simon and the cab driver sitting curbside in handcuffs, feet in the gutter, the entire backseat pulled out of the cab.

"Okay, man, let's see some ID."

In my mind, I saw my passport upstairs on the coffee table covered in crack pipes and the huge pile of used syringes next to it. That wasn't going to be an option.

"I don't have it on me. My name is Mark Lanegan."

The cop narrowed his eyes, took a hard look at me, then said, "Didn't you used to be a singer?"

After walking me back down the street to the surveillance van, he took a small black-and-white photo off the dashboard: a guy they wanted for auto theft and who looked something like me. He had me sign it with a ballpoint pen, then let us be on our way.

1

CHILDHOOD OF A FIEND

WITH THE UMBILICAL CORD WRAPPED AROUND MY NECK, I WAS born by C-section in November 1964 and then came up on the wrong side of the Cascade Mountains in the small, eastern Washington town of Ellensburg. My family were from a long line of coal miners, loggers, bootleggers, South Dakotan dirt farmers, criminals, convicts, and hill-billies of the roughest, most ignorant sort. They came from Ireland, Scotland, other parts of the UK. My grandmother on my mother's side had been born in Wales to Welsh parents. The names of my parents, uncles, aunts, and grandparents came straight out of the Appalachians to the deserts of eastern Washington and every trailer park in between. Names like: Marshall and Floyd, my grandfathers; Ella and Emma, my grandmothers. Roy and Marvin and Virgil, my uncles. Margie, Donna, and Laverne, my aunts. Dale, my father. Floy, my mother. My older sister was given the name Trina. I was the only one who escaped with a non-backwoods white-bread name, a name I hated but thanked God for when I found out my mother had intended to name me Lance. Lance Lanegan. I couldn't think of anything more ridiculous or humiliating and I thanked my father for not allowing it. After that, I could live with Mark. But I always preferred to simply be called by my surname, Lanegan. If I were introducing myself to a stranger, I would always use my middle name, William. As if by telepathy, though, that was how most of my teachers, coaches, and acquaintances referred to me: Lanegan.

Both of my parents came from backgrounds of extreme poverty and cruel deprivation. Both of their lives had been transformed by tragedy when they were young. Both of my parents were the first members of

3

their large families to go to college. Both became schoolteachers. School was something I just could not do.

Caged behind a desk, I never tried to pay attention to what was being taught. I was often lost in daydreams about my first love: baseball. After school, I'd spend hours playing game after game in a makeshift field on a neighbor's property until it was too dark to see. Finally, I'd shuffle slowly home to endure the inevitable torrent of verbal abuse from my mother. The main focus of her rage (although there were many brutal angles to her attacks) was the fact that I was never home. She herself was the reason I stayed away. To avoid her corrosive mental beat-downs, both my older sister Trina and I looked for any excuse to be elsewhere. From my earliest memories, Trina and I were also at each other's throats. Since my father was hardly ever home, it meant I was at both females' mercies at all times. The only thing that ever seemed to give my mother pleasure was bullying and ridiculing me and anything I showed interest in. One of her favorite rote sayings as she slapped me in the face was "You're not my son!" How I wished that were true. As a six-year-old child, she had witnessed her father being murdered on the front lawn of her family home, then had been raised in all-male logging camps where her mother worked as a cook, and had grown into a toxic adult. "A piece of work," as my father would say.

When my parents split, I gladly opted to remain with my father. Though he'd always projected a deep, quiet sadness around him, he was a good-hearted and caring man who meant well. But from the time I was very young, he could not control me.

I shoplifted Snickers, Three Musketeers, Milky Way, and Almond Joy candy bars from the Vail's grocery store across the street from my school and sold them to my classmates at a discount. I became obsessed with playing Quarters, a game where the participants tossed coins off a wall. Whoever landed closest to the wall won all the money. I spent every spare minute rounding up kids to play and would get pissed when the bell rang to return to class. A close friend's father was a gambling-device salesman who traveled to bars and taverns around the state, selling punchboards and other amusements for the drunks to waste their dollars on. One weekend, I stayed at my friend's while his parents were gone.

"Hey, Matt, let's get in and check out your dad's stuff."

That was all it took. We climbed through a window into the barn where his dad kept his merchandise. I grabbed a few punchboards from his stash and took them home. Even then, I was plagued with this devilish obsessive focus, and whenever I saw an opportunity to get over, it kicked in hard. With nothing but time on my hands, I went to work. Over the next few days, I painstakingly split the boards open with a flat-edge screwdriver, extremely careful to not leave any obvious marks of damage. I then spent hours carefully unrolling the tiny pieces of paper inside, removing the ones with $20, $50, and $100 winning numbers, replacing the $1, $2, and $5 winners and other nonwinners back into their slots. Then I carefully glued both halves of the board back together. My handiwork was so tidy that you couldn't tell anything had been done. I carried the boards in my gym bag from class to class all day and sold punches to kids for a dollar a shot. No one ever won the big money, of course, since I had already removed all those slips, much to my friend Matt's amusement.

My obsessive hustling consumed my every day, every action, every thought. It was the first thing on my mind upon waking and the last before sleep. It made me an unpopular figure among some of the other students, who were overwhelmed by my aggressiveness, my willingness to take their money. It never mattered how much or how little money I had. I only came alive with the inventing of ways to get it, and the action of getting it. It would get worse.

While in junior high, I began stealing a few cans of beer from my old man's endless supply and started smuggling them to school in my gym bag. He was also a carpenter and had built a full-size bar and a room to play cards with his cronies in next to my bedroom in our basement. He'd built them out of old wood he'd gotten for free by doing demolition of barns in the area. I drank the purloined beers in an unused janitor's closet between classes or behind some tall bushes on school grounds at recess. I began smoking weed, only one of three junior high kids in my small rural town who did. I became a petty thief. Each class period, I asked to use the restroom and then quickly made my way through our small school, down to the gym locker room. I would rifle through the pants pockets of those kids who didn't lock up their stuff. Change, paper money, whatever was there, I took. The only period of the day I didn't steal was during my own gym class. I was never caught.

My father spent scant time trying to parent me. Due to his own prodigious drinking schedule and his lifelong interest in playing cards all night with his pals and chasing women, he quickly gave up trying to enforce any kind of control. That happily left me to run feral in the streets. After the unpleasant years under my mother's thumb, I loved my father for this new freedom to explore my current compulsions, my wild fascinations, my burgeoning perverse fetishes. I felt like the luckiest kid I knew, no rules, no curfew, no nothing. By age twelve, I was a compulsive gambler, a fledgling alcoholic, a thief, a porno fiend. My porn magazine collection was massive. I'd found most of it by spending hours going through the dumpsters near student housing on the college campus. I had trouble finding a place to conceal it all in the large split-level house I shared with just my father and a couple of dogs.

Hiding anything I wanted kept private had become a necessity when my folks were still together. When I was nine, my mother had discovered a box of unused condoms I'd fished out of a garbage can and she'd hit the roof. Shortly before my folks split up, she'd found a pot pipe in my room and insisted I see a psychologist. He told me, "I think it's your mother that needs counseling, not you." Still, the only thing my dad would not abide was his thirteen-year-old son smoking marijuana. I sometimes hid my weed and smoking apparatus—bongs, papers, and whatnot—in the doghouse under our carport. Several times I discovered my shit not disappeared but destroyed, either stomped by boot or smashed by hammer. I wised up and got the message and found new hiding places.

My dad believed actions spoke louder than words. I could probably count all the conversations of deep importance we ever had on one and a half hands. One evening, he called me upstairs.

"Mark, c'mon up here. We need to talk."

I assumed the cops had come looking for me again, told him what they thought I'd done, and had given him a time frame in which to bring me into the station.

"Sure, Dad. What's up?"

"Well," he said, "I am a teacher and my classes are made of kids who don't have half the opportunities or skills or drive that you have. Every year, one or two new students arrive and I get an overwhelming feeling that they will one day end up in county lockup, prison, or in an early grave. You'd be surprised at how often it comes true.

"Son, I get this same feeling watching you make your way through life just . . . however you please. You think the rules that apply to the rest of us people don't apply to you. I'm talking to you tonight because I have come to the conclusion that even though you've already learned a few tough lessons, you have many more coming. You are going to have to learn them a very hard and painful way. You are exactly like your uncle Virgil. He had nothing but pain, turmoil, and trouble from the day he was born until the day he died."

My uncle Virgil had died of terminal alcoholism in an old folks' home at age forty-three. He had crisscrossed the country for years, hitching rides on hundreds of trains, an actual hobo. As a college student, my dad had been burdened with the task of traveling all around the Northwest to pay my uncle's bail. He'd had to get Virgil out of jail so often that he'd obviously developed some resentments. Virgil rode the rails until one night he fell under a train, drunk, and it cut both his legs off. My father told me he had been in his brother's hospital room when Virgil came to and realized his legs were gone. "What did he say?" I had asked him. With his typical spare language, my father had replied, "Well, he wasn't too goddamn happy." While cleaning out my grandmother's house after she died so it could be demolished, my father and I had found a shoebox full of postcards Virgil had written from every part of the US. Each one started the same, telling where he was writing from, then what menial job he was working. Each one ended exactly the same. Every single one of them sent to his mother.

"Mark," my father said, "you seem unable to change. You refuse to be teachable."

Teachable was one of his favorite words. I forced myself not to roll my eyes.

"So I'm suggesting you start right now to toughen up, and by that I mean smarten up. I'm not talking about fighting. You do that enough already and I'm tired of paying for your broken hands."

It seemed every other altercation I got in, I broke a knuckle.

"You need to toughen up your mind and body. The places you are headed, son, you will need every ounce of strength and all the wits you have in order to survive. I don't know why but you just came out of the box this way. Just like Virgil, goddamnit," he said, shaking his head. It was true. Out of everyone I knew, I was seemingly the most uncanny human-shit magnet manufactured. Brawling had been a constant from grade school through high school. At age fourteen I'd been punched in the face by a grown man outside a small tavern at the edge of a trailer park, after asking him to buy beer for me and my buddies. I even carried a lifelong small black dot of a tattoo on my face from where a kid had buried a pencil in it, attempting to put out my eye one day.

Yet as I remembered being a young child, sitting on the floor near where Virgil sat in his wheelchair, a blanket on his lap, he struck me as the exact opposite of the troubled, morose picture my father had painted of him.

When I knocked on the hollow cosmetic prosthetics he wore under his pants, he'd lean his head back and roar with laughter. His raven-black slicked-back hair reminded me of Elvis Presley.

One day, I saw a strangely compelling photo of a shirtless man on the cover of *Creem* magazine at Ellensburg's lone comic-book/record store, Ace Books and Records. I asked the owner, Tim Nelson, who it was.

"That, my friend, is Iggy Pop."

In the culturally isolated cow town where I lived, all that was played on the local radio station was country music. No one in Ellensburg even knew who Jimi Hendrix was, born only a hundred miles away in Seattle. Tim played me some early punk rock 45s and I was instantly grabbed and fucked hard. The Sex Pistols' "Anarchy in the U.K." was the revelation that changed my life, instantly and forever. I was mesmerized by this aggressive and snarling music. As a little kid, I'd owned one Alice Cooper record and listened to it obsessively, but this was something exotic, something that spoke to me in a way I couldn't articulate. All I knew was I had to have more.

Within a couple of days, I'd traded in all of the comic books I'd collected as a child for records: the Sex Pistols, Damned, Stranglers, and Ramones, Iggy, David Bowie, the New York Dolls, and Velvet Underground. It was a veritable miracle that these albums could even be found here, but Tim Nelson was a unique cat who looked like a hippy but had broad tastes and a curiosity for the new and different. I thanked God I found them and I listened to these records in solitude for years.

Frequent run-ins with law enforcement did little to improve my opinion of authority figures. At fifteen, I was brought in and questioned about some car stereos that had been stolen from a dealership lot. When I failed to give up the name of the guy I knew was responsible, Captain Kuchin himself came in the room and was left alone with me.

Fabian Kuchin was a notoriously hard character. He had performed the job of local enforcer brutally for several years. One arm was in a cast from some rough arrest or bar brawl.

"Son, I'm going to ask you one more time. Who lifted these stereos?"

"I don't know."

The instant the words left my mouth, he clubbed me in the head with the cast on his broken arm, knocking me off the chair and onto the floor.

"Maybe you'll give it a little more thought the next time I ask you something."

It would not be the last time cops would kick the shit out of me in Ellensburg. A few years later, while leaving a Fourth of July celebration, I was whacked in the nuts and the back of the head by baton-wielding deputies who had me facedown on the asphalt.

Kuchin got busted a few years later for selling a couple of ounces of cocaine to some undercover federal agents. He was given a measly $25,000 fine and a year of work release, a prime example of the corruption endemic to my town's local law enforcement, who had always had a hard-on for me. I rejoiced at the news of Kuchin's arrest anyway. I had always wished him the worst.

—

IN HIGH SCHOOL, I PLAYED baseball, which I loved, and football, which I loathed. I was one of two quarterbacks on our team, and we were terrible. Sure, I could throw and the other quarterback could run, but that didn't add up to a winning combo. Our tight end was a giant, already six foot seven at age sixteen, a strong, fast, and powerful player but with hands like a kitchen sieve. Whenever I dropped back to pass in the few seconds I had before being crushed by the opposing defense, he was the only target I could see. No matter how many times I threw a strike, the football bounced laughably off his hands, helmet, face mask, or torso. He went on to a successful decade-long career in the NFL but as a lineman. A brute just there to block and never touch the ball. After most games, we'd limp off the field, defeated, carrying our black-and-blue asses into the locker room in our otherwise useless hands.

And I was the odd man out. Despite playing a position that presupposed leadership, most of my teammates treated me with barely concealed contempt. I could not fathom their concern for their grade point averages, cheerleader girlfriends, and school functions. I laughed to myself when I watched them working so hard together as a group to cheat on their schoolwork. I didn't even give enough fucks to cheat. I never did one piece of homework my entire high school career. I couldn't have cared less if I failed or, by some twist of fate, passed any of my classes. For that, I was treated with a mixture of curiosity, dislike, and fear. I kept to myself and took no shit. That enticed some of the supposed tough guys to try and poke the bear.

On a bus ride home from another loss, someone asked to hear what I was listening to on my Walkman. My punk rock playlist was diplomatically passed around so every member of the team could partake in my ridicule. I'll never forget how they laughed and looked at me as though I were crazy. A running back, one of the most popular guys on the team, threw an ice cube at my head to amuse his friends. I broke my hand punching him out in the rear of the bus and then spent the rest of that season playing running back myself, my throwing hand in a hard cast wrapped in several layers of foam rubber and tape.

In the off-season, I was a full-blown alcoholic. Each day on my way home from school, I got off the bus while still in town, stopped at a grocery store, and shoplifted a pint bottle of MD 20/20, a fortified wine more commonly known as Mad Dog. I would slip the flat bottle down the front of my pants, casually stroll out the door, then walk up the street to the park to drink it. Then I would go back and get another one. Those flat bottles, it was like they were designed to make the rotgut wine easier to steal.

After my second bottle, I'd stop by the college campus to rip off a bicycle. Then it was a drunken, harrowing ride often broken up by a few wipeouts before I came to a canal that ran through the fields about a half mile from my house. There I would toss the bike in the water, cross the bridge, and walk the rest of the way home. This went on for a couple years.

My father was arrested for drunk driving and had his license to drive taken away. This coincided with my passing driving class, and while everyone else my age got their certificates and cars, I had to wait until my father was legal again with fully reinstated auto insurance before I was able to get my own. He spent six weekends in jail and paid a fairly hefty fine. It burned me up that six months after passing my test I still couldn't legally drive. After what felt like an eternity of waiting, I got my driver's license at almost age seventeen. Late one afternoon, I took a girl for a ride down the dirt road adjacent to the canal to drink some beer and hopefully fuck. At one point, she got out to urinate in the bushes. When she came back, she was vibrating with excitement.

"Mark, you've got to come out here and see this!"

She walked me over to the now-dry canal, littered with the rusted-out, reed-covered skeletons of seventy or more bicycles. I felt the thief's guilty flush creep up the back of my neck.

"Weird," I said, then steered her back to the car. All my secret shit. There was no way I was then, or ever, going to give any of it up.

Summer of my junior year, I finally decided *Fuck football*. My only friend on the team, a tough and savvy, streetwise surrogate big brother named Dean "Zeek" Duzenski, had graduated the previous year. He'd been my drinking buddy, advisor, and on a few occasions when I needed it, protector. While going in to suit up for practice one day, I'd found my helmet filled and dripping with soda. The "prankster" had been the biggest, heaviest lineman on our team, an extremely large dark-skinned black guy who weighed well over three hundred pounds named Waddell Snyder. I was a frequent target of his jokes and abuse, and he rarely missed an opportunity to give me shit. The entire team had watched in awe after practice that day as Zeek spent ten long minutes putting the most intense, calculated, physically dismantling ass-kicking I'd ever witnessed on the huge, slow, hapless, loudmouthed bully. He connected punch after pummeling punch to the big kid's face until it was nearly unrecognizable. Needless to say, Del Snyder never so much as spoke to me again. I'd also been completely out of step with my other teammates and their juvenile concerns, and had hated our head coach from the beginning. The way he bossed me around like I was a private at boot camp had never sat right with me.

When I declined to show up for the first day of summertime practice for what would have been my last season, our coach decided to make a personal appearance at my house. When he failed to reel me back in, he got angry, pointed his finger at my chest in my yard, and called me a quitter and a loser. My dad, who was also a teacher at my high school, finally came out of the house.

"Hey, Coach," he said nonchalantly, "why don't you get the fuck off my property before I call the cops?"

I laughed out loud. Although every other word out of my dad's mouth was *goddamnit* or *bullshit*, I'd never in my life heard him say *fuck*. That he had saved it for my coach—his coworker—brought me untold amounts of joy.

—

AFTER DRINKING FOR HOURS AT my house with a friend one night, I talked him into executing a dark idea that had haunted my mind and rolled around my head for several years. We drove deep into the countryside in my friend's Jeep until we found the van that belonged to my probation officer, who I detested. It sat in a field being used to store hay for her husband's cattle, a utility vehicle to cover the several acres of property they owned. While my buddy stole engine parts and tools, I destroyed the van with a sledgehammer. On the way home, the car stereo between the two front seats started to short out; when we both reached down to jiggle it back to life, my friend took his drunken eye off the road, sending us straight down into the deep ditch alongside the pavement.

I was tossed out of the Jeep and thrown violently across the asphalt. I went to brush the hair out of my face and it all came off in my hand. I was partially scalped, the side of my head badly lacerated. My friend, who was driving, had his thumb torn off.

We walked almost a mile to the nearest farmhouse, my pal holding his thumb in place, moaning in agony, blood gushing out of the hole in his hand. It was four a.m. when we banged on the door for help. We were greeted by the homeowner pointing a shotgun at our faces. As we stood in his kitchen waiting for the ambulance, I stared at the huge pool of our blood collecting on the ancient linoleum tile floor. I was read my rights by a cop while lying in a hospital bed.

When my case went to trial, my previous offenses were taken into account: vandalism, car prowling, multiple counts of illegal dumping of garbage, trespassing, twenty-six tickets for underage drinking, shoplifting alcohol, possession of marijuana, bicycle theft, tool theft, theft of car parts, theft of motorcycle parts, urinating in public, theft of beer keg and taps, insurance fraud, theft of car stereos, public drunkenness, breaking and entering, possession of stolen property, and on my second arrest for urinating in public, a disorderly conduct charge. I was convicted on the vandalism, theft, and underage drinking charges, but taking into consideration my long juvenile record, they sentenced me to eighteen months in prison. I would do my time at Shelton, the medium-security prison in Washington. As I stood in court to hear my sentencing, the judge reviewed my rap sheet, then addressed me directly.

"Has anyone ever tried to get you help for your problem, son?"

I said nothing.

"Looking at this record, it's glaringly obvious that you are an alcoholic and drug addict. Every single one of these charges is drug and alcohol related."

I still said nothing.

"Madam Prosecutor, I find it somewhat difficult to comprehend your willingness to send an eighteen-year-old boy still in high school to prison. I am shocked that it did not occur to you to help this kid.

"Mr. Lanegan, I am giving you a once-in-a-lifetime chance. I strongly suggest you do some soul-searching and self-reflection. I am suspending this sentence on the condition that you complete a year of outpatient substance-abuse treatment. You are also hereby ordered by the court to take regular, supervised doses of the drug Antabuse. If you fail to meet these requirements to the T, I'll have no qualms about sending you to Shelton for a year and a half."

I walked out in a daze. I knew the judge had cut me a huge break. But my biggest concern was how I'd be able to drink while taking a drug that existed solely to make you deathly ill if you drank. As a kid, in the middle of wintertime at a local park, I'd seen a Native American man drink after he'd taken it. He'd become wretched, lying on his back on a picnic table, groaning in misery. I knew better than to tempt fate and drink alcohol during my court-ordered year of sobriety.

But in 1982, nobody in my program even got piss tested. I continued to sell and use weed and acid daily. Almost every day before school,
I'd eat a small hit of acid, do a couple hits of weed, and hop in my truck
and head to class. Four nights a week, I went to my program. Many times
in group when the counselor went around the room asking everyone
"Clean and sober today?" I would be stoned or lightly frying on acid.

Two weeks into my final season of baseball, I was having my best year
ever, by far. Even though it was still early in the season, I was nonetheless
hitting .700 and sometimes batting cleanup or fifth, depending on the
opposing lineup, the two power spots in the batting order. Pitching had
become practically effortless. I was brought in as closer in the final couple of innings if we were leading. Throwing at least twice as hard as our
starting pitcher, I either struck out batter after batter or wildly beaned
them in the body or the head, giving them a free ride to first.

With that well-deserved reputation for wildness, I already had the
advantage as opposing hitters stepped in. No one wanted to get hit with
a fastball, and I once or twice closed the game with three straight strike-
outs. Finally, after years of mediocre seasons, my burning desire to win
was being fulfilled. And it was rumored that scouts who worked for college teams had begun to turn up to see us play, although with my seven-
stories-below-average grades it was a virtual impossibility that I'd ever
make it to college. Baseball had provided escape from my mother as a
child, but it was doubtfully going to be my ticket out of the stagnant
puddle of piss that Ellensburg had become to me.

Our high school vice principal turned up at one practice and pulled
Coach Taylor aside. We couldn't hear what they were saying, but when
my coach threw his hat to the ground and got up in the administrator's
face like an angry pro manager arguing a call with an umpire, my teammates laughed. I laughed along with them. Then the coach called me
over.

It had been brought to the school's attention that I had failed a home
economics class the previous semester and thus had not passed the minimum amount of classes required to participate in sports. The vice principal had been informing the coach that my baseball career was over.

Taylor wasn't ready to accept this decision so he went to the home
economics teacher who had blown the whistle on me in the first place.
She made a deal with him. If I would get to school an hour before regular

classes began and take her class again, then I could continue to play baseball, the only thing I cared about. I worried how I'd make it to class at a time when I'd normally be doing bong hits in my bedroom, but I agreed to the deal; I would have agreed to anything to play.

My first day of early-morning Home Economics, Part II, my teacher had a few things she wanted to get off her chest.

"Mark Lanegan. You are one of the students I watch walking around this school who make me sick to my stomach."

This, I had not anticipated.

"I know you think you are Joe Cool, but I'm here to tell you that you're sadly mistaken. What you are is a piece of trash. I only agreed to this because I want you to see what you're really made of, although I already know. And don't think you're fooling me, or anyone else. I'm well aware you are taking marijuana every day."

That last part, she had nailed correctly.

"If you think this is going to be easy, then again, you are mistaken, my friend. You will find this class to be much more difficult now, since the last time you were here you seemed to think it was some sort of joke. It's no joke, buddy. You will have a ton of homework and I will expect you to have it finished every morning when you arrive. If you are ever late with anything, then our deal is off. I wish you the best of luck."

All this at seven in the morning? I was confused at her hostility because, although I'd been absent during much of her class the previous semester, I was never one to cause problems, raise hell, or even talk in class. Sure, I had received an F on my end-of-semester project, the easiest thing to make. It consisted of simply sewing two pieces of nylon material of the exact same length together. But it, like almost anything that involved some bullshit skill I knew I would never need to know, proved to be beyond my capabilities. Somehow, I had rubbed her the wrong way and she took delight in the payback. I was no math wizard but I easily added up the score to this one. She'd agreed not to help me, but to inflict pain. And to make it impossible for me to comply. She may as well have been my own mother.

I felt an unfamiliar sadness welling up in my chest. My lifelong dream of playing baseball was done. Besides punk rock and getting loaded and laid, it was the only thing in life I cared about. Once again, here I was, a piece of detritus, destined for the shit heap.

"Thanks for opening my eyes to your kind intentions, Mrs. Stevens. I guess I have no option other than to decline your generous offer."

I turned and left.

When I showed up late to practice that day and handed my coach my carefully folded uniform, he looked like he was going to cry, or maybe I just felt like I might myself.

"I'm sorry, Coach," I said, "but the deck is stacked. I can't do it. She never intended for me to be able to."

I barely squeezed out of high school with a below-D-minus average on a phony diploma cooked up by some of my dad's sympathetic coworkers. I completed my year's drug-and-alcohol program and a court-appointed attorney then petitioned the court to have my entire juvenile and adult record expunged. I moved into a college-housing duplex project, working for the owner shampooing carpets all day and selling weed and acid and partying all night. One late afternoon, I ate way too much acid and had an extremely long, extremely bad trip. My friends had to roll me up in a carpet to restrain me. The next morning, I took a bong hit and it catapulted me right back into my LSD nightmare. After that, every time I attempted to smoke weed, it would instantly thrust me back into that same terrifying place. My routine of staying off alcohol by constant use of marijuana and LSD went out the window. I submitted wholly to alcoholism.

I blacked out nearly every time I drank. I owned a Yamaha 750. I'd originally had my eyes on a used Triumph chopper but was short the cash to get it, and consoled myself with what I considered an inferior Japanese bike. I loved that 750 anyway, the sense of freedom it gave me while riding. I often rode my motorcycle hundreds of miles while blacked out and, with no helmet law, no helmet. I would come to in some unfamiliar rundown motel, stagger to the front desk, and ask, "What time is it?" and "What day is it?" and then "What town is this?" Head pounding with a terrible hangover, I'd wander around some shitty town I had zero recollection of until I found my bike. Somehow, I pulled off the miracle of this crazed routine over and over again without dying. The only time I'd dump the thing was when I had to stop at a red light. Too drunk to hold it up, my machine and I would fall harmlessly to our side.

My high school girlfriend Deborah had quit college, come back to town, and moved in with me. I resolved to quit drinking and then spent a hellish year attempting to quit and failing. I couldn't get past Friday night. I would drink for twenty-four hours, no drugs, just drinking and not sleeping. Then I'd be unconscious for twenty-four hours. Then forty-eight hours of the DTs. I'd lie on my back in bed with the big black rotary-dial telephone sitting on my chest, just waiting to call an ambulance because I was sure that at any moment I was about to die.

Come Friday, despite my best efforts to maintain sobriety, as the day went on I would find myself coming out of my skin until, at some agonizing point, I'd inevitably fold and do it all again. It was an unbearable roller-coaster ride that took such a toll, mentally and physically, that I actually contemplated suicide. If this was how life was going to be, I'd be better off dead.

While working as a mechanic's assistant during harvesting season in the local pea fields, I made up my mind to leave for Las Vegas, where my cousin said he had a job for me at his restaurant. The day before I was to escape my life of drudgery in redneck rural Washington, my legs got crushed by a tractor in an industrial accident. I was bedridden, in excruciating pain, lost in anger. I'd never make it out of Ellensburg alive.

Deborah had suffered enough by now and left me for her boss at a pizza place. In a fury, I knocked out all the windows in my apartment with the end of one of my crutches, then fell into brooding despair. After three days of no sleep and constant, silent rage, I realized that I'd made it past Friday night. I had been trying to do that for a year.

I had been reviled as a town drunk before I could even legally drink. I'd had a full beard at eighteen years old and started drinking in bars, always blacking out and bringing unwanted attention to myself in ways that often resulted in violence. More than once, I woke up in jail and had to gingerly pull the pillow off my face, stuck to it with my own blood. Now that heartbreak had gotten me sober, I developed a bad case of insomnia and spent my nights wandering around Ellensburg on foot, chain-smoking. At times, I'd be stopped and questioned by the police. They had been on my back since day one and it gave me some small satisfaction when they saw I was not drunk or guilty of anything and had to let me go. Shortly before I turned twenty-one, I found myself in the unlikely role of rock singer in an up-and-coming underground band with plenty of opportunity for female companionship. Thank God Deborah left me.

—

THE FIRST TIME I SAW Van Conner, he was just a little kid lying in a wading pool in his front yard, smiling at me as I walked to grade school. In a town of eight thousand, I always knew who he was after that, but we didn't interact. We met again by chance during a stint I did in detention hall during my final year of high school. He was only a sophomore, but in six years he was the only other person I'd encountered in Ellensburg who appreciated punk. He and his brother Lee were both gigantic, over six foot, maybe three hundred pounds. Van would come to my apartment, buy and smoke some weed, and we'd laugh and listen to records.

I ran into him again after I had quit drinking.

"Hey, man, good to see you! What have you been up to?"

"Nothing, really. Just looking for a job. I need to make some dough and get out of here. I don't sell weed anymore. I don't even smoke anymore. Or drink."

"Hey, you know what? Just today my dad said we needed to hire someone to do repo work for the store. You're perfect for it."

"What do you mean?" He had my interest.

"We need someone to go and take back the TV sets and VCRs from the trailer trash who don't make their payments."

"Fuck yes, I'll do that. When can I start?"

"You can start today. Let's go talk to Gary."

I found it slightly odd that Van only ever referred to his parents by their first names, but they were known around town as an eccentric family. Seven kids and four of them abnormally large for their ages, or any age, for that matter. Gary Conner was an ex-grade-school principal who now ran the most popular video store in town, renting all manner of videos and selling electronics to mostly lower-income people on a rent-to-own plan. He hired me on the spot.

My dad had given me his truck when he'd become a hermit and moved to a cabin deep in the Cascade Mountains, a place he had to snowshoe in and out of in order to reach the road. The truck was a '53 Chevy with three on the tree. I began making daily trips all over the county, taking back what people did not want to give me. I was a pretty big guy, six foot two and a hundred and eighty-five pounds. In rural Washington, violence was just something you grew up with, as common and banal as fast food. I'd learned quickly not to take shit from anyone. As a kid, my friend Duzenski had taught me to throw a punch the minute anyone attempted to bully you. As a loner with few friends, an outcast, and a frequent blackout alcoholic, that lesson served me well. That crucial first punch didn't always settle it, though, and violence became just another way of communicating, a second language I quickly became fluent in.

The rednecks and poor people whose stuff I had to take, they were also made of pretty rough stock. I carried with me on the job an aluminum bat and a stolen .22 pistol with a bad pull to the right. I had confrontations with people almost daily but I usually got what I came for. There were a few times I let discretion be the better part of valor and had to return to Gary empty-handed. He'd have to take the delinquent buyer to court and I'd lose my commission, but fuck it, it wasn't worth killing someone over a TV set.

I would enter the store through a door in the rear that led into a huge back room where Van and Lee, his older brother by several years, rehearsed with their band: Van on vocals, Lee on guitar, a wholesome young churchgoing kid named Mark Pickerel on drums, and some other kid on bass. One night, I stood outside the door and listened to them running through an Echo and the Bunnymen song and thought, *Not fucking bad.*

Eventually Gary offered me a job behind the counter, as I had mainly cleaned up his repo sheet for him and he found it difficult to entice his own kids to work in the store.

"Hey, man, do you still have that drum set?" Van asked one day when it was just me and him in the store. It wasn't a complete kit, only a floor tom, a ride cymbal, and a high hat that a guy I'd worked with at a restaurant had traded me years before in a weed deal.

"No, dude, I got rid of it. Why?"

"Me and Pickerel are sick of playing with Lee. We want to start a new band. He's gonna sing and I'm playing guitar. We want you to be the drummer."

"Van, I can't play the fucking drums. Are you crazy? Sorry, bud, but no thanks."

"It'll be easy. Pickerel can teach you. You're the only guy we know who is into the kind of music we dig."

Young Mark Pickerel was already a very good drummer and a very good singer. Van and Pickerel didn't like Lee and wanted to play without him.

"I'll think about it, man, but I can't promise you it's going to work out."

Their previous covers band had played punk and new wave tunes to indifferent crowds at school functions, church events, and other local self-made gigs. I saw no benefit in that. It led nowhere.

On a night I had to go to their family home to bring Gary something from work, his gregarious wife Cathy insisted I sit down and have dinner with the family even though my friend Van wasn't around.

"Mark, do you enjoy working at the store? I hear that you're a fan of the same music the boys like."

"Yes, ma'am, I like it very much, thank you for hiring me. Before Van, I never met one person who liked the same music as me. So it was a pretty big deal for me to become friends with him."

"Well, you know that Lee writes his own songs, don't you? I think they're very good. Lee! Lee!" she yelled from the kitchen table.

An angry voice came from somewhere in the house.

"What? Leave me alone. For fuck's sake, I'm doing something!"

I presumed the voice belonged to Lee. I'd seen him around but we'd never spoken.

"Lee! You get out here and take Mark into your room and show him your songs!"

Lee came stomping into the kitchen. Without looking me in the eyes, he said, "C'mon, then."

I followed him into his bedroom. It was decorated with cartoonish psychedelia like the set of the show *Laugh-In*, ornate hippy tapestries hanging off walls painted purple and green. What was the deal with this guy—was he a fucking Deadhead?

"So I'm working on this tune right now, you wanna hear it?"

I did, but first I asked, "What kind of cassette player is that?"

I'd never seen someone recording their own music.

"It's not a cassette player, it's a Tascam, a four-track cassette recorder. I record a different instrument on each track and then mix them together and it ends up being a demo."

"What about singing? Do you put that on there, too?"

"Yeah, I can bounce shit over to give myself more tracks, and then use one for vocals," he said, going straight over my head. "Anyway, here's my new one."

He handed me the headphones, I put them on, and he hit play. The music was up-tempo, guitar heavy, raw. The tune was filled with hooks and the vocal part was surprisingly catchy. I couldn't understand many of the words but from what I could make out, they were a bit corny. It wasn't punk or even modern like the tunes I'd heard them rehearse in the back room, but it was rough and aggressive. Despite the silly lyrics, I recognized the demo as something pretty cool, something with rugged potential. I was impressed this weird dude had created this in his bedroom.

"That's great, man! How many of these have you done?"

"Probably fifty to seventy-five so far. I've been recording for a couple years."

"Jesus Christ."

I couldn't believe he'd written so many songs by himself. Van had never mentioned this aspect of his brother's life.

"Can I hear some more?"

I spent the next couple hours alone with Lee in his room, listening intently to a shitload of catchy, rough-hewn '60s-garage-band-styled tunes. I'd had no inkling he or anyone in town was capable of this.

"Hey, man, let me play you this new piece of music." He proceeded to play me one more song in the same vein as the others.

"Do you wanna sing something on it? Van told me about your first band."

When I was fifteen I'd worked as a janitor in a place called the Hi-Way Grill and had been drafted to sing in a lame band with the two cooks. I'd lasted exactly one gig before I'd been fired, a drag of a party where we'd covered Styx, Van Halen, and even "My Sharona."

I laughed when Lee suggested I sing something over his music, but I was intrigued with this four-track machine, this weirdo, and his songs. Over the next hour, he and I wrote cheesy words and a vocal part that felt appropriate for the garage-y throwback tune. We recorded my vocals in his bedroom, an embarrassing song we called "Pictures in My Mind."

I rolled over the experience on my drive home. Van and Pickerel wanted him gone, but I had enjoyed writing and recording vocals for a song with this strange, mostly mute dude. Why were they ditching the only guy making original music, the only guy who wasn't content playing covers like every other stupid band in town? Lee was on to something, and I wanted in on it.

"So I heard you and Lee wrote a song together last night," Van said when I saw him at work the next day. "Are you his new pal? Because you would be the first one he's ever had."

"I wouldn't go that far. He's not very easy to talk to. But you guys are crazy to kick him out. Why didn't you ever say anything about the songs he's written? Seventy-five fucking songs? I listened to a bunch of them, dude. He's got talent. The words need a serious upgrade but besides the questionable 'lead' guitar over everything, the songs are pretty cool. He can write the fuck out of a hook."

Van looked perplexed.

"I never really thought about it," he said. "I always thought of it as his hobby and playing covers was our serious thing."

"You got that backwards, man. Playing originals is the only way to be a serious band. Tell you what, I'll be in a band with you and Pickerel, but only under the condition that you let your brother back in and we play his originals."

Van didn't say anything for a minute.

"Okay. My mom hit the roof anyway when she heard we were kicking him out. You'll have to sing. I'll have to play bass. Pix will stay on drums."

"Deal," I said.

We took our name from an old Electro-Harmonix guitar pedal called the Screaming Tree. The irony was that it was a treble booster and Lee already had the thinnest, most piercing, and shittiest-sounding guitar tone.

In time it became clear that Lee and I could not get along. I tried my damnedest to be friendly with him, but it was like talking to a stone. His only two speeds were mute or enraged. I would often hear him screaming "Fuck you, Gary!" at his dad on the phone. He treated the store till like his own private bank. He would come walking in, grab a couple hundred dollars, tell his dad to fuck off, and walk out again.

Despite how much we'd enjoyed hanging out and recording that first evening, I was never again asked to contribute a vocal part or lyrics to a song. Although I recognized his gift for writing catchy hooks, everything else began to get on my nerves in a big way. His lyrics were the furthest thing from good, filled with phony lines about butterflies, rainbows, smiling cats, just meaningless garbage of the worst kind. I tried every way possible to steer him toward something cool, something of our time, but it was an impossibility. The words were already completely embedded in the song, hook, and melody. Time and again, I tried to change them into something that fit phonetically but that held some sort of personal meaning to me. It was a maddening battle, one I rarely if ever won.

But if Screaming Trees could get me out of Ellensburg . . . From my earliest memories, I had hated this dead-end redneck town, hated the ignorant right-wing, white-trash hay farmers and cattlemen talking constantly about the weather, hated the constant battering wind that blew the putrid smell of cow shit everywhere. I knew there was a world outside waiting for me and repeatedly tried to escape. At age fifteen, I'd signed up for the National Guard and labored through the eight-hour test that may as well have been written in hieroglyphics. I left page after page completely blank, totally unable to understand a goddamn thing. Then I begged my father to rescind his approval after I found out I qualified for only the lowliest jobs, the bottom rung on the ladder. I joined a traveling circus but was quickly fired for, bizarrely, refusing to cut my hair. Poor grades and my prison sentence had destroyed my baseball career to prevent me from leaving. Then my mangled legs had done it again. I felt cursed, trapped in an endless cycle of pointless work and petty crime, circling around town endlessly with a thousand-yard stare, desperate to escape my hometown and the diseased darkness it bred and festered in me.

I had always had a strong fascination with the perverse and strange. In my early teens, I saw a vintage photo of a fully tattooed man and immediately began to tattoo myself with a sewing needle wrapped in thread and dipped into a jar of India ink I had shoplifted from the college bookstore. Crude, jailhouse-looking tattoos, but I knew the moment I saw the photo that someday I'd be covered with them. When I got ahold of William Burroughs's book *Junkie*, I knew then that I would also be a heroin addict someday. Rummaging around underneath the stands at the local college football field at age ten, I'd come across a pristine copy of Anaïs Nin's *Delta of Venus*. I cultivated elaborate sexual fantasies and secret sexual obsessions of every sort and stripe. I wanted excitement, adventure, decadence, depravity, anything, everything . . . I would never find any of it in this dusty, isolated cow town. If this band could get me out, could get me that life I so craved, it was worth any indignity, any hardship, any torture.

2

THE FRAGILE KINGDOM

ONLY SIX MONTHS AFTER OUR FIRST PRACTICE, SCREAMING TREES went into the recording studio Creative Fire in Ellensburg and made our demo with Steve Fisk producing, a blatant '60s garage band rip-off called *Other Worlds*. It was released by the owner of the recording studio on his Velvetone label. The only other record Velvetone had put out was an embarrassing piece of shit called *Winnebago Weekend*, an album of "comedy" songs about the joys of RVing.

Calvin Johnson, a childhood acquaintance of mine who had moved away while we were still in grade school, was now a successful underground musician living in Olympia. His band Beat Happening were a study in cool, catchy, idiosyncratic primitivism. I loved their music and Calvin's singularly offbeat singing and style of performance. He had a cassette-only label called K. Steve Fisk was tight with them and K started to distribute our cassette EP and help get us shows.

It was only moments into the first song at our first show in western Washington that I really understood what I was dealing with. From the first note, Lee Conner went absolutely nuts, stomping, windmilling, and rampaging across the stage and back like a maniac. My jaw dropped at the sheer audacity of his performance, as did that of every member of the small audience. I had never seen it coming. There had been no indication that he'd behave like this once he got in front of people. Of course, the moment the show ended he turned back into the brooding, silent hulk that reminded me of the textbook example of a savant. But that almost didn't matter—I and everyone else in the room had been blown away by his onstage histrionics.

The Conner brothers' father put up $1,000 for us to record a full-length album called *Clairvoyance* that was also released on Velvetone. It was perhaps even shittier than our first recording. But by then we'd met someone who thought we could do better.

The second time the Trees ever played live was opening for a loud and nuanced power trio from Portland called the Wipers. The Wipers were gods in western Washington and Oregon. I hadn't gotten into their records but when I witnessed it live, it stunned me like a kick to the head and I was hooked and after that, listened to their records constantly. Their guitarist and singer was Greg Sage, a leader so charismatic that even his drummer and bass player stared at him with rapt attention throughout their concerts, his snow-white hair always covered by a bandana. Was Sage forty? Fifty? He was at least ten years older than anyone else I knew but still making vital, cool underground rock in our part of the world, the Northwest gold standard.

Much to our thrill, Sage took an interest in the band and inserted himself into our naïve circle. I began to hang out with him from time to time in Portland, glad to be around this genius musician, hoping to learn something from him to take back to my band to improve it.

We'd meet at a bar where he ate lunch in a seedy area of Portland, then we'd walk back to his place and talk. He concocted a plan to get the Trees signed to Enigma, the independent label that put out his records. Then he himself would produce our records. Sage had produced the first Beat Happening album, which I adored, so that was enough for me.

Eventually, we received a huge twenty-page contract in the mail from an Enigma-offshoot label. I was immediately put off by the offer. Pink Dust appeared to be their boutique label for fake '60s psychedelia. Granted, they did have Roky Erickson, the former singer of the 13th Floor Elevators, who we all worshipped. But their assumption that we belonged on Pink Dust with that non-punk, weak-throwback gang of rank imitators made me more determined than ever to change the trajectory of our band. I'd be damned if we didn't transcend that corny hippy ghetto and create something more original and modern. Not only was the money terrible, it was also an incredibly long seven-record deal that could tie us up forever. Still, it was the only offer on the table. We made plans to sign it.

Then while working in the video store one day, I got a phone call out of the blue.

"Is this Mark Lanegan?"

"Who's this?"

"It's Greg Ginn from SST Records calling."

Pickerel had gone to see Black Flag play at the Boxing Club in Seattle and managed to get a cassette of our first EP into the hands of Greg Ginn, Black Flag's guitarist and the owner of SST Records. On our first tour, we had stayed at the apartment of an old friend of Fisk's while in Los Angeles, an employee of SST named Ray Farrell. When Ray had seen us play in a record store in Santa Monica, he had instantly gone from being a silent curmudgeonly dude who was doing a pal a favor to an overgrown teenager, giddy with excitement. Greg Sage had also been in town and we had given him a ride back to his motel after we had performed. I couldn't help but notice how he had played with Pickerel's hair and whispered in his ear during the ride. Ginn had liked the cassette and that, combined with Ray Farrell's enthusiastic report of our live show, had piqued his interest. Now he wanted to sign us. His offer was for only one record at a time, but no one had ever been dropped by SST, so we were free to make records with them as long as we wanted or leave to go to another label. It was such an unreal lucky break that I didn't believe it was actually him on the phone, but someone playing a joke on me.

I called off the Pink Dust deal. Sage was furious with me. The next time I saw him, after a Trees show in Portland, he insisted I go with him to Pioneer Pies for coffee where he spent an hour berating me: "Do you realize what damage you've done to my reputation? My standing at Enigma?" "I personally stuck my neck out for you and you fucked me over!" "Get on the pay phone right now and tell SST you're not signing!"

It was clear from the desperate hostility of his outburst that his interest was in something other than our music. Our just-turned-twenty-one drummer Mark Pickerel was a very handsome kid who drew a lot of attention from men and women both. As a devout Christian, Pickerel was often ignorant of people's intentions, blind to the bounty of sex he could have had. One day, Sage, at his storage unit/apartment/cat-shit-covered-floor recording studio, had told me that he would need the band there for just three days to record our parts, but Pickerel would have to be there alone for two or three weeks to get the drums right. I was far from a genius but I could see his intent from a mile away. I instantly thought, *Right . . . two or three weeks to overdub drums on an eight-track recording? And weren't the drums the quietest, weakest thing on all the Wipers' records anyway?* At every show the Wipers played, Sage was always accompanied by some young-ish dude. I knew a grooming when I saw one and whenever he was around Pix, he acted like a teenager in love. I would always see him touching Pix, talking quietly and intently, staring into his eyes while rubbing his shoulders. Sage just wanted to get with our drummer, plain and simple. Without knowing it, Pickerel had nearly gotten us supremely fucked, and then saved our asses.

—

WE'D BUILT A REPUTATION FOR a crazed, must-see live show, but being the first Washington band to sign with SST brought us instant credibility in the Northwest scene and, with it, hope for the future. SST immediately put us in the studio and then out on the road.

We played a show opening for the SST band Firehose, one of the first things we did as part of the label. Firehose was the new band of legendary Minutemen bassist Mike Watt. The oversized Conner boys reminded him of his late Minutemen bandmate D. Boon. Watt took an instant liking to us, and our first two full-length tours for SST ended up being opening slots for Firehose. Our payment for the first tour was $100 a night, bumped up to $200 for the second tour. It was just barely enough to pay for our gasoline to get us from place to place and the occasional one room for everyone to share at a Motel 6. Watt was such a tightwad that he had the nerve to bum-rush our room some nights and lie there snoring for free, never offering to help pay the $60 bill. But it was a thrilling education for some small-town country boys. I myself had never even been east of the Rockies until then.

The day after returning to Ellensburg from traveling the United States on our inaugural SST tour, I woke up ready to hit the road again. After seeing the rest of the country, Ellensburg seemed even tinier, even more lifeless than I'd remembered. I shuddered as I saw my hometown again for the first time, with the eyes of a stranger: not one business or house over two stories tall. I'd become inoculated to its "quaint" (i.e., empty) downtown with not one thing for a kid to do, much less a man in his twenties who no longer drank or did drugs. Being home again, even for such a brief moment, made me begin to unravel. I had to keep moving or else I was going to lose my mind for real. My girlfriend at the time was distraught.

"I can't live like this. You need to see a doctor and get some professional counseling but you're too sick to see it."

"For what? Give me a fucking break. All I'm doing is going for a goddamned ride, not flying to Saturn."

"Get help or I'm leaving!"

"You're the one who needs help. And keep your fucking voice down; I'd rather not become known as the building wife-beater, if that's all right with you."

I walked out, got into our extra-long Ford Econoline touring van, and drove all day, three hundred miles to far eastern Washington, only returning after midnight.

The monotony of the hours and hours of stultifying boredom that went in hand with SST's aggressive touring schedule was brutal. We were game, at first: young, hungry, and totally unprepared for the rough education that came with endless, thankless touring. We played every shitty dive bar, college student union, record store, and house party willing to have us perform for $100 a night, driving across the US for months on end. If we didn't find someone to put us up or I didn't find a girl to take me home, then that meant getting one room at a Motel 6 for the entire band plus our soundman/tour manager and T-shirt salesman. Bleak nights like these, I opted to sleep on the couch in our van to guard the equipment. Not because I thought anyone would break into our piece-of-shit vehicle with the name of the previous owner's carpet cleaning business still painted on its side. Mostly so I'd not have to lie sleepless next to someone I detested in a dank, crowded room where the snoring was nearly as loud as our stage show.

Violence had been an occupational hazard of Trees live performance from the very beginning. At one of our first shows, someone had called one of my bandmates fat and I had gone out into the crowd to settle it. The Conner brothers almost only ever fought each other. It was like a bad movie I watched through half-closed eyes: the two massive men fighting over money, food, seats in the vehicle, anything, everything, sometimes onstage in full view of the audience. It had become clear that I didn't have one thing in common with Lee Conner and I began to take an unhealthy pleasure in occasionally watching his younger brother beat the shit out of him. He had it coming every time.

Lee was completely inept socially and expected the world to come to him, something that was never going to happen. He comported himself like a fucking prima donna, a hillbilly diva who considered himself a genius. He treated strangers, venue employees, coworkers, fans, crew, record company people, family, and everyone else he encountered like they were shit on his shoes, barely qualified to do his bidding. He was a stone prick and we were constantly at odds over the songs, the direction of the band, his all-important wants and demands, almost everything. He became obsessive with jealousy when he saw me getting laid nearly every other day while no woman would ever approach him. And why would they—with his huge, baggy tie-dyed pant legs tucked into his boots, his '60s-style sunglasses worn indoors, and silent, brooding, menacing affect, he projected an unwelcoming, unhappy, borderline scary presence.

One tour ended with a show in Pittsburgh, leaving us to drive the entire length of the country to get home. As the guys were discussing their future plans, I took that moment to tell them that this had been my last tour, I no longer wanted to be in the band.

Lee, who was driving at the time, pulled maniacally off the road into a gas station. He jumped out of the Econoline and ran to the rear, where he yanked open the back doors and began pulling out all of the equipment and our personal shit, throwing it into the parking lot. I was incensed, as were Pickerel and Van. Van, who never needed a reason to get physical with his brother, ran to the back of the vehicle and began to slug Lee in the face and side of his head as hard as he possibly could, screaming at him the entire time to stop. For the first time ever, Lee didn't cower from his younger brother. Undeterred by the attack, Lee continued methodically laying waste to all of our stuff.

I jumped in and punched Lee several times in the head, but it felt like my fist was making contact with a cinder block. He withstood all of it until every last piece of our shit was strewn across this gas station lot on the outskirts of Pittsburgh. When Lee grabbed his own bag and waddled off into the distance, I took one last opportunity to try to inflict some damage on him. From a backstage catering area somewhere, he had hoarded several round metal tins full of cookies for himself, which he had left in the van. I quickly hurled them after his retreating form, one after another. With a teenage varsity quarterback's precision, I banged can after can off his retreating head and back from a considerable distance away.

Of course, when he sat sullenly by himself at the other side of the parking lot, Van and Pix pleaded with me to tell him I wouldn't quit and coax him back into the vehicle so we could continue home.

"Fuck that. Leave his ass here. Fuck that prick!"

Van sheepishly admitted his mom would kill him if we left her coddled, spoiled, and entitled firstborn favorite alongside an East Coast highway by himself. There was no way he could go home without him. The standoff stretched to over an hour before I gave in.

I finally went over to him, told him I would not quit, and got him back into the van. Of course, I intended to go back on my word as soon as I was home, no longer able to accept his inexplicably bizarre, infantile outbursts. And, of course, my resolve melted when faced once more with my dead-end-street existence in my hometown and I joined again, desperate for a reason to get back out of Dodge.

Lee began trying to sneakily follow me around while on tour if I was in the company of a woman. If it hadn't angered me so much, it would have made me laugh to glance back down the street and see him try to quickly hide his huge body behind a tree or a car, then follow us again when we continued to walk. To me his behavior had all the classic earmarks of a stalker. I caught him clandestinely spying on me while I was having sex in the van, in the backstage area, and once when I was unlucky enough to be forced to share a room with him but had gone ahead and fucked someone anyway. He once made a veiled threat to tell my girlfriend about my cheating because he "felt so sorry for her." I laughed out loud at the ludicrous notion that he cared about anyone but himself and told him if that ever happened, I would make it his last day on earth.

I had a high tolerance for weirdos who exhibited disturbing, ugly, antisocial traits since I clearly recognized them in my own damaged, fucked-up, obsessive behaviors, but the dynamic between the Conner brothers was nearly impossible to bear. The band was sick, violent, depressing, destructive, and dangerous. But my entrapment in Ellensburg had become an infected, weeping wound. I had to fight the urge to stay in bed around the clock, sleeping the days away, a prisoner to sloth and mounting anxiety. Bad as things were, I saw the band as my ticket out of my go-nowhere life in my hometown, my only ticket out.

For that, I endured the constant Conner shitshow, the cornball lyrics, the self-imposed indignity of singing songs written in keys so far out of my natural range that it was a daily headache-inducing bitch to play them live. But I called it right. Through luck and comic/tragic circumstance, Screaming Trees indeed became my way out. I was, in short time, traveling the US and Europe, stumbling from one drunken, drug-fueled mishap to another and taking advantage of whatever sex, drugs, or money that came my way.

—

THE MONOTONY AND SUFFERING OF those early Trees tours was a bad movie, but not one without moments of unintended comedy, however. Our merch man at the time was a childhood friend of mine named Matt Varnum, whose father had been the punchboard salesman I'd stolen from as a youngster. We were being harassed by cops just after leaving a gig in Princeton, New Jersey. As the sirens and lights came on, from my seat next to him on the couch I watched as he took a huge baggie of dirt-dry, shitty, full-of-seeds-and-stems weed out of his pocket, poured the entire contents into his mouth, and then shoved the empty bag under the couch cushion. After the cop had taken all of our IDs back to his car, Matt motioned to whoever was riding shotgun to hand him the can of soda from the tray between the two front seats. He slammed the entire thing, washing down the immense amount of shit weed in his mouth right as the cop walked back up to the driver's-side window. He elbowed me in the ribs and then frantically whispered into my ear, "Lanegan, what is in that can?! Is that chew juice?"

For years I had chewed Copenhagen tobacco all day long, a habit common among men and boys from our backwards red-neck of the woods. I cautiously smelled the can, the cop still at the window talking to our soundman.

"I wish I could tell you that was chew juice, Matty, but that's piss," I whispered back to him. It took all the strength of will I had not to erupt in uncontrollable, hysterical laughter.

It turned out that our tour manager/soundman Rod Doak had sought in vain to find a place to relieve himself and right before the show filled an empty can to overflowing with his piss and put it back in the tray.

A short time later we pulled over at a roadside Dunkin' Donuts where I silently watched with delight as the acne-faced teenager behind the counter repeatedly stuck his fingers through the foam and down into the liquid of the cup of Diet Coke Lee Conner was buying, presumably to see if it was full yet. I roared with laughter at the sight of him drinking it, as I always did whenever he accidentally gave himself the shit end of the stick, and also marveled humorously at Matt Varnum's deep, dark, glassy red eyes and completely stoned countenance, a natural by-product of his weed-eating, piss-drinking episode an hour earlier. It was a comedic double feature, and moments like these were a welcome break from the mostly silent days and months of travel and put the rare smile on my face.

—

SST SENT US ON A European tour, headlining small clubs. One of our first shows there ended almost immediately after it began when thirty seconds into the first tune, singing with my eyes closed, my microphone was smashed into my mouth, bloodying my lips. By then, I had been flattened so many times by Lee Conner rampaging across the stage, knocking anyone or anything out of his way with his three-hundred-plus-pound bulk, that we had a rule: if anyone so much as touched another band member onstage, it meant an immediate fistfight. We were playing on a floor the same level as the audience but with a barrier between us so I knew it hadn't been a fan who'd knocked the mic into my mouth. A minute later, metal again smashed into my teeth and I opened my eyes in time to see Lee prancing away with his back to me, obviously having knocked my microphone stand with his guitar and punched the mic into my face. Infuriated, I picked up the old-school stand with its heavy, round, ten-pound base and swung it like a baseball bat with every ounce of power

I had. It connected directly with the middle of his back and he crashed face first into his stack of amplifiers, taking them all to the floor along with him as he went down. A home run.

I walked off the stage, show over as far as I was concerned, less than two songs in. A few moments later, Lee came limping into the dressing room, having badly fucked up his knee from his much-deserved tumble. Van and Pickerel stayed onstage and the German singer from the opening band joined them for an hour of German drinking songs and Ramones covers, much to the crowd's delight. Lee and I sat silently backstage. I was still enraged and he didn't say a word about what had taken place because he knew it was his own doing.

Crossing the Alps headed to Zurich, someone pulled out a pipe full of weed and started passing it around. Though I hadn't smoked for years, my running joke at the time was to snatch the pipe and pretend I was about to take a hit. The worried looks on everyone's faces at the prospect of my addiction being unleashed always made me laugh. This time, out of sheer boredom, I lit the pipe and filled my lungs with smoke. It went straight to my head and I thought, *Welcome back, old friend. God, how I've missed you*. By the time we got to the club, I was good and stoned for the first time in three years, laughing and carrying on like a kid experiencing his first high.

As we left the dressing room to take the stage, I accidentally broke one of the lightbulbs that framed the Hollywood mirror, leaving it still screwed in but with the filament freed from its glass case and sticking out into the air. I thought nothing of it and we proceeded to play what for me was a fun show, high as hell and Lee only able to play seated in a chair since I'd fucked up his knee. It was the rare occasion where I enjoyed myself. After a couple of wild encores, I left the stage and quickly made my way to the dressing room where I took a seat and put an ice-cold towel across the back of my neck in an attempt to cool down. Minutes later, Lee came slowly limping in and threw his huge body into a chair.

I could not believe my incredible luck as I watched him heave his bulk backwards in his seat and lean his giant, soaking-wet, bare upper arm directly against the bulb I'd broken earlier. He flopped like a fish on a line and I saw blue light coming out of the wall as he electrocuted himself on the open filament. That it was happening because of my actions made it so much more unbearably hysterical.

As he tried to break free of his electrocution, I howled with maniacal glee. The marijuana, his pain as result of my doing, and the sight of it was all too much to take. He finally managed after several seconds to break free of the unexpected shock and screamed in anger.

"You think that's funny, Lanegan? I'll fucking kill you!"

It was a threat I'd heard him make a million times to his own dad, his go-to line. I stood up and backed out of the door, yelling, tears of joy in my eyes.

"Oh yeah? C'mon, shithead! I'll fucking annihilate you, you fucking prick!"

Watching him struggle to get up and chase me with his fucked-up leg just made me laugh harder and double down on my taunts. Like a wounded rhino, he burst through the door, out into the narrow hallway lined with some radio-contest winners who had secured the dubious honor of meeting the band personally post-show. He knocked out of his way several kids, their parents, and the always-present weird older men with their stacks of records and photos to sign as he determinedly raged down the hall while I continued to ridicule and threaten him. Needless to say, the meet-and-greet was a disaster, but for me it was one of the funniest chain of events I could have ever been witness to. And again, knowing it was me, myself, who'd set it in motion made it so much sweeter.

Van's jovial, good-natured, yet huge and rebellious personality, and especially crazed sense of humor, was my saving grace throughout my time in the group. In backstage dressing rooms all around the world, with every wall commonly covered with the ugly graffiti and band names of the hundreds of groups who had been there before, the Trees never wrote a thing. Except for the one drawing that Van put on a wall everywhere we played. It was an uncannily accurate picture of his brother, pants down and fucking some kind of unknown animal, maybe a dog? A goat? Was it a llama? I would never be able to discern what group of species the beast was of, but the drawing of Lee was unmistakable, and him fucking it from behind was the only calling card we ever left anywhere. Anyone who ever knew him, or had seen him, could instantly tell it was Lee pictured doing the deed. I loved Van for that.

Van quit the band. After marrying his pregnant sixteen-year-old girl-friend, he took exception to the new band rule that no girls were allowed to ride in our van to gigs. He took it personally, of course, because it was personal: no one else in the band even had a girlfriend. But his wife was unbearable. At every show, she would stand directly in front of Van and scream at the top of her lungs throughout and in between every song as though we were the Beatles at Yankee Stadium. Van made no attempt to control her behavior, so we instituted the new rule. And with that, my lone ally in the band was gone.

I got a phone call from a friend, a guitar player I knew, Dylan Carl-son. I'd met him a couple years earlier at an outdoor show near a lake in Olympia. The heat was unbearable that day and not knowing his band at all, I had asked them if I could get in their air-conditioned car to escape the oven-hot sun. I quickly became enamored with his mellow, offbeat, contrary slant on life and his sharp, dry sense of humor. The singer in his band was an over-the-top motormouth named Slim Moon. He was dressed like Olivia Newton-John in her "Physical" video: pink sweat suit, pink headband, the whole nine. I remember being impressed that Slim rhymed *stupider* with *Jupiter* in one of their songs. But what struck me most was Dylan's guitar playing. He was on another plane.

Dylan's best friend was in a band that was booked to play a show in the Ellensburg Public Library with some local bands opening and he asked if I would go down to meet the singer as he was a fan of my band Screaming Trees. Knowing the very small scene of bands playing original music in my town and the very likely miniscule turnout for such a show, combined with my current state of deep, clinical unhappiness, it didn't sound like much fun but I agreed, thinking I was doing a friend a favor.

At the time I was living in a seventy-five-dollar-a-week, one-room studio pad with no kitchen, one bare lightbulb that came straight out of the wall, and a terrible '70s-style shag carpet permeated with the stench of the previous tenant's pet ferrets. A grim, mold-covered shared bath-room down the hall had the only sink in the place. In other words, a complete fucking outhouse toilet hole. My only piece of furniture was a couch that was also my bed. The only door to the outside from my room led into an alley at the end of which was the elaborate two-story house where my most recent ex-girlfriend stayed with her new man. Half the time I left my place, the first thing I'd see was the two of them making out on the swinging chair on his decorative, pillared front porch. My only respite from my pseudo-suicidal/homicidal preoccupations came from near-constant masturbation and my used Radio Shack cassette player and the lone tape I owned: Neil Young's *After the Gold Rush*. I played it around the clock, morning till night.

The evening of the band's show, I skipped the openers and instead spent a few minutes guiltily jacking off while watching my ex through an uncurtained window of their house fucking her boyfriend in a brightly lit room. I might have missed the last band, too, if I hadn't seen a cop car crawl around the corner a couple blocks away. I hid in the bushes for an agonizing moment, then furtively screwed off to the library and showed up just as the band were going on.

As they took the stage, I was immediately struck by the bass player, a six-foot-seven-inches-tall giant with a fierce intensity obvious before even playing a note. He looked pissed off and I was instantly drawn to him. I admired his openly angry countenance since that was how I felt every time I was onstage, like I was going into battle.

Upon seeing this enormous guy tuning up, my first thought was here's my bass player. Because of the unique physicality of the Trees, it would take a supersized person with a special charisma to retain the visual balance and fill Van's shoes. This guy had all that in spades. I began to formulate a plan to steal him away from this band I'd not even heard yet.

Once the three-piece group began playing, however, the wall of noise, the raw catchiness of the songs, and the voice of the left-handed guitar-playing singer made me realize I was witnessing something special. Perhaps one of the best bands I'd ever seen, in the fucking Ellensburg Public Library no less. The show was shut down after only three or four tunes due to a typical small-town curfew and timing fuck-up and the giant bass player stood there throwing his bass all the way up to the high ceiling, catching it with one hand and angrily tossing it back up, over and over again until the lights in the room were finally turned off.

Leaving the library, I was approached by the singer.

"Hey, man, thanks so much for coming out to the show."

"Dude, you guys are great! What a fucking drag that these idiots shut you down. But that's Ellensburg for you."

"I want to tell you, I'm a huge fan of yours. If you ever need an opener or want to do something musical together, please give me a call."

We exchanged phone numbers, ballpoint pen on the back of a flyer for the show.

"Definitely," I said, "I'll take you up on that. Seriously, I was completely blown away in there."

"Thank you so much. And please, give me a call whenever you want."

"I'll do that," I said. For once, I meant it. I looked down at the scrap of paper for his name: Kurt.

I walked back to my depressing hovel with an electricity in my step and a newfound buoyancy of spirit. I couldn't shake the notion that I had just experienced something touched by greatness.

A couple weeks later I picked up the phone to a voice I didn't recognize, a somewhat nervous, anxious-sounding voice.

"Mark Lanegan?"

"Yes . . . ?"

"Krist Novoselic here, I play bass in Nirvana. Are you still looking for a bass player? I can't stand playing with Kurt anymore. I'm sick of everything always having to be his way."

I was silent for a moment, thinking it over.

"Yeah, man, we're still looking. I love your style and it would be great to have you in my band. But if I were you, I'd get past your problems with Kurt and make it work. You guys got something special there."

I never mentioned the call to Kurt. It had been easy for us to become friends, just a couple of long phone calls talking about girls, music, life. I loved Kurt, and I envied him because Nirvana were fully developed from the first moment I heard them. The difference between Nirvana and the Trees was so clear to me. Nirvana were who they were from the first time I saw them: great songs, great singer, great look, everything.

The Trees, on the other hand, were always fighting: fighting each other, fighting fans and promoters and bouncers, fighting to find a direction. Three records in, we still didn't know what the fuck we were. We had no identity beyond our notoriety for our unhinged live show. Lee Conner would go insane and tear up the stage with a ferocity never before seen in a guy that size. People would gawk and stare and then go back to their beers and go on with their lives. Lee's nightly grand mal–esque fits made us a curiosity, a freak show to be experienced only in that setting, nowhere else. Our records were a shitty mishmash of half-baked ideas and catchy tunes derailed by the stupidest of lyrics. I fucking ached when I thought of all the opportunities we missed as we churned out shit record after shit record. I longed to make music that could be taken seriously, music that I could take seriously, instead of just the tall dumbass singing on the same stage as the lunatic, Falstaffian guitar player. Our mess of a "career" had become only a source of embarrassment, frustration, and turmoil. Worse yet, I myself had set the wheels of this machine in motion. I had idiotically insisted that Lee remain in the band and that we play his songs, a move I cursed myself for almost daily. But beyond all belief, we were still upwardly mobile, and I'd be damned if I was going to quit before the ride was through.

We found Van's replacement in a woman from a band we had previously done shows with. Her name was Donna Dresch. She had the most compelling stage presence of anyone I had ever seen, like a more energetic, female Keith Richards, lit smoke hanging out of her mouth, swinging her bass from side to side and banging her blond-haired head from start to finish of every show. When she was onstage, it was hard to take your eyes off her. I came to love playing live just because she kicked so much ass. Somehow, the symmetry was perfect and the combination of Lee's three-hundred-pound Angus Young impersonation and Donna's total rock-and-roll charisma on either side of me and Pix's eye-catching stick-tossing and -twirling routine behind me made it an outrageous spectacle. Night after night, I watched from the stage as people thrilled to our new lineup. Donna had that rare quality of true magic rock appeal. I liked Van a lot and had enjoyed having him in the band, but Donna lifted our live performances to heights we had never reached with him.

Like me, Donna preferred the companionship of women, so the minute we came offstage, the two of us were on the prowl for girls to if not sleep with, then at least talk to, look at, and lust after. She was as cool off the stage as she was on it, and before long we were tight pals. Meanwhile Pix and Lee suffered through the long days silently, not part of Donna's and my gang and Pix never leaving the shelf in the back of the van, unhappy because he couldn't stand Lee either.

Lee had been solely responsible for generating our music and always acted as though he were the focal point, the center of the universe. With his huge superiority complex and kindergarten-esque demands and behavior, it had always taken a huge amount of restraint on my part to not kick his ass. When Van had been in the band, he had functioned as a natural border between Lee and me. With Van gone, I often found myself counting the seconds before I strangled Lee to death in a rage. The young, heavily Christian Pickerel had made silently obvious his distaste in my extracurricular pursuits. He also took quiet exception to the way I ran the show like a self-appointed dictator, so Donna became my only compadre in the band, taking Van's place in more ways than one. That was fine by me; she was by far the coolest member of the band. I didn't consider how our connection and Donna's natural magnetism marked her as a threat to Lee's fragile kingdom.

—

ONE NIGHT, I'D GONE TO Seattle to hang out with Kurt and catch a Nirvana show at the Vogue, a popular small, dark, and dingy rock dive. They were first on a bill of three Sub Pop Records bands but I was really only interested in them, with just a slight curiosity to see the second act, Tad. Sub Pop owners Bruce Pavitt and Jonathan Poneman sidled up to me together pre-show.

"When are the Trees gonna quit SST and start making records for us?" Bruce said with a smile.

"So you came over to check out Blood Circus, huh?" Jon said.

Blood Circus were the headliner.

"No." I'd heard their music and found it not to my liking.

"Tad?" Pavitt asked.

"Tad's cool but I'm here to see Nirvana. They are the best band you have. By far. They're one of the best bands I've ever seen."

I'll never forget the puzzled look they gave me and then the way they looked at each other. It was as if they found it unfathomable that someone would love Nirvana. I found it unfathomable that they were unaware of what greatness they had in their hands, that they had Nirvana opening for such obviously inferior music. They weren't the only ones who didn't get it.

Kurt asked me to try and get Greg Ginn to sign Nirvana to SST because they were a cool label with lots of bands he liked, but mainly because of the freedom; they allowed their artists to do whatever they wanted. SST had never asked to hear anything or see any artwork until we gave it to them and Kurt's experience with Sub Pop had been the polar opposite. They told him what songs to record, what the album cover would be, and even the title of his record. To my utter disbelief, Greg Ginn was not interested at all in having Nirvana make records for SST. I sent him a cassette of their music twice and had three difficult conversations with him on the phone trying to convince him of their brilliance. Conversations difficult not only because of his aversion to Nirvana, but because any conversation was difficult with the notoriously nonverbal Ginn. His sentences were broken up by lengthy, uncomfortable silences as he made normal communication all but impossible. Yet the worst part of these interactions was that he simply and stubbornly just didn't get it, period.

As we started making plans to record what would be our final record for SST, Lee and Pickerel blindsided me. Van had not found married life to his liking. Lee and Pix had easily lured him back in behind my back. One day, they bluntly informed me that Donna was out. Van would be making the record with us, not her. It was three against one, they said, so I lost the vote.

"Three? How the fuck did Van get to vote himself in? You fuckheads never gave me or Donna a chance to vote! Fuck all of you! Don't you guys know how great we are with her?"

"I don't like her and I'm not playing with her again" was Lee's sullen, slow-witted response.

People were magnetically drawn to Donna. At best, people were morbidly curious of Lee, but more often simply repulsed. I knew full well his true feeling was one of jealousy. It was that simple and that stupid.

I had begun to rely on the band more and more as my stepladder to a different future. Even though I was in hell, it was a hell that might lead to a less intensely heated one, and I didn't want to quit before it got me there. It came down to me to give Donna the call to tell her she was out. I was disgusted with my bandmates for betraying me and disgusted with myself for caving in to these imbeciles' demands so that I had to betray my friend, a talent like no other. In my heart, I knew beyond all doubt that the band was losing the only natural true star it would ever have. It was a move that undermined not only me, but the Trees' own success, as we were never as great as what we'd become with Donna.

I was furious and sad. Fuck this dead-end town and the doomed, self-sabotaging weakness it had instilled in us all. I was done. I stashed my meager belongings in a storage unit my dad still kept in town, one

I'd actually lived in one winter with only a couch, sleeping bag, and space heater for comfort. I told the band if they wanted to continue with me as their singer they could find me one hundred miles to the west. I climbed on the back of a friend's motorcycle and fled the boring, brown-dirt, shit-hilled wastelands of eastern Washington state for Seattle—a dope fiend in the waiting, a hillbilly, an idiot know-nothing sex freak, game for the city and every dark thing it had to offer.

3

SEDUCED, FUCKED

"BABY, CAN YOU PLEASE LEND ME A BUCK FIFTY?"

"When are you ever going to have your own money?" she screeched. "Here, take it, you scumbag! You'll just steal it from me anyway!"

She winged the handful of change at my head with the awkward motion of someone who'd never thrown anything other than insults, missing me completely despite the close quarters. I scooped the coins off the ground and walked quickly out the door, slamming it behind me.

"Go fuck yourself," I muttered.

I stepped outside into the rain and walked to the bus stop to wait for the 26 bus to carry me to my low-wage job in the University District. I fondled the dollar-fifty's-worth of change in my pocket, enough for two hard-boiled eggs off the food truck at morning break, an acute reminder of my need to alter my intolerable living situation. I couldn't wait to be free of this woman and her weird-smelling apartment in a building that was 90 percent geriatrics.

When I had first met my girlfriend, she told me she could read people's minds. Thinking *Sure you can, honey*, I had asked her to read mine. She said she never did it anymore because it disturbed her to know people's thoughts. Several months later, I was tossing around in bed with evil, debilitating insomnia, wet with sweat, thinking about a pretty dark-skinned girl I had slept with in Texas who had given me a lift in her car between Austin and San Antonio while on tour with Screaming Trees. Suddenly my girlfriend rolled over, grabbed my arm, and said, "I just had the worst dream, you were in Texas fucking a black girl." An electric jolt went through me. I stammered that she was just having a nightmare, urged her to go back to sleep, and tried to clear my mind of any more incriminating thoughts. But the relationship was never the same after that.

Now things had degenerated to the point where a dollar and a half brought on this kind of drama. No matter how much I earned, I was perpetually broke. If not for her and a couple of soft-touch coworkers, I would never have eaten at all. Still, this had to end.

Of course, I was going to miss the sex. In between our furious fighting was lots of furious fucking. Three, four times a day, sometimes. But fuck it, I could no longer tolerate her bullshit; it was time to move on.

—

A FRIEND OF MINE NAMED Dean Overton had given me a job as a grunt in the warehouse of a local Seattle record store chain. It consisted mainly of filling orders from the stores around town, loading boxes with records, stocking shelves, and making deliveries in a van. Compared to the demeaning, physically and mentally taxing agricultural and restaurant work I'd suffered through in eastern Washington, this was cake. The crew were mostly good-natured, funny people, including several other local musicians, and I warmed to the comradery of my coworkers. Despite being by nature an introvert and loner, I slowly came out of my shell and made some friends.

One day, I unpacked a box set with a haunting black-and-white cover photo of a lone figure walking on a beach in a long coat while smoking a cigarette. It piqued my interest and I asked a quiet but friendly fellow employee named Justin Williams about it.

"That's Nick Drake, man! It's great. I'm gonna make a tape for you."

The next day he handed me a cassette. When I got home and put it in my player, I was introduced to the music of Nick Drake, Leonard Cohen, Tim Buckley, Tim Hardin, and others. It captivated my imagination. I had listened to the first four Nick Cave and the Bad Seeds records often and this music was in a similar vein, dark and beautiful. As I immersed myself in it, I felt transformed. I loved the Velvet Underground, the Saints, Captain Beefheart, the Groundhogs, Kraftwerk, New York Dolls, Joy Division, Gun Club, Wipers, the Fall, Lou Reed, the Stranglers, the Birthday Party, the Damned, John Cale, Bowie, and the Stooges and many more . . . but this mainly acoustic, personal, and confessional music seemed to tell my own story back to me. It hit me in some deep grieving place I'd heretofore been unaware of. It changed my musical perspective in a profound way. Soon, I wasn't listening to anything else.

I had already been greatly dissatisfied with what my own band was churning out. Immersing myself in this intimate, deeply moving music made it even harder to invest in the swill Screaming Trees were producing.

—

AFTER A PARTICULARLY VICIOUS ARGUMENT where my mind-reading girlfriend made it clear what a toxic, lying piece of shit I was, she finally kicked me out. Once again, I found myself at loose ends and in need of a place to crash. Dylan and Slim had recently moved to the city so I moved into their cheap, decrepit, rat-infested three-story house a couple of blocks from north Seattle's Green Lake. They used the basement for rehearsals with their new two-man band. The music was extreme. Extremely loud, extremely slow, a strange and beautiful glacial guitar drone, unlike anything I had ever heard before. It was unclear what role Slim played in the band. He had been the singer in their old band, and I had coproduced a single for another group he sang with that didn't include Dylan. I could never hear any vocals over the din coming from the basement but assumed he must have been singing, unheard.

My room was on the third story and when they practiced, the vibrations from their holy noise slid my bed across the floor. I found it soothing; I had always found noise soothing. As a child, I had been constantly yelled at by my mother for turning on the clothes dryer down the hall from my bedroom in order to fall asleep. While living with Dylan and Slim, I often fell asleep only to wake to find the crusty, fractured futon I had stolen and dragged out of a Goodwill bin wedged against the door at the opposite side of my room.

The first few months in our new dive were a bleak exercise in shared low-grade unhappiness. The place was cold, damp, depressing. We spent each evening listening to records in the living room we had named "the waiting room at the morgue." None of us had girlfriends, just ourselves for company. Each morning, all three of us woke up covered in flea bites. We devised a coordinated plan to set off flea bombs one day before work. On the target morning, Dylan and I set off our bombs and left the house at precisely eight a.m. as planned. It suddenly occurred to me that Slim might not have exited. He was a chronic oversleeper who always slept fully clothed in polyester slacks and wide-collared polyester shirts, using the rest of his wardrobe piled on top of him as a primitive blanket. After a moment's hesitation, I ran back inside to make sure he was up.

The second I opened his bedroom door, I was met with the eruption of a powerful insecticide blast from a flea bomb that had detonated at that very moment, blinding me and choking me and covering my clothes with its rancid chemical smell and blistering, venomous toxins. I slammed the door and staggered out of the house, collapsing to my knees with tears streaming from my eyes, having received the brunt of its noxious cloud full in the face. "Fuck me!" I said out loud to myself and, having missed the bus, walked to work, coughing the entire way.

As soon as I got there, Dean took me aside.

"What the fuck is wrong with you? Are you fucked up? Or do you have the flu?"

I relayed the morning's comedy of errors. Despite my protests, he insisted on calling the Poison Control hotline and they strongly urged me to seek medical attention. Given the rest of the day off but with no money for the clinic, I spent the afternoon lying in the wet grass under the freeway overpass a block from our house, vomiting up bile intermittently. When I started to feel a little better, I bought a chocolate bar from the gas station up the street and promptly puked that up, too. I gave up and lay there, occasionally dry-heaving, waiting for the eight hours to expire until it was safe to go back inside the house. It was only much later that we discovered the huge rats that shared the house with us and figured out where the fleas had come from in the first place.

Eventually, Dylan confided in me that Slim was contributing nothing to this new band that Dylan had named Earth. It was such a slow drone that Slim, who had previously sung in somewhat boring trad punk bands, could not find a way to fit himself into the music. He was also opposed to any real work so picking up a bass or guitar was not going to happen. His impotent dissatisfaction began to create a fissure between the two. By this time, a friend of mine from Ellensburg, Nate Hill, had moved into our giant house. A guitar player with such an uncanny resemblance to Axl Rose circa 1988 that everyone in the Burg had called him "Little

Axl." He'd asked me what was up when Slim, who always unsuccessfully tried to assume the mantle of alpha dog in his bands, began to sulk, then bitch around the clock. In a fit of anger, he told Dylan, "If you're not going to play something I can sing to, I quit!"

Dylan was the most loyal of anyone I'd ever known and would have taken a bullet for Slim or any of his friends. He did not argue with Slim but neither did he attempt to tailor his music to accommodate him. Dylan was a true original. A genius whose vision was stubbornly forward-facing and springwater clear, he was in the process of inventing a new genre of rock music, one to become known as drone metal. Finally, Slim left, bitterly and unilaterally ending his years-long friendship with Dylan in the bargain. He went on to say publicly years later that it was because of the "danger" in the house, that we were obsessed with firearms. That was a joke. We had exactly two firearms: Dylan's rifle and my piece-of-shit .22 pistol. Ironically, Slim had spent much time proudly bragging about his rough upbringing and the prevalence of guns among his relatives back in Montana. The truth was he craved being a top dog, and since he was finding that to be an impossibility in Seattle, he went back to Olympia, tail between legs, to become a big fish in a goldfish bowl.

By now, the rest of the Trees had one by one emigrated to Seattle: first Pix, then Lee, and finally Van, his short-lived, ill-advised marriage over. Our manager Susan Silver had rented a house for her assistant and we began rehearsing in the basement along with a couple of Susan's other bands, Soundgarden and Alice in Chains. As I was coming in one day, I was met at the door by a stunning black-haired girl in glasses named Anna, the girlfriend of an acquaintance of mine.

My mind went straight back to a night several months earlier when my previous girlfriend and I had gone out to eat at a local restaurant where Anna had waited on us. My girlfriend had been borderline rude to the smiling and friendly waitress and hadn't spoken a word to me throughout the entire meal. In the car afterward, I couldn't take any more of her scowling silence.

"Okay, what's your problem?"

"I don't want to talk about it. You'll just say I'm crazy anyway."

"Goddamnit, I can't take this shit! What in the fuck is it now?"

"You're going to be with her," she said, starting to cry.

"What are you talking about? Be with who?" I had obviously missed something along the way and now I was genuinely steamed. "Please enlighten me as to what you are talking about. Now."

"That waitress back there. You two are going to be together someday."

True, I had thought the girl was hot and I was attracted to her, but only in the way any normal person might be ten times a day when they encountered an attractive member of their preferred sex. There had been zero flirtation, almost no conversation, nothing. I hadn't given it a moment's thought.

"Anna? That girl is going out with a friend of mine. You are out of your fucking mind. I'm over it. You need to check yourself into the psych ward, you've fucking lost it."

Months later, the second Anna opened the door to the rehearsal house her beauty hit me like a hammer. I tried to shake it off, went downstairs and rehearsed with the band, but I couldn't stop thinking about her. I still wanted to consider the entire scene with my last girlfriend as mere unwarranted drama, but I knew my ex had that fucked-up "gift" for knowing things a normal person would not. She'd read my mind in her fucking sleep, for chrissakes. I was going to have to explore Anna's situation.

I went to use the bathroom during rehearsal. She was curled up on the couch, reading a book. She looked up at me and smiled.

"Aren't you Eric's girlfriend?" I said. "He and I go back a ways."

"Oh, that didn't turn out so well. We're not together anymore."

"I'm sorry to hear that," I said, thinking the exact opposite. "It's really none of my business, forgive me for prying."

She laughed out loud and said, "Come on, man! Give me a break."

I smiled at her and said, "Do you smoke weed?"

She laughed again. "Sometimes. Why? Do you wanna get me high?"

"I actually do, yeah," I said with a slightly evil look of intent.

"Come up and see me when you guys are done, hotshot," she said, smiling with an equally smoky look. It was on.

We hooked up that afternoon. I got immediately, deeply addicted to her sexually, and to her quiet, smart, and funny bookish manner. We would stay in bed for hours at a time. On the occasions I could get her to smoke weed with me, she would laugh and laugh. It made me happy. I started spending quite a bit of time at her place.

When I was home, my roommates and I fell into a routine of work, listening to records, and going out to an occasional show at one of the local bars. Sometimes Kurt would come down and stay with us for a couple days. Sometimes I'd hang out with him in Olympia, listening to the old blues records we both loved. One afternoon at his place, we started talking about making a record.

"We should do a record of this stuff," one of us suggested.

And then the other, "We should do a record of all Lead Belly covers."

Lead Belly was a legendary folk-blues musician, a twelve-string-guitar-playing ex-convict. We'd spend hours at a time listening to his records and nothing else. I casually mentioned the idea to Mark Pickerel, who was by then working for Sub Pop Records, the label that had signed Kurt's band. After one rehearsal with Pickerel and Krist Novoselic as rhythm section before we'd really even thought it through, we suddenly found ourselves in the studio to make a record for Sub Pop.

Being pals was easy but creating together turned out to be more difficult as our respect for one another turned it into an oddly unproductive exercise. Neither Kurt nor I were really willing to grab the reins. Despite being the least musically proficient member of Screaming Trees, it had become obvious to me early on that I had to be the default leader of the band, simply due to force of personality. I was used to directing Screaming Trees recording sessions, only because it was a chaotic, unproductive shitfest unless I took charge (and even then, it still often went nowhere). I couldn't bear to do that in this situation, I was too awed by Kurt's genius. He was also strangely reticent. Dylan had joined us in the studio just to hang out and ended up offering more direction than either Kurt or me, but in the end not much was accomplished. No one was willing to be the shot-caller.

It was years later that I realized Kurt didn't take the lead out of respect for me. Part of me knew he saw me as a sort of big brother, but I struggled to get my head around that. I felt like Screaming Trees' work was second-rate, everything dragged out or cobbled together, every unsatisfying song the result of too much toil, and I saw everything through that prism. It was impossible for me to accept that someone else could find worth in what I did because I could not. How could Kurt be a fan when I saw in him a talent that was genuinely not of this place and time, like

Bob Dylan, John Lennon, David Bowie, or Jimi Hendrix? I simply had the heart of a packhorse.

A few weeks after figuring out that neither Kurt nor I were interested in continuing our Lead Belly experiment, I got a call from Jonathan Poneman, co-owner of Sub Pop Records. He had a proposition: Would I like to make a solo album for them? His offer was a three-record deal, $13,000 for the first with substantial advances for the second and third.

I had never picked up an instrument in my life. My only contribution to Screaming Trees songwriting had been attempting to change the most egregious of Lee Conner's lyrics to something less embarrassing to sing. But every record the Trees had made for SST had come with a strict $1,000 advance. I could probably make a solo record for three grand at the most and pocket the rest. *Ten thousand dollars.* By far the most money I had ever had in my life. I took the deal.

I carried in my head two different musical inspirations for this first record. The Trees had recently played in San Francisco opening up for Henry Rollins. Van Conner had once again punched Lee out onstage, and Lee played the last fifteen minutes of the set with a nosebleed, the front of his white shirt quickly soaked in blood. Afterward, while waiting for my ride, I watched with strange admiration for Rollins's high-testosterone intensity and huge balls as he did one-armed push-ups next to the stage in full view of the audience before going on. Donna Dresch was now living in SF and picked me up and drove me across town in time to catch a band from Boston, Galaxie 500, playing their encore. It was stunning. A room packed with people were silently intent on this band playing slow, quiet, beautiful music. At the end of each tune, the crowd erupted in enthusiastic cheering, then became stone silent again as soon as the band delicately began their next song.

It was an epiphany for me to witness. Trees played at top volume nightly. Head throbbing from the terrible-sounding high-pitched guitar amp pointed straight at me and the pounding of the cymbals directly behind on the tiny stages we most often played, I was being deafened every show. It had never occurred to me that it was possible to play quietly in a rock club and people would enjoy it.

My other musical inspiration was *Straight Ahead*, the largely acoustic solo record of Northwest legend Greg Sage of Portland band the Wipers. Despite his now-obvious deception and his somewhat comical, desperate attempt to intimidate me at our last meeting, I nonetheless remained a huge fan of his music. His solo record pointed me in the direction I wanted my record to take: quiet yet powerful dark tunes.

I bought a cheap used piece-of-shit acoustic guitar and a Mel Bay guitar chord book. I began to learn the simplest chords, began to try to teach myself how to write.

Every day at my warehouse job, I would start making up a melody and some words in my head. When I came upon a combination I liked, I would memorize it through silent mental repetition all the way home on the bus. As soon as I got home, I'd get the guitar and book and search until I found the chords that fit under my melody and vocal part, almost always the same three or four chords. Dylan Carlson also showed me a chord that was useful, the B. I've probably employed it on every song I've written since. I came to realize much later that my caveman style of songwriting was the complete reverse of what's normal. Most songwriters write music first, then find the vocal part to go with it.

Paranoid that Sub Pop would realize they had made a mistake and void our deal, I wrote with a maniacal urgency, my eye ever-focused on my huge upcoming payday. My virgin fingers raw from the thick strings that had probably never been changed on the instrument, I managed in my primitive, idiosyncratic way to put together a group of songs to record in just over a couple weeks. I enlisted the help of my friend Mike Johnson, who played guitar in a Eugene, Oregon, band called Snakepit, to come to Seattle and play on the record. He put intros, middle sections, and outros on all the songs since I wasn't proficient or savvy enough to do it myself. It was then that I discovered that my simplistic guitar parts were actually maddening for real guitarists to play due to the awkward way I would jump from chord to chord, following the vocal part instead of doing it in a normal way with natural timing. It was at the outer range of my musical knowledge just to find the chords that fit under my singing.

After running through the songs with Mike for a few days at my house, we entered Jack Endino's Reciprocal studios to begin recording. Jack was an enthusiastic, eccentric guy who had produced almost all of Sub Pop's records as well as the previous Screaming Trees album. He and I shared a love for the music of the British trio the Groundhogs and wasted a lot of valuable studio time chattering like teenagers about our

favorite records of theirs. We began with Mike laying down guitar, playing along to a click track. I would then lay down a scratch vocal. Jack
recorded all the bass parts, then finally Mark Pickerel would overdub
the drums. It was a backwards way of recording but necessary due to the
nature of my weirdly constructed tunes and the limitations of the ancient
eight-track recorder. Sub Pop's records had all been loud, raw rock and I
started to have serious misgivings about making a quiet acoustic record,
but Jack and Mike kept reassuring me that what we were doing was
great.

After I had tracked all the vocals one night, Steve Fisk dropped by the
studio to say hello and to put some minimal piano parts on a track or
two. Steve had recorded all the early Trees records at a studio in Ellensburg. He and I had had a minorly contentious relationship from the
beginning of our association, as he was always irritated by my paranoid, suspicious questioning of his every creative decision, but that night
I greeted him as an old friend. He started messing around on an organ
and I quickly wrote what I thought was a funny little song to his organ
riff. Because of the sad and serious tone of the record, I felt like it needed
some comic relief at the end. Jack rolled his eyes and Johnson outright
hated it: "Why make a beautiful record and then shit on it?" I included it
on the album anyway. "Juarez" may be the only song in history to mention crack, heroin, blow jobs, and diapers, all in a minute and a half. Kurt
came in and sang on "Down in the Dark," a more electric tune. We also
ended up using a recording of one of the heavier songs from our aborted
Lead Belly record, "Where Did You Sleep Last Night?," an acoustic tune
Kurt had electrified, which had compelled me to take my performance
into the familiar rock territory of the Trees, doubling my voice to harmo-
nize with myself and singing the last couple of verses in the very utmost
registers of my limited vocal range, as though Lee Conner himself had
written the part.

With the record done, I did the first of what were to be many photo
sessions with Sub Pop house photographer Charles Peterson. They were
mostly shots of me walking around the rubble of what had been the
Western State Hospital, the psychiatric hospital hellhole that had once
housed the famous actress Frances Farmer in the 1940s. My own grandmother had been a patient there during World War Two when my father
was a young boy. During that time he had lived alone with his father,

an older man who was working in the shipyards to assist the war effort, having already fought in the trenches in France during World War One.

Back in Seattle, Sub Pop co-owner Bruce Pavitt insisted I sit for some close-up portrait-type shots. I was reluctant. After much back and forth, I only agreed when he said, "If you don't like them, I promise not to use them for anything."

A few weeks later, Pavitt and Poneman scheduled a meeting so we could review the contact sheets from the photo sessions together. I arrived after working hours to meet Jon and Bruce in the Sub Pop stockroom. As I approached the door, I could hear the two of them in a heated discussion.

"Goddamnit!" Pavitt said. "Is Nirvana the only band we have that is ever going to sell any records?"

By this time, Nirvana had started to become an underground sensation, taking the English and European rock press by storm. All the UK music rags were going crazy for them and so were the kids. I shook my head as I recalled how little they'd esteemed Kurt's band just a couple years previously. As it turned out, it was a good thing Nirvana stayed with Sub Pop. The two label bosses turned out to be genius marketers. The way they promoted the label turned it and all their bands into an underground phenomenon with Nirvana as the brightest star in their universe. Not that Kurt had been wrong about how Sub Pop tried to control their artists. "Watch out, they will fuck you if they can," he had warned me.

At that meeting where we looked at the contact sheets of possible cover photos, Pavitt quickly became enamored with one of the portrait shots he had insisted upon. I hated it. To my punk rock sensibilities, it screamed PRETENTIOUS. There was no way I would agree to let him use it. After a lot of hemming and hawing, he finally said we could use one of the photos I deemed acceptable for the cover if he could use the portrait shot for promotion. I begrudgingly agreed to that deal, relieved it wouldn't be the cover shot but still mortified it would be seen at all. Shortly thereafter, the Trees went on tour. My record, which I had titled *The Winding Sheet*, was to be released a couple days before we returned.

When I got home, there was a box of albums waiting for me. When I opened the box, there on the front cover of my first solo effort was the fucking photo Pavitt had been in love with, the one he had sworn to me would not be used. I was incredulous, then livid. No one in my music career had ever fucked me like that. I could not believe he'd had the balls to do it. I couldn't look at it without feeling humiliated and violently pissed off at the same time.

Just home from tour and exhausted, I borrowed my roommate's car and drove down to Sub Pop, overcome with murderous anger, fully intending to beat Bruce unconscious. When I burst through the office door, the secretary stood up and then, gauging how dark my mood was, sat right back down.

I walked straight into Pavitt's office where he sat behind his desk, talking to someone on the phone. I crossed the room in a couple of long, fast strides and came directly at him, fists clenched. He dropped the phone and threw himself to the floor behind his desk, his arms up over his face.

"Mark! Wait a second! Please wait a second!"

I stood over him as he cowered on the ground, barely resisting the urge to kick him in the face.

"I know you're angry and you have every right to be! I'm sorry about the cover, I should not have done it."

"Fucking A right, you shouldn't have done it! We had a deal, mother-fucker. Who the fuck do you think you are? And who do you think you're dealing with? Some Seattle-band pussy? Where I'm from, people end up in a ditch somewhere for shit like this. I should kick your fuck-ing head in."

"Please wait a minute and hear me out," he whined. "I thought I was doing what was best for you and the record. And the label."

"Yeah. I know. We had that discussion the day you promised not to use that photo. Dude, not only have you shit on our deal, fucked me, and lied to my face, but now I have to live with this terrible embarrassing album cover for the rest of my life. I'm gonna have my lawyer sue your ass and keep you from ever releasing this piece of shit."

"We've already shipped out a couple thousand copies," he said in a hoarse, choking whisper.

"Then I'll have them pulled off the fucking shelves, I don't give a fuck." Finally exhausting my blinding rage, I turned to go with a final "Eat shit, Bruce. You don't know how lucky you just got."

With him still on the floor of his office, I turned and left, mute and dazed with shock that he'd really done it. Although I was loyal to the few close friends I had, in those days I would have freely lied and screwed anyone else over to get what I wanted, and now here I was, totally enraged that someone had done it to me. I was furious at myself for falling for his con before I was in a position to con him.

I had vowed to myself early on in life to fuck anyone before they had the chance to fuck me, and I had walked backwards right into this fucking. I made a mental note to pay this son of a bitch back if ever given the opportunity, swallowed what felt like a mountain of shit, and filed his betrayal away in the back of my mind. I was prepared to wait as long as I had to until the opportunity came someday when it would be my turn to force the shoe onto his foot and see how it fit him. At least I had the $13,000 for a balm. If there's nothing else handy, money is always a sufficient lubricant.

4

IF YOU START AGAIN, IT WILL BE AS THOUGH YOU'D NEVER STOPPED

I REFUSED TO DO ANY PRESS OR SHOWS TO PROMOTE *THE WINDING Sheet* but it nonetheless received a decent response and quite a few positive reviews. *Spin* magazine (the biggest music magazine in the States besides *Rolling Stone* at the time) could not be bothered to ever write about the Trees but they gave *The Winding Sheet* a good notice. I was privately relieved it didn't get slaughtered in the press.

Now willfully estranged from Sub Pop, I turned my attention back to the Screaming Trees. Our manager Susan Silver had miraculously secured us a major label deal with Epic Records. I had initially been put off by the over-the-top manner of their extroverted A&R man Bob Pfeifer. When Susan picked me up after I'd met Bob for the first time, we rode in silence for five minutes before she finally asked how it went. I said, "If I'm ever alone with that guy again, I will kill him or myself." Though Bob and I were almost complete opposites personality-wise, I came to trust and value him as a friend and advisor and the two of us formed a tight bond. He and the rest of the band, not so much. Lee couldn't bear to acknowledge the contributions of anyone but himself and was completely, childishly deaf to any sort of constructive criticism. Susan sadly confessed to me much later on that only one other major had been slightly interested in signing us . . . under the condition that we "lose one of the big guys."

We settled on big-time Northwest producer Terry Date for our first major label recording. Since we'd made several terrible-sounding records on rusty old eight-track machines, I was eager to make a great-sounding album in a big professional studio. Even so, I was leery of losing our edge, desperately afraid that we'd end up sounding like one of the terrible hair-metal bands I despised, the current kings of popular music. Because of my reticence, Soundgarden singer Chris Cornell, who I liked and respected, was brought on board as coproducer to basically hang out with me, function as a go-between for Terry and me, and generally assuage my fears about the process.

Like all of our recordings, it became a musically challenging head-fuck, but it was ultimately a pleasurable experience for me simply because I hit it off with Terry and loved hanging out with Chris. Chris was a solitary creature and presented a quiet, thoughtful, and serious front to the world but had a sly, somewhat perverse sense of humor not unlike my own, with a gift for making me laugh. He was highly intelligent, wise beyond his years, and possessed zero fear. He was always up for anything, silently focused and fiercely competitive. I had a terrible cold one day and Cornell insisted I allow him to lick my bare eyeball to test his invented-on-the-spot theory of virus transmission. I was, of course, delighted to take part in the experiment. Chris never got sick. I can't recall if this proved or disproved his theory, but it was an effective way of making me laugh.

On another occasion, Chris played me some home demos he'd done, just acoustic guitar and singing. I was blown away hearing the earliest, raw version of "Say Hello 2 Heaven." He had an extremely powerful voice and was technically the most gifted singer I'd ever heard. He laughed when I said in complete seriousness, "That's a fucking hit, man!"

Every day, Terry cajoled Van and me into playing two-on-two basketball against him and Chris, a game they hardly, if ever, won. With Van at six foot four and nearly three hundred pounds and me at six foot two and a hundred and eighty-five, we had a serious size advantage. Chris was slightly shorter than me and Terry several inches shorter than Chris. Every time we had the ball, Van would simply set an unmovable pick on whoever was guarding me. I drove around them to an easy lay-up or pulled up to hit a jump shot or passed it to Van for an easy close-to-the-hoop shot as he rolled to the basket after the pick. As the recording session went on, each day their intensity raised incrementally as they stubbornly attempted to beat us. Van and I would get up from our seats in the studio and slowly walk out to the court where, playing in our heavy boots, we would inevitably kick their asses yet again.

Terry tried hard to make me comfortable, and to help us make a Trees record I'd be proud of. I was so conditioned to being horrified by the finished results of our previous recordings that not being ashamed of one was the best I could hope for. I had never enjoyed any of the records we'd made because, despite being the dominant personality in the band, from the very beginning my creative role was limited to merely singing the songs written and arranged by the prolific, controlling, obsessive guitar player Lee Conner. With no friends, relationships, or social life of any kind, Lee churned out as many as three or four demos of songs a day, complete with lyrics and singing. He was a machine. I was overwhelmed by the sheer mountain of material. It was much catchier and more "rock" than anything I'd written, so there was never a question of using any songs but his—that was all we'd ever done. It was a constant battle just to keep him from soloing from start to finish through every song and then demanding his shrill, atonal, uninteresting playing be the loudest thing in the mix. It often seemed like the bulk of the band's creative energy was devoted solely to tamping down Lee's worst narcissistic impulses.

I privately thought of Lee as a copycat revisionist of the cheesiest kind, his entire persona and songwriting style a cornball expression of the terrible '60s-garage-band revival briefly popular in the '80s. He was a slave to the *Nuggets* collection, a compilation of obscure '60s garage and psychedelic music curated by Patti Smith's guitar player Lenny Kaye. I could not relate to the fakeness of it all, it had no connection to my experience, but Lee worshiped at that altar. He tie-dyed his own pants and shirts, wore square, purple-lensed sunglasses indoors, and wrote literally hundreds of songs with bullshit faux-psychedelic lyrics about tripping on LSD. The great irony in all of that was that he had never once in his life taken acid or even smoked pot. He was most definitely a casualty, but not from acid. That had been my experience, not his.

It was all a terrible, shit-stained charade, a fucked-up and ridiculous farce orchestrated by a man nearly thirty years old with no real human experience outside of his lonely life of solitude, with us but without us, on the road. If I happened to be somewhere and one of our songs came on—one of Lee's songs, a Screaming Trees song, not anything I would claim any part of—I would cringe and leave immediately. In the recording studio, I was driven by sheer embarrassment and my unflagging admiration for raw, edgy, and meaningful music to try to make Lee's songs into something I could endure with my head up, but I would never enjoy singing them.

Yet against heavy odds, through dogged, determined obsession and sheer force of will, I kept trying. With Van Conner as my likewise-handcuffed, like-minded conspirator battling his sullenly stubborn, broken, savant-like brother residing somewhere on the spectrum in fantasyland, both our only hope and most glaring hindrance, I kept trying. Trying to shape our music into something I could not only live with, but also something that might give the band continued upward success. So that I could keep running from the painful mire of my past, the uncomfortable reality of my present, and, of course, mainly from myself. Toward where or what, I did not know or care.

—

WE FINISHED OUR FIRST RECORD for Epic in late 1990 and *Uncle Anesthesia* was released early the following year to little, if any, fanfare. As hard as I'd worked in the studio, as hard as Terry and Chris and I had fought to drag the band forward, our major label debut was more of the same shit we'd always done, it just sounded better. Not long after the record came out, I was displeased to see one of our tunes included on a Sony Music compilation CD with several different boring hard rock bands. Epic couldn't really find another way to market us other than to try and tie us in with late '80s and early '90s hair metal, soon to be replaced in the public popularity contest. I had a conversation with our product manager at the company, an enthusiastic, positive, forward-thinking man in his forties named Al. "Mark," he said, "I'm gonna work my ass off to get you guys to the same place as the Psychedelic Furs or Midnight Oil." He saw us as an outlier, and not hangers-on of some metal scene with which we had nothing in common. That he had used the Psychedelic Furs as a point of reference made me feel like he got it. Despite their name, the Furs had nothing in common with the fake psychedelia I had fought so hard to distance Screaming Trees from. The Furs were an English post-punk band that I personally loved because they were unique unto themselves. With Richard Butler's one-of-a-kind voice and their sometime use of instrumentation uncommon in rock music, their sound was unlike anything else out there yet they had several worldwide hits. They were an example of what I hoped we'd become: an original, not an imitator.

We hit the road. One of the very few upgrades since our SST days was that we now had two vans instead of one, in part to accommodate our three new crew members. I rode in the equipment van with our guitar tech and lighting guy while the rest of the band took the other, more comfortable passenger van with our tour manager/soundman Rod. Mark Pickerel had become involved in a serious relationship and, still in his early twenties, realized the dysfunction in the group dynamic wasn't worth it any longer and quit the band shortly after we finished the record. Dan Peters, a hilarious and sweet-natured good-time Charlie who was also the drummer for local Seattle stars Mudhoney, took his place.

Only a couple days into the tour, guitar tech Jim Vincent was driving our crew van down a snow-covered Wyoming highway when we hit black ice. The van swerved, then began to weave from side to side. I was riding shotgun and the van took so long to finally swing out of control that I had time to put a big bag of clothes in front of me like a crude airbag and brace my feet up on the dashboard. After what felt like an unbearable eternity of mounting panic, we skidded off the road into the snow-blanketed median. As the van flipped suddenly, violently, end over end, I was thrown into the windshield, and with my face up against the glass, I saw the ground come rushing up and smash into my head again and again as we toppled through the highway divider, my corner of the van taking the brunt of the contact. Finally, we came to rest upright on the shoulder of the opposite side of the highway. We sat in shock for a few seconds, all three of us still in our seats. Then, realizing the ass end of the extra-long Econoline was still sticking out in the path of oncoming traffic, we scrambled to get out before a semi truck came through and finished the job.

I looked at Jim, blood streaming down his face on the side of the highway.

"Jesus Christ! I'm so sorry, guys. Fuck!" Jim was a staunch perfectionist at his work. I knew he felt personally responsible.

"Hey, what the fuck, Jim? You couldn't have done a goddamn thing. It's okay, man. As long as you guys are okay, I'm okay."

I looked at our wisecracking light man Jimmy Shoaf and he nodded his agreement. He had been riding in the back and was virtually unscathed. They both assured me they were fine but I wasn't convinced. They were both white as a sheet and blood was pouring off Jim's head. I looked back on four lanes of highway and divider and saw our drums, guitars, and amps strewn across the entire distance. My head began to pound with what I felt but wouldn't see until later, a large, ugly blue-black bump starting to raise above my right eye.

There was no way to get in touch with the rest of the guys, who had been driving ahead of us when it happened. But, by chance, one of them had been looking back at a critical moment and noticed we'd disappeared. They eventually turned around and arrived in time to see the van being towed off by the emergency road crew, then located us in the local hospital where we'd been taken by ambulance. To our luck, Jimmy was untouched, Jim took just a few stitches to his head, and I walked away with a concussion, at one point stopping to vomit in a hospital toilet while wandering the hallways in a daze looking for the guys in the waiting room. After staying awake all night in a local motel by doctor's orders to make sure I didn't die in my sleep from a brain hemorrhage, the decision was made to continue on. We'd rent new equipment and another van in Chicago, where our next show was scheduled.

At this point, I'd not had a drink or done hard drugs for nearly five years. I hadn't even smoked weed for the first three years. But eventually I had fallen back into what had seemed to me to be a harmless routine of smoking pot. I was unhappy much of the time, my mind consumed by the band and its demands, not to mention the pressure I put on myself to steer it away from the music we'd been rehashing for five years toward something greater. I'd done my own record, written all the words and the bulk of the music myself. I now knew how to do it. Although I felt the songs weren't great, they were a true representation of myself and had some personal meaning. I had managed to create a mood, I'd become comfortable in my own skin, and had sung in my natural range and my authentic voice. And it made coming back to the Trees that much harder.

Life on the road was dreadful, dreary, and mind-draining most of the time. I sat there like a zombie in an unending, boredom-induced trance brought on by the complete lack of any remotely interesting interaction between us. Half the time, I felt like I was mindlessly staring at a black-and-white TV after it had gone off the air, sucked into the static, trapped between the horizontal and vertical lines.

Always a two-pack-a-day smoker, I'd developed a cold and nasty case of strep throat by the time we got to Chicago. That on top of the lingering effects of my car-crash concussion had left me in a terrible mood. When it came time to go onstage for our late-afternoon matinee show, my usually robust singing voice was diminished to a faint, painful, red-raw echo. I sounded like Peter Brady in the episode where he goes through puberty. It was impossible to make enough sound to be heard above the roar of the band. After three embarrassing songs I walked offstage, furious that I couldn't sing. I took off running down the stairs to the backstage to grab my coat and split, anxious to get the fuck out of there and back to my hotel room. In my haste, blinded by anger and humiliation, I did not see a low-hanging beam halfway down the staircase. When I smashed my head into it, I knocked myself out cold.

I came to with a club employee holding an icy wet rag against my forehead.

"Holy shit, man, are you okay? Should I call an ambulance?"

For several seconds I had double vision, but I finally regained my sight. In my tiny, barely-there voice, I croaked, "No thanks, man. I'm okay." I slunk off into the dressing room and sat down for a second to steady myself.

In the span of four days, I'd taken several heavy blows to the head. I had lost my voice, and with it, the will to continue. My friend Garrett Shavlik, drummer for the Denver band the Fluid, my Sub Pop label-mates, burst through the door behind me. I'd not even known they were in Chicago but he was drunk and he was pissed off.

"What the fuck are you doing, Lanegan? Those guys are dying up there without you."

"My voice is fucked, Tidbit," I said, using the nickname I'd invented for him with my habitual method of finding a fucked-up near-rhyme to or perversion of anyone's name. Geoff Templeton became the Tough Gentle-man, Blair Underwood, Blood Underwear, etc. A quirk that inexplicably gave me great joy. "I can't sing, brother." Without thinking, I reached out to grab the bottle of booze he held in his hand. He wasn't buying it.

"Bullshit, dude! What the fuck?" he yelled and yanked the bottle out of my hand.

I had a soft spot for the usually entertaining and sweet-natured Garrett but he was obviously sloshed. When he suddenly shouted, "You're not Morrison, motherfucker!" it took a great deal of restraint on my part not to knock the holy fuck out of him. If my head were not already throbbing painfully, I probably would've done it. He had said out loud what nobody I knew dared say to my face. I found it sad and demoralizing. If even my supposed friends were convinced I was a rank Jim Morrison imitator, then I had no friends at all. For the first time in years, I needed a drink. If my unsympathetic pal wasn't going to share his bottle with me, I was splitting.

"I ain't got time for this right now," I croaked. Grabbing my coat, I slipped through the back door and hopped into a cab, my already fucked-up head now much worse.

On my way to the hotel, I thought, *Fuck it, I really do need a drink*. In my state of severe depression, physical and psychic pain, what I was really saying was *Fuck it, I want to die*. The five years in hell I'd not drank or drugged had been a cursed and crazed walk on a tightrope, one I always knew I was destined to fall from.

—

BEFORE I HAD LEFT MY far-right-wing hometown, my excessively long hair and fuck-the-world attitude were a statement of rebellion that had nothing to do with rock music. In a place where many people (including many of my high school classmates) wore cowboy hats and boots as their everyday attire, where tattoos were only seen on the occasional biker rolling through town, I stuck out like a sore red dick. I got into frequent fistfights with strangers in broad daylight if they made a cutting remark or looked at me the wrong way. While waiting in line at the post office one day, a man standing behind me wearing a cowboy hat said under his breath, "Fucking faggot." I punched him in the face. As he staggered out, holding his blood-gushing nose, the forty-something male government employee behind the counter smiled and, with a look of unabashed glee, said, "Nicely done."

So there was a faction of more progressive thinkers in Ellensburg, too, mainly older hippy types or immature young college art students. It was from that small pool of art students—overly dramatic girls living away from home for the first time—that I had habitually fished for sex partners/girlfriends. They often acted as if they were on an imaginary stage with bohemian affectations like using cigarette holders, throwing theme parties, and droning on and on in mindless, boring, pretentious conversation with friends while clutching the latest ridiculous cocktail popular among their group. New exotic names they'd given themselves after leaving home to go with their newfound freedom, an excess of lame bracelets and necklaces, jewelry some ex-boyfriend had inevitably "crafted" for them . . . I was instinctively turned off by these girls but I needed sex and they were easily had and heavily preferred over the homegrown Ellensburg girls who wouldn't have touched me with a hundred-and-fifty-foot pole. Nor would I, them.

I was by nature drawn to and got hooked hardwire-hardest to the feral, streetwise, tatted, dark and sultry Goth girls in black fishnets, short skirts, heavy boots, and heavier eye makeup that I would come across in my travels. Should they happen to wear glasses, that was a plus. Since childhood I'd also had, among a thousand other kinks, a somewhat predictable fetish for the classic "nasty librarian" look. As a fifteen-year-old doing seventy-five hours of court-ordered community service at the public library for one of my teenage misdemeanors, I would jack off a couple times a day in the employee restroom just from the thought that I was actually in a library, never mind that the only women who worked there were in their fifties and anything but sexy. Women who were smart, dirty, and open to any sort of nonmainstream but legal and consensual action in the bedroom were who I sought. In short, the kind of woman I never came across in my hometown. Because of this, I was always eager to hit the road.

In this tiny college cow-town, I was forced to work with what was available. Without my medicine of drugs and booze, I became very dark, wide awake all night, and open to trouble. I went through a succession of these girls who, after the initial novelty thrill of dating the only semi-known underground rock singer in town wore off, quickly became unhappy. Their complaints were always the same. I was cold and distant,

I only interacted when I wanted sex, the intensity of my sexual behavior worried them, their friends were afraid of me, I never wanted to hang out with their friends, I never wanted to go out, I would never agree to let them throw a party at my house nor ever accompany them to a party elsewhere, I would never say what was on my mind or talk about my feelings, I did not appreciate their art, I stayed awake all night and slept all day, all I cared about was music, etc., etc., etc.

The homegrown aggressive darkness I cultivated during this period of will-driven sobriety followed me everywhere in those days. When someone hurled insults or objects at me or anyone else in my band, I'd be the one to go into the audience and trade punches. The minute someone overtly crossed the line, I was down. At one of our earliest shows, some guy standing there with a drink in his hand had yelled out, "Come on, fat boys! Make some fucking sound!" before we'd even had the chance to start our set. I leapt from my perch into the crowd and punched him a couple of times in the head, putting him on the floor, knocking off his baseball hat and soaking his shirt with his drink. I'll never forget the surprised look of shock and admiration on the faces of my bandmates while climbing back onstage that first time. I wasn't having it. I wasn't being paid twenty bucks a day to stand on a stage and take shit from some drunken frat boy, or anyone else for that matter. In those days, no one pressed charges or tried to sue me for dough I didn't have, but the river ran both ways and my angry soldier-on-the-wall routine onstage also made me the target at times. On more than one occasion, I was the one whose ass was kicked. While walking behind my road manager/soundman through the crowd to get to the dressing room post-show one night in Daytona Beach, Florida, without warning a big college-jock-looking guy stepped out of the crowd in front of me. With a huge smile on his face, he suddenly crushed my nose with a straight right that immediately dropped me to my knees, down for the count. It was three days before we got to Atlanta where I was able to get my broken nose set and by that time I'd sung a couple of shows with it throbbing in pain, a black bruise covering my face like the mask of the Lone Ranger, or that of a raccoon.

That intensity I wore like a suit of armor had carried me a long way, but it could only carry me so far. During that cab ride in Chicago, I had finally been beaten down to a place where I surrendered. I was exhausted to the point where willpower wasn't gonna see me through. I had to get loaded.

By the time my girlfriend Anna called the next morning, I'd already been drinking for a few hours. It felt so good, all the misery it had caused me in the past forgotten. All the beatings I'd received or given, the insanity of the constant blackouts, waking up in unfamiliar towns with no memory of having ridden there hundreds of helmetless miles on my motorcycle, coming to in bed with people I'd never have fucked sober, all the jail time and subsequent prison sentence, the year-long rehab, all of it erased in the beautifully familiar warmth of the liquor on my brain.

"What's wrong with you? You sound funny," she said.

I admitted I had been drinking. Anna freaked out, no doubt recalling the stories I'd told her of my difficult past with alcohol.

"How long are you in Chicago? I'm coming out there!"

With a three-day break in this hotel before moving on to our next gig, I had anticipated a good long drunk and did not want that interrupted by her or anyone else.

"Don't worry about it, baby, I'm fine. It's not going to continue after this weekend, I just needed to relax for a minute."

She insisted on coming anyway. About four or five hours later, she knocked on my door and walked into my hotel room. Seeing me standing there with a bottle of vodka in my hand, she dropped her bag on the ground and said, "Oh my God." I braced myself for what I assumed was the coming confrontation, but instead she put her arms around me and quietly whispered, "Oh my God, I can't believe it."

"What can't you believe?"

"You look ten years younger." She sounded honestly baffled.

I looked into a mirror and was woozily surprised. After several hours of drinking, instead of looking like a disheveled bum, I looked much younger. The hardness I'd developed over five years of white-knuckling, the lines that had been etched on my face from my depression and quick-to-ignite violent firestorm of anger . . . it was all gone. The unmistakable disappointment and dark concern always written on my features, born from the lifetime of failures, had slipped away. I looked at peace.

When I came to three days later, phone ringing, head pounding, alone on the hotel bed, I plunged deep into immediate regret. Both myself and the bed were covered in hundreds of pieces of broken glass from a mirror I must have smashed, but I had no memory of what had transpired in the preceding days. I was to find out much later it had been broken not by me, but by Anna. She'd thrown an ashtray at my head when I'd inevitably gone into a blackout and become dark and threatening. The unfortunate consequences of my fucked lapse in judgment and moment of weakness had only just begun.

A warning sprang instantly to my muddled mind, one I'd heard so many times during my year of court-ordered drug and alcohol treatment. The voice of Hoppy, the man who had run our group, rang suddenly in my head: *When you are an alcoholic and quit drinking, even if you stay sober for years, if you begin again, it will be as though you'd never stopped.* Meaning you would not just start off at the level you were at when you quit; instead, you would be at an advanced state of addiction, at the level you'd have sunk to had you never quit at all. Judging from this first experience of drinking again after so many years, that seemed to be true. I had been an advanced, hardcore blackout drunk when I'd quit at age nineteen. At twenty-four, I was already so much worse off that it scared me.

I choked down the last two miniature bottles of vodka left in the minibar in an attempt to steady myself enough to collect my shit. I had to get down to the van in time to leave for the next city on our tour.

5

MEATLOAF

I CONTINUED TO DRINK ALMOST DAILY. BOTH VAN CONNER AND Dan Peters were also daily, heavy drinkers but they were comical, playful. I was a wild-card drunk, blacking out through entire shows, entire days and nights lost in the haze of my unquenchable, around-the-clock thirst for booze and chaos. I drank throughout our shows, then walked straight up to the bar to drink with the audience. I came to while having sex in a bed/in an alley/in a car with women I had zero recollection of ever meeting, total strangers whose names I never knew, whose faces I forgot the minute I left their company.

One night after our set in a tiny bar in Grand Rapids, Michigan, before I could even get off the maybe half-foot-high stage tucked into the corner of the quarter-full place, two young-looking girls approached me.

"Hey, man, what are you doing right now? Do you wanna come party with us at Blackie's?"

I considered these girls for a moment. They seemed too cute to be eighteen, let alone twenty-one . . . but then they had to be of age to be inside the bar.

"Sure. Who's Blackie?"

The better- and older-looking of the two grabbed me by the hand and pulled me impatiently off the miniature stage. She led me to a table where a mustachioed dude who seemed at least fifteen years older than me sat alone with a drink.

"Hey, man, cool tunes," he said, shaking my hand. "I'm Blackie. You ready to go?"

I looked around to see if anyone else in the place was coming along to this "party." Nope. I guess it was just gonna be me, these two possibly underage girls, and this strange older guy. I got our road manager to write on a bar napkin the phone number and address of the hotel where the rest of the band were staying, then followed my three new friends out to the parking lot. The younger of the two girls hopped in shotgun, and I got into the backseat of Blackie's large American sedan with the older of the chicks. She held my hand tightly and squeezed my thigh as we drove. Finally, we pulled up to an old, impressive, foreboding house, large but just shy of a mansion.

"Hey, Blackie, cool pad. What do you do for a living, if you don't mind my asking?"

"I do some acting," he said, and left it at that.

I didn't recognize him but, then again, I was no fan of Broadway plays or anything like that. He could very well have won a Tony Award for all I knew. As we followed the guy into his place, I thought, *How weird is this gonna get?*

"C'mon, let's drink in the library," Blackie said as he turned on the lights and led us up a flight of stairs into a circular room with shelves of books covering three-quarters of the walls. The only section that wasn't covered with bookshelves was covered with photos of Blackie himself. I always found it gross whenever I encountered someone who adorned their place with odes to themselves. Our boss at Peaches, the Seattle record store where I worked, had maintained in his office what we called his "Wall of Shame." It was covered with photos of himself, smiling with lame musicians, including not one but two large framed pictures of him with Billy Joel, easily my most vehemently disliked singer ever.

I again asked myself, *Who the fuck is this dude? Some kind of dealer, criminal, famous actor . . . what?* He obviously had some dough if he could afford to live in this huge old house, even slightly run-down as it was. I looked at the books on his shelves and didn't recognize any of the titles, but that was no surprise since I was not much of a reader. I didn't expect to find Cormac McCarthy, Peter Matthiessen, or Robert Lowell, or any of the predictable French poets whose works I'd devoured: Rimbaud, Baudelaire, Apollinaire, Corbière. Nor did I see any of the beat poets I'd become enamored of: Burroughs, Norse, Ginsberg. I continued to slowly circle the room, silently perusing his large collection as he put on some music and began to pour drinks for the four of us.

When I finally sat down, the girl who'd been next to me in the car sat herself uninvited on my lap while the other sat on Blackie's lap. Blackie looked up and with a huge, toothy grin, lifted his drink and said, "Cheers!" We all clinked glasses.

Before I could even take a drink, the girl on my lap grabbed my dick through my pants and shoved her tongue into my mouth. Out the corner of my eye, I could see the other young girl and Blackie also making out passionately. *Okay, they brought me along for a fuck-fest.* That was fine by me.

For a half hour, my girl and I fumbled like teenagers in a car outside a school dance . . . except we were in a brightly lit room with no beds or couches, just a couple of uncomfortable chairs. And I was painfully aware that the forty-something owner of the house was making out with a girl who struck me more and more as a child. Was something going to happen? Was anything going to happen? Did I even want anything to happen?

"Hey, man," I said to Blackie, interrupting his reverie, "where's the pisser in here?"

"Right through that door."

He pointed to a door directly off the room. I pulled the girl off my now nearly asleep legs, stood up, and gingerly walked over to take a long-overdue piss. I entered the closet-sized toilet, pulled the light string hanging from the ceiling, and was instantly overcome by a profusion of photos plastered on all four walls of the claustrophobic restroom. Childhood photos, family Polaroids, grade-school class pictures, all of the same boy. A boy I instantly recognized as Red Hot Chili Peppers singer Anthony Kiedis. I knew nothing of his personal history but he was a well-known rock star and I quickly realized that there was a family connection between him and my gracious but weirdly creepy host. When surrounded so oppressively with this huge multitude of photos in such a small, enclosed space, I finally recognized the strong physical resemblance between the two.

Confronted by Blackie's tribute wall to himself, I had winced at his unseemly narcissism, but now I found it much sicker that he'd chosen a tiny, cabinet-sized room dedicated to the excretion of human waste to display the photos of his son. I got the eeriest feeling that this would be the exact place my own mother would stash pictures of me, except that I knew she had none. There were childhood photos of my sister around her house and many of my stepbrothers and their families but none of me. This fucked-up, ghoulish photo gallery and the fact that I was apparently meant to fuck this girl under the bright lights where this slippery dude could watch snapped me to my senses. I needed to leave. I was normally up for anything—the weirder, the more shameful and depraved, the better—but something about this struck me the wrong way.

I walked out of the restroom, closed the door behind me, and said, "Hey, it's been great meeting you folks but I gotta run. Take care."

Blackie didn't stop kissing and groping his girl, just raised his hand and made a dismissive action with his arm, sort of a "Shut up, already! Begone!" The girl I'd been halfheartedly making out with hung on my arm the entire time I made my way down the stairs, begging me to stay. Finally, I shook her off and stepped out into the now sub-zero night wearing only my still-damp black denim jacket for warmth. I ran down long, endless streets, shaking uncontrollably from the cold, searching for a pay phone I was never to find. Just when I thought, *This is it, you're gonna freeze to death for bailing on a weird orgy,* a taxi pulled around the corner, hustled me in, and cranked up the heat for the ride back to my hotel.

I had been to many more questionable parties than that one and had participated in much heavier scenes. But something about that toilet shrine to his kid had stitched cold fear into my soul. This cat was a different breed of freak and somehow I felt I had gotten out in just the nick of time.

—

AS THE TOUR PROGRESSED, SO did my drinking. My wild, unhinged alcoholism had always been a source of deep shame and heartache but now that I'd stepped back on the merry-go-round, I found it impossible to step back off. I was out of control but I usually had a slight awareness that I was among friends, not foes, so we were spared the violence that had often accompanied my blackouts in the past. I would drink to escape the brutal hangover and the demoralization from the preceding night's bizarre behavior and unsavory situations. I would wake up and walk into my hotel-room bathroom to take a piss, only to come to the realization that I was standing barefooted in a puddle of piss that covered half the bathroom floor, a by-product of yesterday's blackout. I would come to nude on the floor of some unfamiliar room and, hearing voices from another room, would silently pull my clothes on and, carrying my boots, quietly sneak out without ever knowing where I'd been or who with. After a show at Saint Andrews Hall in Detroit, I stood in a blackout at the window of the upstairs dressing room throwing beer bottles and screaming insults at the audience members as they were leaving the gig. Someone had shouted, "Hey, Mark! We love you! Why are you doing this?" Only then had I come to and realized where I was and what I was doing. I drank myself blind every day, only to emerge from a blackout into a new variation on the same nightmare. It was an obsessive, crazed cycle: waking in hollow, booming pain, then seeking relief where there was only more emptiness and pain to be found.

One night, I was met after the show by a pretty blond German girl now living in the US. Her boyfriend was the singer in a band that had opened for us a year earlier and he and I had become friends. The boyfriend was out of town doing a gig and had sent his girl down to say hello. She asked me out for drinks, one thing led to another, and I soon found myself following her up the six flights of stairs to their apartment at the top of an old row-house-style apartment building in some Midwestern city. We began having sex in their one-room pad with the ceiling slanting down hard, echoing the angle of the roof. After we'd been messing around for an hour or so there was a loud knock on the door. In my inebriated state, I struggled to stand up to get dressed. She grabbed my arm and pulled me back down.

"Please! Don't say a word! Quiet, please!" she whispered frantically in my ear in her sexy German accent.

"Is that your boyfriend?" I drunkenly whispered.

"Yes. We just moved in and I have the only keys. He'll leave in a while."

"Okay," I whispered and lay back down.

But the knocking didn't stop. *This is fucked*, I thought. Her boyfriend had been so friendly, so genuine. We'd become such good buddies the first time we'd met, I could only imagine what would happen if he were to find me in his place right now, doing this. The blond sat there naked, holding on to me tightly, sometimes putting her hand over my mouth when she thought I was about to blurt out some alcohol-fueled profanity and get us busted. After a half hour of intermittent knocking, the phone began ringing, from a pay phone on the street below, I assumed.

"He'll give up soon and go to a friend's. I'll tell him I was at my girl-friend's all night," she said. Yet the ringing continued for a very long time. Sobering up, I looked at the clock. I was able to focus enough to see it was five a.m. I needed to get out of there, our ride was due to roll out at seven a.m. How was I gonna get past her boyfriend without some confrontation? She had informed me as we were climbing the stairs that there was no way out other than the way we'd come in.

Finally, the phone quit ringing for twenty minutes or so. I knew I had no other choice than to go for it. I carefully crept down the stairs to the ground level, then burst through the door and sprinted drunkenly down the sidewalk and across the street to where a row of cabs sat sleepily waiting for the early-morning crowd. I got back to our hotel just in time to grab my shit and hop in my seat in the van, pull my watch cap down over my face, and fall asleep.

When I came to around five hours later, still en route to our next show, Van was looking at the tour book. He turned around and said, "Hey, Lanegan, remember last year when we played with that band and you became such great pals with their singer and he dragged you along while he went out hell-raising all night? They're opening tonight. Better get ready for a party!"

I woke up immediately, realizing that when we arrived at the gig in less than an hour, I'd be in the company of the very guy who'd spent the night before trying to get into his place where I was fucking his girl. *Jesus Christ.* This thing could only turn out one of two ways. Either my friend was going to attempt to beat the fuck out of me, or I was going to be forced to drink and make merry with my old pal all night, sick with guilt the entire time. I would have signed up for a beating but I knew that my bent-backwards pride wouldn't allow me to tank a fight, even when I knew I was dead wrong.

When we arrived, I slowly trudged up the prodigious stairway to the venue, still slightly hungover. As soon as I stepped into the dressing room area, there was my good buddy. I tensed up in case I was gonna have to defend myself. He looked at me. Then a huge grin spread across his face and in two seconds he had me in a tight bear hug, swinging me around, kissing me on the cheek and overjoyed to see me again. We played our sets that night and then, at his insistence, we went to a popular bar, filled with many of the kids who'd attended the gig. One tall, hot blond had taken a shine to me and sat uninvited on my lap, much to my friend's delight. Happy that I was now drinking, he egged me on to take this chick somewhere to fuck but I was too twisted up by the previous night's escapades. A black cloud of exhausting guilt lurked over me as I sat with the friend I'd burned less than twenty-four hours earlier. Finally, I told him I had to go. He followed me outside, a friend to the end. The evening was knocked on the head with the two of us drunkenly throwing a garbage can full of empty fifth bottles, one by one, against a brick wall near some railroad tracks. Mine had a little extra juice on them as every one I threw, I imagined I was throwing at myself.

He and I were staying in different hotels so as I burned with guilt, he gave me a long embrace and we went our different ways. Depending on how angry he made his girlfriend someday, I gave myself a fifty-fifty chance that he'd be much less enthusiastic to see me the next time. Or more enthusiastic, if it was an enthusiasm born from a furnace full of betrayal-induced anger to kick the holy fuck out of me.

—

THE TOUR ENDED EARLY, ABRUPTLY, in Florida. It was clear to me and everyone that I was too fucked up to continue. My old friend Gus Brandt, who had promoted our shows and put us up whenever we played Pensacola in the '80s, took me to a small airport somewhere in Florida to send me home.

Once, years earlier, Gus had taken the whole band to the Pensacola Interstate Fair on a day off. The fairgrounds featured a booth where, for a couple bucks, you could be recorded singing to backing tracks of any number of popular songs and then receive a cassette recording of your efforts to treasure forever. Of course, Lee Conner couldn't wait to get behind a mic for his star turn. The minute he locked the door to the see-through-plastic-walled booth, I went into carnival barker mode, yelling, "Meatloaf! Come see international recording artist Meatloaf sing! Meatloaf! Hey people! Come hear Meatloaf!"

Within minutes, a large crowd of adolescents and then adults gathered around the fairground booth. When Lee stepped back into the bright sunlight after finishing his ecstatically applauded and enthusiastically received performance, he was swarmed by the crowd, clamoring for a moment with Meatloaf. Though he glared daggers at us, we couldn't hold back our laughter as Lee stalked away clutching his cassette, ignoring the requests for autographs. Being mistaken for Meatloaf was a semi-common occurrence, one that he hated more than anything.

Florida was darker this time around. Gus drove me to the airport during a massive storm. I lay on the grass outside his car for half an hour, puking violently in the pouring rain.

"C'mon, bud. Please, Mark, you've got to get up or you're gonna miss your plane."

"I can't do it, Gus. Can't I just sleep here for a while?"

"Mark, it's freezing out here and you're completely soaked. C'mon now, let's get you up off the ground," he said, trying to gently coax me up.

"Gus?"

"Yes, Mark? What, buddy?"

"Can I just stay here in Florida and live with you?"

"You've seen my place, man, you know there's no room for you. Where would you sleep? In the kitchen?"

I said nothing. I was drunkenly heartbroken he had denied me. I loved Gus.

"All right, that's enough of this horseshit, now *I'm* drenched. Get the fuck up or I'm leaving you here for the cops to pick up."

And with that, he pulled me up off the ground and walked me into the tiny airport. He had to do some negotiating with the ticket clerk, but eventually smooth-talking and hyperintelligent people-person Gus convinced them to let this obviously shitfaced, soaking-wet drunk on the plane. After enduring a long, drunken embrace from me, he turned to go, and I was left alone.

I began to dangerously weave out onto the runway carrying a ridiculously large umbrella they'd given me at the gate. The gale-force wind instantly, savagely, tore it from my hand. I stood for a second and watched it fly a mile away in the blink of an eye. Pushing against the blasting wind, I traced a wandering, serpentine path toward the waiting plane. I climbed unsteadily up the stairs, fell into the first open seat I came to, and passed out. I was awakened by the pilot shaking me by the shoulders at some other airport where I was to catch my connecting flight, the last person left on the plane.

6

TINY DAGGERS

IN THE '90S, MAJOR LABELS SPENT SICK AMOUNTS OF MONEY making videos that might never be seen by anyone, putting their bands on the road, and especially recording albums. Almost all of it was paid from recoupable advances that bands would ultimately be on the hook for, so unless you were lucky enough to have a hit and sell a shitload of records, you were simply racking up a huge debt with the company, money that would eventually come out of any royalties you might make but also money that was in most cases never recouped. Record companies spent vast amounts of dough signing a bunch of bands, only to throw them like wet dog shit against a wall and wait to see which ones stuck and which would slide to the ground, out of sight, into oblivion.

Despite the disaster that was our first tour on Epic, we were shortly thereafter booked on another tour of the US. After six years as a band, we would have our own tour bus for the first time, an expense paid for by the record company as "tour support." We were to meet the bus early one morning in the same Green Lake, Seattle, neighborhood where I still lived with Dylan and where, by now, nearly the entire band lived within a few blocks of each other.

The night before leaving, I started searching through my stuff to find my sleeping bag, one thing I always took with me on the road. After scanning the place, I could find no trace of the brand-new one I'd recently bought and planned to take with me the next day. I had slept in a bag on the road for years: on the couch in our van, while forced to share a motel-room bed with a bandmate, even if I got my own room. I disliked sleeping on the suspect sheets of the shitty subpar motels we frequented, and there was no way I was sleeping on a tour bus in some cum-stained bunk where hundreds of scumbag rockers had jacked off into their socks without a sleeping bag now. When evening rolled around and I'd still not located it, I asked my roommates if anyone had seen it.

"Oh fuck, man, I forgot to tell you. Your sister came by and grabbed some of your stuff a while ago. She said it was okay with you."

I straightaway hit the roof. For years, my older sister Trina had been coming by my place and simply taking whatever she pleased from my room for herself. I'd once stopped by the place where she lived with her darkly deranged husband and had been pissed off to find a lamp, an antique standing ashtray, and some of my other belongings in their front room. We'd had a violently tempestuous relationship as children, as teenagers, and into our young adulthood but had slowly become friends. By this time, I considered our relationship to be a close one. This just made me that much angrier when I found out she'd taken an item essential to my touring comfort. I called her on the phone and demanded she return it at once. To my acute vexation, she told me she didn't have it but had taken it out to her husband's sailboat, currently moored in the middle of a bay on Bainbridge Island, a ferry ride from Seattle. Determined to have it back, I demanded she go get it.

"No can do, bro, I'm all tied up. Just go buy a new one."

I had just bought this bag and would be damned if I was gonna turn around and spend money on another one. Plus there was nowhere open that time of night to get one.

"How do I find the boat?" I asked impatiently.

"It's not really easy but here's what you do. Take the ferry to Bainbridge, drive around the island to Eagle Harbor Drive Northeast. There you take a left and will eventually come to a dirt road. Follow that to the end and you'll come to a chain-link fence with a shed on the other side. There's a small hole in the fence but if you can't fit through it, just climb over. Then, next to the shed there's an old rowboat that belongs to whoever owns the property. Take the boat, get in the water, and row out to the middle of the bay. You're gonna need a flashlight to find our boat because it's just one of many that are moored out there in the water. It's white with a green roof."

I was so pissed off that I hung up the phone before she was even done talking, but I had scribbled down her vague directions. If I wanted to get over there and back before the last ferry of the night, I had to leave now. My girlfriend Anna had planned on spending a final romantic evening with her touring, ne'er-do-well boyfriend. She grumbled but eventually agreed to join me in my quest to retrieve the sleeping bag.

After exiting the ferry, we followed my sister's directions all the way to the fence. The hole was so small neither one of us could fit through, so I hoisted Anna to the top of the fence and then followed her up and over. Not knowing who or what we might encounter, I quietly searched for the rowboat we had been instructed to "borrow." We slipped it into the water and began rowing for what seemed like forever out toward the shadowy figures of these hulking vessels in the middle of the bay. With only the wholly insufficient illumination from the tiny flashlight we'd found in the glove compartment of Anna's car, we finally came upon a large, decrepit sailboat that, judging from the peeling white-and-green paint job, I figured must be my sister's boat. After rowing completely around the outside of it, we finally found a way up to the deck and after tying the rowboat to the ladder, climbed aboard.

I brought the flashlight down into the dank, terrible-smelling cabin and there on the floor, covered in the hair of my sister's Great Dane and soaked in some kind of foul-smelling boat motor oil, was my previously pristine sleeping bag. Had they been there, I would have murdered my sister and her creepy husband both and hoped for a manslaughter charge.

Back on deck, as I ranted in psychotic detail about the revenge I planned for my sister, Anna tried to calm me down.

"Hey, baby, sit down for a minute and check out the lights. It's a beautiful view."

I sat beside her on the roof of the sailboat's cabin. Determined as I was to not allow anything to puncture my murderous anger, I had to admit that the view was nice. Across the water, the lights of downtown Seattle glimmered and pulsed. We sat quietly for a few minutes before I took a pipe out of my pocket and filled it with weed. We shared it, silently enjoying the still beauty of the water, the lights, and the night. At some point, we began to make out. My pants came down, she got on top of me, and we began to have sex. She knew from much experience that that was the quickest, easiest way to divert my attention from anything that irritated me. I loved being with her as I was so completely hooked on her body and her ability to quickly reason through things that sent me off on an angry tangent. I loved her talent to quiet my mind.

After fucking, we realized it had gotten late. We got back in the row-boat and I began to work with some power to get us back to the car and then to the ferry before it quit running for the night. I noticed some heat and slight discomfort in my ass cheeks and thighs—maybe just the action of my ass against the seat on the rowboat? By the time we reached shore, it had become acute irritation. Halfway to the ferry, my ass and legs were burning. By the time we got off the boat in Seattle, I was in screaming agony, my ass totally in flames, itching and burning intensely, just the weight of my jeans bringing extreme pain.

I called Poison Control as soon as I got home, sure I'd sat in indus-trial solvent or some such irritant. I explained in detail to the woman on the phone exactly what had taken place directly preceding this excruci-ating episode.

"Well, I don't know how else to say this," she said, "so here goes. What I'm understanding is that you rubbed your bare butt fairly hard back and forth on an unfinished fiberglass surface for twenty minutes. You're going to have to go to the emergency room where they will remove as many of the microscopic slivers as they can. But it's likely you're going to be in some pretty major discomfort for at least a week or more."

It was two a.m. and we were meeting the bus at six thirty. There was no possible way I was going to the emergency room for several hours of fiberglass removal. I threw away the jeans I'd been wearing, then soaked in the bathtub until six a.m. Then I grabbed my suitcase and walked gin-gerly the two blocks up the street to the waiting bus.

By the end of that first week, my entire ass was covered in a huge painful scab. I felt it every step, every minute of every hour of every day of that uncomfortable tour as the tiny slivers of fiberglass worked their way to the apex and out of my skin. I was able to get a script for some Percocet 10s at a clinic somewhere along the way, but the bottle of ninety was gone in a couple days. They didn't do much for the pain in my ass, but I did enjoy the way a handful made my head feel.

That was my life in a nutshell: a stolen moment of desperate plea-sure, an assful of tiny daggers, then an eternity of agony. That theme had repeated itself over and over again, a constant throughout my entire time on earth. As quickly as my mind jumped from one scheme to another, I was, at the end of the day, a slow learner, an extremely slow learner afflicted with the lack of self-awareness to even realize it. I always thought I knew it all, but I was only ever motivated into action by one of two things: pleasure or pain.

7

FIRED, REHIRED, AND A THOUSAND FORMS OF FEAR

WHEN I RETURNED FROM TOUR, ANNA AND I MOVED INTO OUR OWN place, an apartment one block from Harborview Medical Center, a major emergency trauma hospital on Seattle's First Hill (or Pill Hill as it was commonly known due to the multitude of hospitals in a relatively small area). With Harborview one block to the west, Swedish Hospital three blocks to the east, and Virginia Mason about five blocks to the north, we were surrounded by the sounds of ambulance sirens and all manner of other activity on all sides. Desperate to mitigate the damage from my uncontrollable drinking, I had begun secretly dabbling in heroin. My alcoholism had become so raw that I would have tried anything to save me from its expanding horrors. Heroin neatly disappeared my need to drink while I was using it, and I picked up a small habit pretty quickly.

———

WHILE I WAS WALKING THROUGH the shadowy yard of a Capitol Hill dope house one night intending to score some heroin, I chanced upon Layne Staley, the charismatic and switchblade-quick singer of Alice in Chains, the first Seattle band to hit it big. Though we'd never formally met, we knew each other by sight so we quietly shook hands. Layne shot me a sly smile.

"Are you here for what I'm here for?"

"Yeah, I am, but my girl can't know about it," I said because Layne's girlfriend, Demri, was an acquaintance of Anna's. We entered the stairwell together but when I headed up, Layne turned to head down.

"There's better shit down here. And cheaper," he said over his shoulder.

So Layne hooked me up with a new, better connection in the same building where I'd already been scoring. It was, as they say, the beginning of a beautiful friendship. He was one of the most naturally hilarious, magical, mischievous, and intelligent people I'd ever met. At times, he had a mystical, otherworldly aura. We spent days and nights on end together, making each other laugh until we lost our voices. Then he would fall into elaborate comedic pantomimes, eliciting more painful laughter. Once, while we mindlessly watched a late-night rerun of *Jerry Springer*, I began to howl at the fucked-up, totally bizarre expression on the face of one of the guests. Layne, who had been sitting on the floor in front of me, suddenly turned around. He had the exact same seemingly impossible-to-imitate expression himself. I lost my mind in hysterics. His perspective on life, love, and everything else had a profound influence on me. He was the first friend I'd ever had with the ability to calmly change my mind and patiently show me there was more than one way to view every situation. Before Layne, I saw everything in strict black and white. He was every beautiful shade of color on the wheel, as well as many that had never been seen before. It often felt that he was not of this earth but instead some spiritual being from elsewhere. After a while, Layne felt like the brother I'd never had.

—

I NO LONGER NEEDED SCREAMING Trees. As things had worked out, shortly after returning from our last tour on our first disc for Epic, Sub Pop had reached out to me and we had repaired our fractured partnership. I'd begun making another record for them with a substantially bigger advance than what I'd received for the first. Not having to split it with three other guys nor being forced to spend it all on an expensive producer and studio, I knew I was gonna be fine.

But halfway through making my second album for Sub Pop, Bruce and Jon invited me for lunch and, curiously, arrived carrying the canned spools of analog tape from the recording sessions I'd been working on, not a great sign. Without ordering any food or even being seated, they dropped the tapes on the table.

"Mark, we don't want you on the label any longer. You can have your tapes and do whatever you want with them, but we're finished and we're not paying you the rest of the advance."

"May I ask why?" I inquired, but I knew I had given them a million reasons. I was a pain in their ass, I was never willing to toe the company line, I had never toured to support my first album, and I'd become accustomed to raiding the Sub Pop warehouse on a regular basis and then taking the records I'd snagged to local used record stores and selling them for drug money. Most glaringly, I'd never mended the fence from when I'd threatened and humiliated Bruce in his office. (He had told Dylan Carlson that he was sure there were bodies buried under my house, to which Dylan had replied, "Well, that would be my house, too, so . . .") I came to find out that the real reason was that the company was broke: I was just the first deadweight to be jettisoned.

"Your records don't sell and, frankly, we can't pour any more money into your projects," Jon replied.

I noticed a slight smirk from Bruce, as he was obviously enjoying springing this unwelcome surprise on me. They turned and exited the place and left me sitting there with a pile of tapes in metal canisters, slightly confused, slightly bummed, but immediately formulating my next move. I estimated it would take $2,000 to complete the nearly finished record, so I began to search for an independent label willing to give me that small pittance. It was fruitless. None of the connections I'd cultivated through the years were willing to sign me, to license my record, nothing. My prospects were dim enough that I began to hope that Epic would pick up the option for another Trees record, something I'd previously dreaded.

Early one morning around six a.m., my phone woke me up and I groggily answered it. It was a poor connection and I nearly hung up before I heard a faint, unfamiliar, and obviously English voice on the other end of the line.

"Hello, is this Mark Lanegan?"

"Who's calling?" I asked gruffly, irritated at being awakened in this way.

"Hi, Mark, it's Ivo Watts-Russell here from 4AD Records. I was wondering if you'd be willing to have a conversation with me. I've not called too early, I hope?"

I was instantaneously wide-ass awake. 4AD was a highly respected UK label, a much cooler British version of what Sub Pop was in the States. All of their bands had a dark, moody beauty, and each of their records had unique packaging that somehow adhered to a singular aesthetic. To me, 4AD was the gold standard of indie record companies. I also felt like the quiet music I'd been working on had more in common with 4AD's roster than it did with anyone on Sub Pop. My mind raced. What was the genius owner and architect of this label doing calling me at six in the morning? Could it be possible he was interested in signing me?

"Hey! Of course not! What can I do for you, sir?" I asked in my most sincere ass-kissing voice.

"Well, Mark, first off I've called to tell you that I and everyone here at 4AD are huge fans of *The Winding Sheet*. It's the most beautiful, real recording. I simply adore it."

"Oh, thank you, man, that means so much to me. I'm a huge fan of your label, your bands, and all your records," I gushed. Could my luck really be this good? Was this guy going to actually step in and offer me a deal right at the moment I had exhausted every angle to put together a lousy two grand and find someone to release my album? No way! It couldn't be possible . . . but it happened before . . .

"Now, the reason I've called is I wondered if you'd mind talking to me a bit about how you achieved this beautiful record? How was it recorded? How did you get the wonderful space and wonderful sounds?"

If he wanted to know how the sound was achieved, he was talking to the wrong guy. Only Mike Johnson and Jack Endino could tell him the specifics; I had just been along for the ride. But I nonetheless imparted what I could about the instrumentation, recording process, and analog equipment we used.

"If you don't mind, why are you so curious about this stuff?"

"Well, Mark, we have an artist on 4AD named Brendan Perry—you might know him as one of the singers from Dead Can Dance. We're preparing to record his first solo record and I'd very much like to use *The Winding Sheet* as a sort of blueprint for how I'd like it to sound."

Motherfucker wakes me up at six in the morning to grill me about how to rip me off? I was bummed yet undeterred. I had to pitch him my current record, only because I was out of options at that point.

"That's very flattering. I love Dead Can Dance and Brendan's voice. What an incredible singer; I can't wait to hear it when it's finished. By the way, since I've got you on the line, I wonder if I could send you a cassette of what I've been working on for a second record. It's nearly finished, I'm just trying to scrape together a couple thousand dollars and find someone to release it. If you like *The Winding Sheet*, then I'm pretty sure you'll enjoy this one. I think it's so much better."

"Certainly! I'd love to hear what you're doing. Send it on over and I'll let you know what I think."

He gave me the address to 4AD and I sent a cassette of the roughs out that day, knowing I was pissing in the wind. Since they already had a singer under contract with whom they wished to make a record that sounded like mine, my chances at becoming a part of their ultra-cool, ultra-stylized stable of bands were slim to none. A couple months later, still with no one willing to help me finish and release my record, out of curiosity and desperation I gave Watts-Russell a ring. I was of course sure to call during proper business hours at his office in London, as it was the only way I'd have a chance to catch him. To my surprise, they transferred me straight to him once I'd announced who was phoning.

"Hello, Mark, what can I do for you?" was his curt, borderline unfriendly comment when he picked up the phone.

"Hey, I'm just calling to see if you'd had an opportunity to listen to the tape I sent?"

"Yes, I did. I have to tell you it really isn't right for our label, but thank you for calling. Goodbye."

Click. Silence. End of conversation.

"What a fucking prick!" I said out loud.

"Who?" Anna asked.

"Nobody, baby, just some stupid asshole, never mind."

—

WHILE TREES SEEMED TO BE spinning our wheels, my friends' bands had shifted into high gear. A couple of months before they went into the studio, Kurt had played me the demos for his band's next record, *Nevermind*. I told him I thought they were brilliant. We had been playing acoustic guitar together at his place in Olympia a couple of years earlier when he'd written "Something in the Way," the dark and brooding tune that was to close the record. I had always known Kurt possessed genius and believed him destined for greatness, but nothing could prepare me (and especially him) for the instantaneous, explosive popularity and blinding spotlight that was about to hit him with the heat of a desecrating sun. In late September of that year, Nirvana released *Nevermind*. The record blasted them from the basement of the music world to the penthouse suite with the force of an atomic bomb, replete with toxic, billowing mushroom cloud. That explosion carried Seattle's music scene with them to the worldwide stage.

In the early days of Nirvana-mania, Kurt and I were lying on the huge bed in his room at the Hotel Sorrento in Seattle. It was just down the street from my place but it might as well have been the moon to me, the one room twice the size of my entire apartment, equal parts tawdry tackiness and out-of-reach opulence. He was living in Los Angeles by then but had come back to Seattle for some reason or another and had called me to hang. "Smells Like Teen Spirit" had taken off and suddenly Kurt could go nowhere without being harassed.

He was on the phone, arguing with someone over some financial issue. As I lay there stoned watching MTV, he got particularly angry at something that was said to him. He slammed down the receiver, pulled the cord out of the wall, and yelled, "Fuck!"

At that very moment, the video for "Smells Like Teen Spirit" came on the TV. Kurt grabbed my boot lying on the bed between us and threw a perfect strike at the television, hitting the power button and turning it off. In that same instant, we heard through the open hotel window a car rolling by three stories down blasting "Smells Like Teen Spirit." Kurt looked stricken. He groaned "No way" and buried his head in the pillow.

Nirvana's sudden celebrity coupled with the earlier success of Alice in Chains and the subsequent massive popularity of local band Pearl Jam had the brass at Epic seeing dollar signs. Epic were suddenly keen to keep the Trees around. They wanted to land us on the coattails of our friends and peers for this previously unheard-of chart takeover by so many bands from the same small, provincial city. Had the Nirvana phenomenon not been in full effect, they would have dropped us without a second thought.

After the Nirvana boom, Sub Pop were also flush with cash from suddenly selling shitloads of copies of Nirvana's first record and the rights to their contract to their new label, DGC. They had also reportedly done a deal with a major where they'd sold a piece of the company for millions. Around that time, someone at the label decided I was still under contract. Months after our lunch where they'd unceremoniously dismissed me, I got a call from Jon Poneman.

"Hey, Mark, you ready to finish that record for us now?"

I would have absolutely been within my rights to tell him, "Fuck you, man, you guys told me to get lost." But having wasted the months following our humiliating non-meal in an empty, hopeless search during which not one label had been willing to pick me up, I didn't think twice before responding.

"Yes I am! Thanks, man!"

And just like that, I was back in the game. I was so grateful to be given another chance to complete what I intended to be a masterpiece a million times more artful than my flawed first effort (and also to collect the balance of my now-restored advance) that I began happily working on the record immediately.

But with Nirvana ascending the charts worldwide, Epic also began asking us about another album. I was already five records into my unsatisfying run with the Trees and, despite my friends' success, I knew one thing for certain: the next time the Trees stepped into a recording studio, it would be done to my satisfaction . . . or not at all.

When we met up, Lee and Van were openly excited to make another record with all the attention Seattle was getting at the moment. They were also, like myself, broke. The increased money due to come our way for a second Epic offering was serious enticement for them.

"I'm sorry, guys," I said, "but I think I'm done with the band. I've been trying for years to make this thing into something it was obviously never meant to be. Lee, thank you for giving me the opportunity to sing your tunes, but I can't do another record singing your lyrics. I have no connection to them and anything I do from this moment on will be authentic or else I won't do it."

Van nodded his head in acquiescence. He had ridden that lame horse with me every inch of the way; he completely understood my point of view. Lee's reaction was, of course, to throw a childish fit, tossing stuff around in his own apartment. It was as predictable as everything else he did, the exact same behavior he'd exhibited many times over the years. I used that opportunity to leave.

A couple of weeks later Van asked me if I'd come over and have another discussion with him and Lee about a possible second record for Epic. I agreed out of curiosity. What kind of pitch could they possibly have dreamed up that I would agree to? But I also knew my history of quitting and rejoining probably had them just feeling me out. When I arrived, Van did all the talking.

"Look, man, we are as tired as you of making the same record over and over. We have been talking about it and both of us truly want to create something great."

Since they were officially drummerless and singerless at the time, it was just the two of them to have their discussions. Lee chimed in and immediately blew my mind.

"Mark, you are a great singer and we aren't going anywhere without you. If you do this record, I promise we will create it with all three of us involved at every step of the way. The lyrics will be in your hands. We will start and finish songs together as a team, not the one-man band you guys have had to be a part of all these years. I realize that we have to do things differently if we are ever going to get anywhere and make something timeless."

It was the first time he'd ever acknowledged my contribution to the band. After years of battling him for inclusion and growth, he was now, in an open and intelligent manner, saying he needed our help if we were ever going to make something great. It was also the first time he'd ever uttered the word *timeless* in conjunction with our music, and I was totally taken aback by that. It was as though he'd finally allowed himself to admit what we had seen the entire time, an epiphany years in the making. For the first time, I saw another side to this man. I had for so long considered him a monster and I was humbled in a profound way by his newfound honest appreciation of my contributions. It was like finding a stream of cool water in the desert when you were about to die of thirst.

Once again back in the band, I put my solo project on hold. We began to develop the music and form the songs that would become our breakthrough record, the album that would take us as close to mainstream success as we'd ever get: *Sweet Oblivion*.

Working in Lee's cramped one-room Capitol Hill apartment, Lee and Van would play around with riffs on acoustic guitar until we heard something pleasing. Then I would begin formulating vocal melodies and partial lyrics. The brothers had hired on the spot the first drummer to try out, Barrett Martin, Jack Endino's former bandmate in Skin Yard. They'd called to tell me about him and, sight unseen, I'd said, "Go ahead and hire him if he's that good." He was a young, talented player with crazy Afro-like hair and the huge personality to go with it, one that ran the gamut from extreme naïveté to outright pretentiousness. He had loud opinions on every subject that came up, no matter how misinformed or off the mark he might be. I was shocked at his lack of knowledge of underground rock. After a conversation about his influences, he informed me his record collection consisted of Zeppelin, Rush, and other run-of-the-mill trad hard rock but that the bulk of his listening habits had been informed by his vast knowledge of jazz. That was an art form I had zero connection to and I wondered, *How's this gonna work?*

It took a while for me to warm to this big kid, almost as physically large as myself. He attempted to out-intimidate me a couple of times, once throwing a full sixteen-ounce can of beer at my head and missing from close range. I instantly collapsed in a fit of laughter. That had diffused his anger and made him start laughing as well. His keen sense of humor, his ability to poke fun at himself, and his heartfelt compassion for people won me over. But mainly it was the ferocious artistry of his jazz- and hard-rock-influenced drumming that made me accept him with open arms. Who gave a fuck that he'd never heard the Velvet Underground or most of the shit I loved as long as he got the job done? And get the job done he did.

Barrett was a powerful and nuanced player like the Trees had never had before. After years of playing with drummers who had their own particular style but were never able to adapt, we'd learned to accept what we got, no matter how inappropriate their parts might be for any particular song. Playing with Barrett was a monumental revelation. He could not only pound like John Bonham, he could also play sensitively, with a musical sense of the big picture. And he played in time with correct and steady tempos, a talent some of our previous drummers had lacked or at least not given a damn about, probably due to the chaotic, noisy quality of our early years. Here was yet another completely different weirdo thrown into our dysfunctional mix, but that, coupled with his proficiency at his instrument, made him the perfect complement to our newfound focus and dedication to excellence. His playing was a huge influence on the hard rock sound of *Sweet Oblivion*.

After putting together a batch of tunes we felt good about, the music ironically turned out to have a more organically classic rock feel than any of our previous work. Still, we were lacking a standout, an obvious single.

One day, Van gave me a cassette he'd recorded of himself fucking around with the guitar in his garage while tripping on acid. I tried to pay attention to it with headphones on but most of it was unlistenable crap. I thought, *Van plus acid plus guitar equals shit.* As I was about to fall asleep, a short, probably minute-and-a-half-long piece of a song jumped out. It was an extremely brief, catchy riff. I could hear his drug-addled voice repeating far off in the distance "I nearly lost you" a couple times and then it was over. I rewound and listened to the snippet of a song probably twenty times. That catchy little riff was unlike anything Lee would ever write. From the two or three times Van had repeated that one line, "nearly lost you," I could clearly envision how the vocal should go. I was sure we could fashion it into a single. I phoned Van on the spot: "Van, you don't know it, but you've written a hit."

With the album's lyrics still incomplete, we played what we had for Bob Pfeifer. After I assured him they'd be done in time, he agreed we were past due to get into a studio. The decision was made to record in New York City where Pfeifer was based so he could keep a watchful eye on what for the band was a make-or-break record. We hired producer Don Fleming, who booked us into a studio with a talented engineer named John Agnello, who had begun his career as an assistant on Cyndi Lauper's huge breakout hit *She's So Unusual*.

Where Don was a methodical, studious type we all liked and respected, John was a good-natured, foul-mouthed New Yorker with a keen eye for hilarity, a classic ballbuster. We all fell in love with him and his wicked sense of humor. We began to lay down basic tracks—drums, bass, guitars. I'd sing a scratch melody with the band with whatever words I had to help them get the instrumental tracks down. I listened to the roughs in the hotel at night and wrote until I had the lyrics done.

Unbeknownst to the band, I would sometimes go down to the Lower East Side and buy a few bindles of heroin. Since it was powdered East Coast dope and it was impossible to legally buy a syringe in NYC in those days, I would simply snort it. When I was unable to get out to score, I drank heavily. Fleming actually encouraged me to drink because he was convinced he'd get a better performance out of me. I sang almost the entire record drunk, high, or hungover. But it didn't seem to matter to anyone which state I was in as everyone involved was enthusiastic about the results. For the first time ever, I sensed that we were actually making something special.

There had been a sea change in Lee Conner, something I'd previously thought impossible. It was strange and cool to witness. He had a newfound dedication to tone, and to when to play and when not to. His openness to everyone's ideas, flexibility as to song arrangement, and general good-natured spirit of cooperation were inspiring. He had been true to his word. I was finally glad I hadn't given up before we were able to collectively pull off what, until then, had seemed would never happen.

While in the city, I took full advantage of the use of record company car vouchers. On a day off, I drunkenly took a company voucher limo out to New Jersey to see a woman from Georgia I barely knew who was staying out there with her band for the night. The next thing I was conscious of was waking up in the burning-hot backseat of a small car, windows rolled completely up, baking in the hot sun with my head pounding from an obviously brutal night's or days-and-nights drinking episode. I stumbled out of the car, no idea where I was or how I got there. I heard music playing faintly in the distance and started to stumble in its direction. I was so parched and dehydrated that I wobbled into the first business I saw, seeking water. It turned out to be a cheesesteak place—I must be in Philadelphia. As I stood in line hoping to buy a bottle of water, a huge winged insect of some indiscernible variety flew into the place, landed on the hot grill, walked around on it for several seconds, then took wing up and out the door again. Seconds later I was drawing stares, dry heaving uncontrollably on the curb until I thought something was going to burst inside me, nothing in my stomach left to puke up.

I finally found the bar where my acquaintance's band were doing their soundcheck. It turned out I'd drunkenly ridden along with them to Philly and arrived passed out in their car. They'd just left me there to nearly suffocate in the airless, boiling-hot interior of the tiny vehicle. I got on a pay phone and called Fleming in the studio.

"Where the fuck are you, Lanegan? It's your night in here! Get on the fucking train and get your ass to the studio!"

He was pissed off for sure, but the hungover performances I gave that night delighted him to the point that he proclaimed them to be "the greatest vocals you've ever done! Guaran-fucking-teed!"

When we finished recording, we turned the record over to mix specialist Andy Wallace, the same man who'd mixed *Nevermind*. When it was done, I thought, *There—we finally made a good record.*

Back in Seattle, I got a frantic call from Pfeifer.

"You have to take a cassette of 'Nearly Lost You' to a hotel downtown and give it to Pearl Jam's A&R guy Michael Goldstone right now!"

"What the fuck for? What's he got to do with us?"

Bob went on to explain that Sony was putting out the soundtrack to a movie called *Singles* based on the Seattle music scene and "every Seattle band is on it but you guys!"

"Who gives a fuck? That sounds incredibly lame to me," I replied.

"Don't you get it? They're trying to fuck us! Every Seattle band on Sony and several others but not you? And you're part of Sony! It's an intentional fuckover!"

"From who, Bob?"

"I don't know, but I refuse to let it happen. Now get your ass down there with that cassette!"

Pissed off that I had to be the ambassador as well as messenger boy for the band (especially for something I considered to be weak as fuck), I nonetheless walked over to the hotel, not far from my apartment. I walked up to the counter and asked them to call Goldstone's room, a further humiliation because Bob had insisted, "You do not leave it at the counter! You put it into his fucking hands personally!"

When he came down to the lobby, Goldstone smiled and introduced himself as Goldie. We shook hands and he thanked me but then he asked, "Are you okay? You look like you're in a terrible mood."

The idea that I had to pitch something to my own record company was sitting very poorly with me. My uncontrolled displeasure must have been written all over my face.

"I'll be honest with you, man. Bob seems to think we're being intentionally fucked over by someone who wants to keep us off this soundtrack, and it's something I personally couldn't give a damn about. I'm embarrassed that I'm the one who was forced to come down here, hat in hand, and beg for something I don't even care about. It sounds totally cheesy to me."

Goldie leaned his head back and let out a loud, authentic laugh. He stuck out his hand to shake mine again and said, "I appreciate your honesty, man. If someone's trying to keep you off of this, I promise to not let that happen. I can see this was hard for you but I thank you for bringing this to me. I hope we see each other again soon. Give my best to Pfeifer."

I walked away from our meeting feeling slightly better. Goldie had been a warm, welcoming guy with a sense of humor. Who knew if we'd ever see each other again, but I had genuinely liked Goldie.

I had begun using heroin on a more regular basis, still carefully trying to not get too strung out, but I found its appeal overwhelming. It was everything that booze was not. I did not black out, get into fights, or come to with head pounding painfully in embarrassing, inexplicable situations. Heroin made me calm and relaxed and quieted my always screaming mind. I could write songs and carry on with a fairly quiet, normal life. Where my band, girlfriend, and almost everyone I encountered while drunk had loathed being in my company, everyone seemed to be happy with this new mellow version of me. But living with me day and night, my girlfriend began to get suspicious.

"What's up with you? You're acting weird," Anna would ask me in the beginning.

I would attempt to deflect her magnifying-glass-eyed attention or guilt her into silence on the subject.

"Nothing, I'm just tired," I would say, or "I'm just happy. Is that a crime?"

"What are you doing locked in the bathroom so long?"

"I'm taking a fucking bath, trying to have some peace and quiet and a minute to myself to think!" Or when I'd wrung that line dry, "It's the only room in the apartment where I can be alone and write."

My only way to deal with what I deemed an attack (and I might deem anything an attack in those days) was to attack more aggressively in return. The level of hostility in my offensive depended on my level of fear. Fear of being caught, fear of having to tell the truth, fear of being exposed as the lying, cheating fraud I was. But it was the fear of showing my true heart, at times either so full it might burst or so empty I could cry, that hounded me most viciously.

There had been a perpetual war between myself and the costume of persona I'd donned as a youngster and then worn my entire life. Petrified that someone might discover who I really was: merely a child inside the body of an adult. A boy playacting as a man. My lifelong hard-ass exterior and, underneath that, ironclad interior were all an intricately constructed, carefully cultivated, and fiercely guarded sham. I was, in reality, driven by what I'd heard referred to in rehab all those years ago as "a thousand forms of fear." Sadly, somewhere deep in my soul, I knew that was probably me.

8

NICE WARDROBE

DURING THE EUROPEAN FESTIVAL SEASON OF 1992, VAN CONNER, Mike McCready from Pearl Jam, and I got wasted together, drinking all day long in the backstage at the Roskilde Festival in Denmark. Denmark's football team was in the World Cup and the entire festival had been shut down halfway through the evening in order to show the game on a huge screen to the several thousand enthusiastic audience members. We were supposed to play earlier on the night but Kurt, who was fighting dopesickness, had insisted we play last, after Nirvana. I had tried to argue with him as he lay uncomfortably under a blanket on a couch, being administered to by a doctor, in his dressing room.

"Please, brother, we can't play after you. That will be a fucking nightmare—nobody will stick around and everyone will be pissed off that you guys didn't headline! Don't do this to me, Kurt!"

We'd had to play after Nirvana once before and were, of course, blown off the stage. In this huge setting, now that they sat atop the rock world, this was going to be much worse.

"It will be great, Lanegan. I want everyone to see how fucking great you are. I've made up my mind, you're playing last."

It was one of those rare situations when he stubbornly refused to listen to my wishes. Most days, he would patiently consider my viewpoint, even when it wasn't something he wanted to hear or do. He almost always bent somewhat to my will or at least met me halfway, treating my advice like that of a respected mentor. Not this time. I knew it was because he disliked it when I was visibly drunk. He was sick and holding all the power; his word ruled the day.

When we finally took the stage in front of the disappointed 50,000-plus concertgoers, I was beyond shitfaced. First song in, I had no monitors nor could I hear myself through the gigantic PA that blasted the music out into the audience, a singer's nightmare scenario. I realized I was singing to nobody because my microphone wasn't even on! I dropped it to the ground and sat down on the drum riser, pulling a huge drink off the bottle of booze I'd had our crew set there for me, as the band dutifully played on.

I watched as our longtime tech Jim Vincent scrambled to set up another mic stand. He then came over and shouted in my ear, "It's fixed! You can sing now!" Now in a nearly complete blackout after the ten or twelve hours of drinking leading up to this fiasco, I wobbled back up to the mic and began singing the second song of our set. Again, nothing. No voice in the monitors and if it was coming through the mains, I sure as fuck couldn't hear it. Are you fucking kidding me? This was such large-scale embarrassment that I started to lose my shit.

In a drunken fury, I tried to shove the heavy monitor in front of me off the stage. The stage crew tried to stop me but every time they came close, I lamely squared off as if to fight, looking like some phony boxer from an old silent movie. I finally succeeded in rolling one off the stage into the pit full of photographers, destroying thousands of dollars' worth of television cameras in the process. While I tried to push another monitor off the stage, the rest of the band began to ritualistically lay waste to their equipment, as much in anger toward my drunken antics as to the futility of our attempt to just play our fucking set. Lee Conner smashed his guitar to pieces on the stage and Barrett Martin did the same to his drum kit. It was carnage. Only Van, who had joined in and encouraged my and McCready's all-day drunk, stood holding his bass with eyes open wide. I recognized that he was on guard, looking to protect me should the burly stage crew actually get their hands on me.

The whole scene onstage resembled an episode of *Tom and Jerry*, a total cartoon, but the damage I caused was real. Just as the crew was about to take me down en masse, out the corner of my eye I saw Krist Novoselic rush onto the stage to intervene. He and Van Conner kept me from getting crushed, Seattle watching out for its own.

Kim White was our manager at the time, someone I'd hired on the advice of Bob Pfeifer. I trusted Bob implicitly by that point. He had taught me a shit-ton of valuable lessons about the music business, song-writing, and basically just living as an adult. Even though Kim had zero experience in management, she had been employed by major labels and had worked with some big-name "troublesome" bands in that capacity, the Red Hot Chili Peppers and others. I had parted company with Susan Silver, our first manager, at the insistence of the rest of the band who felt she didn't "understand" us. Whenever it came time to bite the bullet and do what no one else wanted to, it fell to me. Now nobody was happy as Kim continuously dropped the ball, needlessly spending band money to follow us all over the world only to do . . . virtually nothing. Too emotionally caught up in our personal problems and running vainly around trying to clean up our trail of garbage to do any real managerial work, she was out of her depth. She had, however, managed to capture that whole Roskilde debacle on a video camera. Watching the footage later, I felt mounting shame. It was a pitiful comedy of errors, brought on by the hours of hard liquor Van, Mike, and I had indulged in, and it got us banned from the rest of the festivals that season.

Nirvana was headlining the legendary Reading Festival in the UK later that summer. Kurt said they would not play unless Screaming Trees were allowed back on the bill, so we were grudgingly restored to the lineup. I made myself scarce around the stage crew, who were the same as in Denmark. All of them would have loved to have beaten my head into the ground. I would certainly have deserved it.

We went on early, one of the first acts on the main stage, right after our Washington state cohorts the Melvins. The wind was blowing crazily and my ridiculously long hair flew in a circle around my head, stinging like a whip whenever it hit me in the face. All the bands onstage early that day were pelted with shit thrown by the crowd. At one point during our show, Lee Conner stood alone at the edge of the stage, windmilling his guitar a la Pete Townshend, when a roll of toilet paper came flying toward him from the audience. As it descended, he kicked it perfectly out of the air mid-windmill without missing a beat, sending it far back into the crowd to where it had come from. The British, obsessed with football, let out the biggest cheer we ever received in appreciation of the athletic dexterity of our three-hundred-pound guitarist.

The rain hit shortly after we finished. Now the bands had to dodge baseball-sized hunks of mud flung from the crowd. When LA band

L7 were being hit with mud balls, I watched from sidestage as badass singer Donita Sparks pulled out her tampon onstage and threw it at the audience, one of the best responses to rowdy crowd behavior I'd ever seen.

As the day went on, the rain poured down relentlessly. While heading to the beer tent that night with legendary Sub Pop in-house photographer Charles Peterson, I tripped on one of the heavy ropes holding down the tents in the artists' area and went face first into the mud. I came up completely covered head to foot in the thick black shit, my face encased as if in a mask at a beauty spa. As I looked up from the ground, I saw Charles frantically clutching for the camera always worn on a strap around his neck. For some reason, he had left it inside the tent where Mudhoney had their backstage room.

"Goddamnit!" he yelled. "Of all the times to not have my fucking camera!"

"If you took a picture of me like this," I said, "I'd kill you."

Nick Cave and the Bad Seeds and Nirvana played historic sets. After drinking all day, I wound up in a bar late that night with Mudhoney singer Mark Arm and some other Seattle guys. A girl walked into the bar wearing the most outlandishly garish, neon flower-covered jumpsuit and we all fell into hysterical laughter. When I walked past a table where sat former Vaselines singer Eugene Kelly, the band Teenage Fanclub, and several other Scottish musicians, I heard some guy make a wisecrack regarding my mud-covered clothes. Never one to take the high road, especially when drunk, I pulled up short.

"You got something to say to me, fuckhead?"

"Yeah, I do," he replied, "nice wardrobe."

"Why don't you come on outside with me so you can get a better look at it while I beat the fuck out of you, wise guy?" I said, that familiar angry fire igniting in my head.

"Sure, hold on a second," he said.

I watched as, to my horror, he struggled to get to his feet from behind the table, crutches with handholds on his arms. He was obviously disabled—not injured, but afflicted with something he'd been born with, like polio. I immediately felt the burn of humiliation on the back of my neck. I'd fallen into a trap and painted a picture of myself as an ugly thug for everyone there.

"Hey, man, it's cool. Please have a seat and accept my apology," I said gently, trying to put a stop to this embarrassing scene.

"Oh no, man, I'm coming outside so you can beat me up," he replied, obviously hell-bent on shaming me. Now I started to get pissed off all over again at this shithead who was using his disability to full advantage in a confrontation that he'd actually begun by talking shit in the first place.

"Okay, dude, everyone has seen that I'm the fucking bully, point made. Take a fucking seat, I'm going back to the bar." With that, I turned and went back to my seat at the bar with the Mudhoney gang.

After a couple more drinks, I saw Mark Arm reacting to something he saw over my shoulder. He burst into laughter, spitting out his beer and almost hitting me in the face with it. I turned to see what was so funny and nearly spit out my own drink. Mudhoney road manager and well-known ballbuster Bob Whittaker had come walking through the door dressed in the same crazy outfit the girl had been sporting earlier. He obviously had convinced the girl to give him her clothes and it was an outrageous and hilarious sight.

Whittaker, long ensconced in the Seattle music community, was known as a local comedian. He was also a bit of a celebrity. Named after Robert Kennedy, a close friend of his dad Jim Whittaker, the first American to scale Mount Everest. He was also someone I always did my damnedest to avoid. Otherwise, I'd have to endure a meaningless conversation with someone whose entire purpose was seemingly to irritate me. Whenever I was trapped in his presence, he unfailingly gave me what appeared on the surface to be good-natured ribbing, but always with an underlying edge. He never gave me sufficient fire to justify a legitimate ass-kicking, but he'd gone right up to the edge with backhanded compliments and sarcastic, smart-ass comments so often that violence had naturally crossed my mind several times over the years. Bob was a king of passive aggression; he had the comic insulter's instinct and fearful intelligence as to where the line he dare not cross lay.

After the laughter died down, we continued to drink until the place closed. I found myself outside with Mark Arm, the sun coming up, the last two men standing, the still-bitter wind blowing a mini-twister of garbage, paper tickets, and all other manner of shit around our heads.

Since my band and crew had headed to our London hotel several miles away hours earlier, I had few options.

"C'mon, man, we have a room nearby, you can crash there," Mark offered. As the almost twenty-four hours of drinking had me exhausted, I took him up on it.

At that point things became a blur. I remember entering an empty room, Mark falling onto one bed and me onto another.

I came to I don't know how many hours later to the uncomfortable sensation of someone rubbing something hard against my ass, through my mud-encrusted jeans. I groggily opened my eyes. As they began to focus, I discovered I was looking at Arm, facing me a few feet away on another bed, passed out. I then noticed I had someone's arm around me. I was being spooned by some unknown person behind me. I threw the arm off me, wriggled out of this mystery person's grasp, and sat up on the edge of the bed, my alcohol-tortured head splitting in agony as though I'd been axed in the face. I finally looked over my shoulder to see who my bed partner was.

There lay Bob Whittaker, still dressed in the girl's comically festooned jumpsuit. I couldn't help but smile painfully at the sight of him in the outlandish costume, still dry humping the air in his sleep, my ass no longer within reach of his dick. As I silently sat there, wiped the fuck out and totally hungover to the verge of nearly puking, Arm opened his eyes. He looked at me and slightly shook his head with an expression that spoke of momentary horror and regret, as though he couldn't believe how damaged he was and what we'd done to ourselves. He turned over and went back to sleep. I stumbled outside, found a shuttle going into London, got in, and passed out.

I woke up at some fancy hotel in the city, got a cab, and rode over to the dump of a bed-and-breakfast in Shepherd's Bush where we always stayed. I had arrived with just enough time to change my clothes before catching a ride to the airport with the rest of my bandmates, then onto a flight headed back to Seattle.

9

YEAH, THIS IS THE COPS!

AS I WAS LEAVING A WELL-KNOWN HEROIN DEALER'S PLACE LATE one rainy afternoon, I came face-to-face with one of Anna's friends, a coworker at her Mexican restaurant job, on her way into the house. A friend who, although there to buy the drug herself, was predisposed to disliking me for my increasingly public indiscretions, my sleeping around, my staying out all night, my thoughtless and rude treatment of Anna. Now she had me cold. If she was willing to give herself up to my girl as a junkie, I knew I was going to feel some pain from this brief encounter. Sure enough, a couple days later I came home to find Anna sitting on the couch, arms crossed and as visibly upset as I'd ever seen her. On the coffee table sat a couple of used rigs, a blackened-bottomed spoon, and a small amount of dope I'd stashed inside a small canvas sack under the insole of a shoe inside my closet. My feeble ruse was clearly done, dragged out into the sadistic light of day. I had been busted with fire-red hands, and I instinctively went straight to the front lines.

"What the fuck are you doing searching through my shit? That's totally fucked!"

"Don't put this back on me, you son of a bitch! You've been lying to me for months. You made me into somebody who has to search to get to the fucking truth, liar!"

My praise for heroin's calming effects on my mind and the positive role it was playing in quelling my urge to drink fell on entirely deaf ears.

"If you can't quit drinking, you go to AA, you don't become a fucking junkie! What is wrong with you? Your thinking is so incredibly messed up."

"You're right, baby. The last thing I need right now is to get strung out on dope," I finally confessed.

What I did not confess, however, was the fact that I was already strung out. Not with a huge habit yet, but if I ever attempted to take a day or two off from using, I definitely felt it in an unpleasant way. I could control it. I was sure I could control it. I told myself I could control it.

Sweet Oblivion came out in the fall of '92, two months after the *Singles* soundtrack that had been such a big deal to Pfeifer, and apparently to everyone else at Sony. Our first single, "Nearly Lost You," became the only song of ours to ever make the charts, as well as the only video we ever had in MTV's regular rotation. Not only had I grudgingly gotten it included on the hugely successful soundtrack, "Nearly Lost You" became one of the most popular singles from it. It was a double-edged sword. Our song, in heavy rotation on MTV, spurred sales of the soundtrack, but by the time our record came out, it was already old news. I later learned that all the bands on it had also gotten hefty pay-days for their tunes. Mudhoney received twenty grand for the use of their song but we had been forced to waive our sync fee for the fucking "privilege" of being included at all. In other words, we'd given them a hit single for absolutely nothing.

Our album went on to sell somewhere around 300,000 copies, well short of the half-million sales required for a gold record. I remember reading somewhere that we were raised to our peak in record sales due to the soundtrack. I knew the reverse was true. We'd shot ourselves in the dick for the sake of the soundtrack, a soundtrack we'd helped to sell, never receiving a single penny in payment at the expense of our own album. A soundtrack to a film that I had been told by friends who'd seen it was just as corny as it sounded when Pfeifer had first told me about it, a lame and sap-filled farce of a movie. It was supposedly set in the "Seattle Scene," but sounded like an episode of *General Hospital*, an obtuse bandwagon jump if ever there was one. To me, it may as well have been the Spice Girls film. Seeing a poster for it featuring actor Matt Dillon in a terrible wig was as close as I ever got to watching it. That poster, plastered all over town, told me more than I ever cared to know on the subject. Years later, while drinking together post-gig in a NYC bar, I stuck my lit cigarette into the pocket of Matt Dillon's suit jacket when his back was turned and set it on fire while I walked away.

—

SOON AFTER THE RELEASE OF *Sweet Oblivion*, the Trees found our-selves touring America again. During an East Coast swing in October, we were scheduled to appear on *Late Night with David Letterman*. A couple nights before the show, we had a day off in the dying tourist town of Asbury Park, New Jersey. I woke up in our shitty waterfront hotel near the empty boardwalk. With no drugs to speak of and too hungover to go up to NYC to get some, I started drinking gin. I could always drink gin. By eleven a.m., I was fairly messed up.

When evening fell, after a half dozen phone calls from Anna where I repeatedly denied drinking or using, I finally decided to go out and get the lay of the land. I thought I might prowl around and scare up some dope but quickly put that idea out of my head: this place was as quiet as a tomb. Walking through a cavernous empty building along the seaside in the dark, I suddenly felt a chill run up my spine and started shaking like a wet dog in the thick and misty cold sea air. I glanced down and noticed I had not one, but two used condoms stuck to my boot. It was time to quit sightseeing and get the fuck inside, someplace warm.

Back at the hotel, I found out that some of the band and crew were going down to the Fast Lane, the bowling alley where we were booked to play the following night. I went along and started drinking for real, throwing back double after double, having a rare good time out with my bandmates.

In the haze of a near blackout, I thought again about scanning this stone-dead neighborhood for drugs and headed for the exit, still carry-ing my drink. As I passed through the door, a rotund bouncer grabbed me by the throat with one hand and batted the drink out of my hand with the other.

"Goddamnit, I told you idiots, no drinks outside!" he yelled.

Without thinking, I immediately clubbed him in the face with my fist, knocking him backwards off his barstool and down the three or four steps out of the place. Another bouncer then shoved me down the same steps. Right behind me came Trees drummer Barrett Martin, suddenly caught in the fray. As I drunkenly scrambled to get up in the street, I grabbed a large piece of wooden signpost lying in the gutter.

Barrett and I found ourselves back-to-back, surrounded by four very round, very large goons. The weight of the two-by-four was too much for me in my inebriated state and I dropped it just before it pulled me over. The bouncers closed in and the six of us began trading punches. It was a long couple of exhausting minutes before an armed security guard appeared out of the gloom and broke it up.

The guard took us back inside to have the manager decide whether or not to call the cops. When he found out who we were, he let us go but also refused to let us play the next day. I later discovered what had primed the pump for our fight: Van Conner, the Screaming Trees' massive bass player, had come out the door right before me. When asked to leave his drink inside, he had told the doorman to go fuck himself. I welcomed having a day off and went up to NYC that next afternoon to score some heroin and cocaine.

The next night we made our national television debut performing on *Late Night with David Letterman*. I had a bruised black-and-blue eye and Barrett was unable to play because his shoulder had been dislocated in the brawl. Sitting in the greenroom where we were required to hang out during the afternoon hours before our performance, I drank from a pint bottle of gin hidden in the inside pocket of my jacket. I looked on with a kind of curious bemusement as the featured guest, actor Jeff Goldblum, read aloud from some book in a huge, affected, obnoxious voice as he walked quickly up and down the empty hallway alone for at least an hour. It was like being forced to watch some bizarre preparation of an audition for a role in a tedious, weird Shakespearean play.

I thought, *What the fuck man? Is he on coke? Is this how a serious thespian prepares for a talk show?* I concluded that he was just a weird fucking dude. I put some headphones on and listened to Suicide's *A Way of Life* on my Walkman. I loved them and that album in particular always got me jacked up. There were many days I would take my first shot of heroin with Alan Vega's creepily affected voice saying, "Yeah, this is the cops, yeah, she's wild in blue" over a propulsive industrial electronic beat as the soundtrack to my morning fix. Just as the Dead Kennedys were the only thing I wanted to hear while on acid as a kid, I had my favorite music for shooting heroin. While shooting coke, I needed total silence.

Finally good and drunk, it was time to play. With Steve Ferrone filling in on drums, smiling stage manager Biff Henderson held my drink as we galloped unsteadily through our current single and still best-known song, "Nearly Lost You," while Paul Shaffer chicken-necked behind us. Letterman, with a well-known propensity for ridiculing heavy people, liked us enough that he called us out again at the end of the show to avail ourselves of the catering. While the Conner brothers dug in, I took the opportunity to wing some food at Lee's head, accidentally catching an unamused David Letterman with the shrapnel. It devolved into a full-on food fight ending with Van trying to force a carved pumpkin onto Lee's head. It would be seventeen years before I'd be allowed back onto the show.

10

HOUSE OF PAIN

IN NOVEMBER OF 1992, WE BEGAN ANOTHER TWO-MONTH TOUR OF the States, this time playing in the middle slot on a bill with Seattle band Gruntruck opening and Alice in Chains headlining. Offstage, it was an insane, dark, drug-and-alcohol-fueled frat party from start to finish, with Layne and I raising hell, behaving like teenagers, staying up days on end. We partook of whatever drugs came our way: heroin, cocaine, painkillers, anything. On one particularly pleasing night, Alice in Chains bassist Mike Starr pulled Layne and me aside.

"This chick I was hanging out with gave me this and told me you guys might want it." He pulled a large bottle out of his coat. "She said it's called Dilaudid."

Layne and I both grabbed for it at the same time while trying not to look too eager.

"Thanks, Mike. Yeah, we can probably find something to do with it."

We spent several days shooting the Dilaudid in a hazy bliss. When it was gone, we resumed drinking like madmen until we were able to get our hands on some opiates again. One night while riding on Alice's bus with Layne, we got so shitfaced we tore apart the back lounge of the bus in a drunken frenzy, leaving a huge mess. Susan Silver had come out and joined the tour for a few dates in her capacity as Alice's comanager; the next day I was ashamed to receive a kind yet stern talking-to from my now ex-manager who told me that Layne and I were to clean up the mess immediately and that I was no longer allowed to ride on their bus.

I witnessed some of the greatest performances I had ever seen, by anyone. Alice in Chains was like some massive apocalyptic machine onstage. No matter what shape Layne was in, no matter how little sleep we'd had, he would fucking kill it every night. Guitarist/singer/ songwriter Jerry Cantrell, the architect behind their sound, delivered nuanced but powerful vocal harmonies that gave their songs their unique, haunting, one-of-a-kind quality. Layne was such a monster vocalist. I was amazed that after partying with me the previous twenty-four hours, Staley could get up and roar in a voice so painfully powerful you could feel it physically while watching from sidestage. He was the most singularly impressive hard rock singer I would ever hear, up there with some of the greats from my youth—Rob Halford, Brian Johnson, and even Freddie Mercury, all guys I'd seen play live as a kid. In my mind, Layne was in their league.

We found it effortless to meet girls to hang out, have sex, and party with. On a weekend off somewhere in Florida, Layne and I were having a round-the-clock party with three cute girls we'd met after a show. Every couple hours, I would leave the hotel, go out to our tour bus, and grab some beer. At the time we had a temporary bus driver, a total redneck. Each trip to the bus to grab more booze, I had to walk past him and a tough-looking, mannish woman seated next to him in the front of the bus. She wore a denim vest covered in dozens of truck-stop buttons with corny country witticisms written on them.

After I grabbed what I'd come for, I would leave through the same door, say, "Thanks, Roscoe!" and then head back up to the party. On the way out after my umpteenth beer run, I said, "Thanks Roscoe!" once more. This time, his female companion angrily heaved herself up, blocked the exit, and yelled in my face, "His name is Royce, goddamnit!"

Another bus driver we used had been a part of country singer Sonny James's band in the '60s. He was now a hardcore Christian evangelist and he tried his damnedest to convert us to the ways of Jesus. One day, I heard the Righteous Brothers tune "Unchained Melody" for the first time and was so captivated by it that I listened to it nonstop on my Walkman the entire day. While parked at a truck stop, the driver had come up to me, talking and gesticulating wildly, as I sat smoking a joint. I was irritated that I was obliged to take my headphones off for a second to hear what he was saying.

"You sick SOB! You owe me a Bible, MF-er!"

His angry, abbreviated expletives drew huge laughter from everyone on the bus. Turns out I had been rolling joints with pages torn from one of his personal Bibles. I'd not known where the book had come from and used it because it was all I could find.

"Whatever," I said and went back to the song.

He quit that day.

We had a show in Philadelphia on November 25, my birthday. To celebrate, Layne and I went back to the hotel to get high. We ran into the guys from the rap group House of Pain, who were staying in the same hotel. Their single "Jump Around" was a huge hit at that moment. Lead rapper Everlast was a nice guy, and with a wide smile, he invited us to come hang out and party. Before we joined him, we each did a shot of some powerful East Coast white powdered heroin. By the time we got up to Everlast's room, I was in such a heavy nod that I could barely lift my head off my chest. I remember Layne telling Everlast, "It's cool, he just smoked some great weed" and not much else.

While playing a show in Boston two days later, I got so drunk that I was like a rag doll on rubber legs. At one point, I found myself on my knees in the crowded dressing room going down on a hot red-haired stripper. Whenever the door opened, a group of audience members could clearly see what I was doing but I didn't care. Whenever I was drunk, all decorum went directly out the window.

On the tour bus driving to Montreal that night, I noticed a slight tightness and heat in the crook of my arm where I had injected the dope in Philly. By the time we arrived in Quebec, my entire arm was swollen twice its normal size, flaming hot, and apple red.

My road manager first took me to see a doctor in a seedy medical building. The moment I took off my shirt, the doctor said, "You have to go to the hospital immediately. You have a blood infection. You'll be lucky if you don't lose that arm."

Later, on a gurney in the basement hallway of the French-speaking hospital, a doctor hooked me up to IV antibiotics. With a ballpoint pen, he drew a line around the inflamed, scarlet area from my shoulder to my wrist and said, "I'm gonna come back in twelve hours. If the redness has gone outside the line, I'm afraid we're going to have to amputate your arm at the shoulder."

At the show that night, Layne got up onstage with the Trees to sing some of my songs in my absence. Afterward, he came to the hospital to see me. He broke down in tears for a minute at the sight of me lying in the hallway with my huge, bright-red swollen arm.

A cute French girl I often hung out with when in Boston had traveled with me on the bus to Canada. She came to see me as well. After speaking to a doctor in their native tongue about my condition, she looked at me with profound sadness and shook her head before also breaking out in tears. I was starting to feel like this might not turn out in my favor.

Sleeping that first night was next to impossible with the constant crying and moaning of the elderly woman in front of me and my mind racing about the possibility of losing my dominant arm from the shoulder down. Late at night, as I was almost asleep, out of the break room directly opposite me in the narrow hallway came a rousing version of "Happy Birthday" in French. I snapped and yelled, "Shut the fuck up!" The break room door slammed shut.

I awoke the next morning to something heavy landing on my chest and some hot liquid hitting me in the face. I opened my eyes and saw the large male orderly who had just dropped a breakfast tray on me, splashing hot coffee in my face. With an evil smile, he leaned down and whispered in a heavy French accent, "Still happy, rock and roll?"

I was never to get into a room, just a gurney lined up with several others in a subterranean hallway. Every twelve hours for the next eight days, someone came by to look at my arm.

"It looks like it's getting better. We may be able to let you go tomorrow," one doctor would say.

Hours later, a different doctor would say, "If this thing isn't better by tomorrow, we may have to take it off."

I tried to console myself with the pitifully small doses of painkillers they gave me, and I became obsessed with getting head from one of the street hookers outside before I lost my arm. My close friend John Hicks, who some people not unfairly referred to as my "bagman," was working as the Screaming Trees' drum tech. While the rest of the band kept traveling with the tour in case I was released and could rejoin them at some point, Hicks had stayed behind in a flea-bitten motel near the hospital to keep me company. He had been my close friend for years. I'd met him in Seattle, where he'd come from Johnson City, Tennessee, bringing with him the thick, heavy Southern accent many Europeans, and even some Americans we'd come across, found confounding to decipher. I loved him and his balls-out courage in his role as my surrogate and closest ally. He was one of the first people I'd ever done heroin with and we traveled together for years.

Every day he tried to get a hooker past security with the idea that I would roll my IV stand down the hall to the stairwell to receive one final blow job as a two-armed person. Much to my consternation, it never happened—the security guard at the door was particularly vigilant and immediately wised up to Hicks's game. In a stagnant fury, I envisioned Hicks in his motel room, getting endless rounds of oral sex from the hookers outside, scoring dope for himself and not sharing it with me, while I was laid up in this grimy, soot-covered hallway, amputation imminent, bored to fucking death with sick, elderly French-speaking homeless people as my only companions. Unable to get off their gurneys, most of these unfortunate souls were faced with the indignity of having to shit in bedpans in plain view of everyone else. The whole place constantly stank like a hole-in-the-floor Italian gas-station toilet. I thanked God I could at least walk to the restroom when I had to. By the end of my stay, Hicks steered clear of me to avoid my wrath at his failure.

Finally, the swelling subsided. After eight days—during which I did nothing but hit up nurses and doctors for painkillers, berate Hicks, and obsess about sex, drugs, and amputation—I was released. Not for one moment did it cross my mind that I had done this to myself. I wasn't built like that. God forbid I should change my way of living. John and I rejoined the band in Cleveland, where he and I spent our first evening back partying with two strippers all night in the hotel sauna, which we'd broken into after hours. I eagerly accepted the first blow job one of them offered and the next day immediately started shooting dope again. Self-reflection and soul-searching were not in my limited vocabulary.

A few weeks later at a show at Los Angeles's Palladium, Everlast tracked me down backstage before the concert.

"Hey, man, I got something for you," he said with a huge grin.

I quickly ushered him into an empty room where he broke out a large bag of pungent weed. I couldn't hide my disappointment.

"Oh damn," I said, unable to mask the letdown.

"What's wrong, bro?" he asked with a puzzled look on his face. Suddenly I felt like an asshole.

"I'm sorry, man, I just thought it was something else."

"But you were so high in Philly . . . I thought you'd appreciate it."

"Dude, I so appreciate it . . . but I just quit smoking."

11

DRINKING BLOODY WATER

IN EARLY 1993, WE HEADED FOR EUROPE, AGAIN OPENING FOR Alice in Chains. After doing my last shot in the restroom on the plane several hours earlier, I arrived in London on the edge of dopesickness. Layne and I hooked up with an American guy we knew named Craig Pike, our London connection at the time. He had previously done a brief stint as bass player in Iggy Pop's band. Now he squatted in a large decrepit house with no electricity or running water, playing bass for London band Thee Hypnotics, strung out and scoring drugs for people to feed his own habit. Though I liked Craig, I found his predicament pathetic. I would certainly never sink that low, you could fucking count on that.

We stayed strung out the entire tour. The effort it took to stay well was a full-time job. We were entering a new country almost daily and clearing customs could be a several-hour affair. Drug-sniffing dogs were brought on board our busses to go through every bunk and snuffle around in every corner while their handlers emptied out our pockets and went through our wallets. Sometimes we were compelled by border agents to unload everything out of the trailers—equipment, personal stuff, everything—and have customs officials with dogs search through it all, looking for contraband or unreported merchandise. It became a regular practice for us to try to finish as much of the drugs we had on us before leaving one country and entering another. We'd stop a few miles before a border crossing so we could dump anything we still had: drugs, paraphernalia, syringes and spoons, etc. Unless we had a connection already lined up, this meant hitting the streets to score immediately upon arriving in the next city. Since my junkie pal John Hicks from Tennessee was still traveling with us at the time, it meant we needed heroin and works for all three of us. It was often easier to find the dope than the needles and we were loath to snort the powdered dope. We'd become so accustomed to shooting the black tar heroin we used back home that unless it was going straight into a vein, you were just wasting good gear. Not only did we need outfits and dope but you also had to use citrus to break down European dope before injecting it. It was rumored that if you were to use lemon juice instead of the powdered citric acid found in shops, you risked fucking up your eyesight, possibly losing it altogether. Nonetheless, there were several times we arrived at a hotel late at night with no bar or room service open and we found ourselves prowling the hallways, looking for a slice of lemon left in a glass on someone's room service tray placed outside their door.

Eventually, I found a hiding place. Inside one of the bus's bunks, there was a tiny, unnoticeable crack in the wall of the huge vehicle's interior where I was able to conceal just one syringe, carefully bleached to remove any scent. It was a good thing, because due to timing or circumstance, we were unable to procure any new rigs for several days. Layne, Hicks, and I used that same syringe often enough that it became so dull we took to sharpening it on the rough part of a matchbox before every use, like an ancient knife on a primitive whetstone. It was critical we were never caught with it while going through a border. Getting caught meant probable incarceration, a permanent ban from the country, and the confiscation of the bus and all the equipment by the state authorities—a massive fuck-up with the most serious consequences.

One late night after arriving in a new European country, the three of us quickly found some heroin on the street, then went back to my bus to retrieve the syringe. We used my key to get in, but as the bus wasn't connected to any electrical source, the interior lights didn't work. Carefully, and out of habit, quietly we fumbled and felt around inside until we finally found the bunk by illumination of a cigarette lighter. Hicks had the skinniest arms so he got up in the bunk to try to fetch our needle. Though he tried and tried, his sweating, trembling dopesick fingers just could not latch on to the rig in the darkness. Several minutes passed with mounting anxiety: we *needed* to get well. Finally, Hicks succeeded in extracting the outfit from the tiny crevasse and took the cap off to confirm the needle itself was intact. We collectively let out a yell of jubilation. From the bunk directly below our hiding spot came a blood-freezing scream as the bus driver, who unbeknownst to us had been sleeping there, awakened in fright. Startled, Hicks swung his arm out and buried the needle in my upper arm.

"Goddamnit, Hicks!" I shouted in pain.

"The fuck's going on in here?" yelled our British bus driver in the darkness of the hallway.

"Nothing, man, so sorry to wake you," I said through clenched teeth while pulling the needle out of my arm, relieved to find it still usable.

Our Benny Hill routine finished, we got off the bus, went inside, and proceeded to get well, once more holding at bay the sickness that now dogged us every minute of every day.

Like any traveling addict trying to stay ahead of the devil of withdrawal, we found ourselves in many situations where, due to our obvious need, we spent what sometimes felt like an eternity in the company of unsavory, damaged, or borderline dangerous people, some of them legitimately out of their minds. People we'd not willingly have hung out with under any other circumstances, like the couple of elderly hoarders who sold dope out of their council flat in the UK, so impressed to have musicians in their place.

"So you lads are musicians, then, how exciting it must be. You know, we have nearly every Cliff Richard record ever made. Sweetheart, sweetheart! Go find the Cliff records to show these lads."

"Oh, piss off, Johnny. You go find them. I can't find a bloody thing in this house!"

No surprise there. I grew more and more dopesick as we were forced to sit among the huge piles of squalor for an hour and a half, drinking tea out of filthy cups before they finally broke out their wares. They let us do a shot in their utterly disgusting, never-cleaned bathroom, then tried to entice us to stay even longer with the promise of some "surprise" supposedly on its way. We did not hang around, as I felt it might end up being like the surprise Lincoln got at Ford's Theatre. And so we split.

There was the surreal, comically entitled Swedish couple we forced ourselves to sit with in the back lounge of the Alice bus outside a concert hall in Ghent, Belgium. A nonstop stream of pretentious, mind-anesthetizing drivel poured from their mouths like the putrid liquid poison you simultaneously shit and puked while kicking dope cold turkey. In agony, we listened to the young blond girlfriend, as narcissistic as she was physically beautiful, work slowly through the incredibly long list of bands she'd partied with who were, in her estimation, so much better than us. I nearly lost my shit, my personal patience well exhausted by the time they finally produced a bag of heroin and another of coke to sell us. Our disdain for them was so great that, when we were finally rid of them, we nicknamed them "the King and Queen of Sweden" and they became our touchstone for the worst Europe had to offer. It was people like these—two sides of the same agenda-ed, opportunist and condescending, cat-shit-encrusted coin—that we were forced by our circumstances to spend time with on a regular basis, along with every other stripe of hustler, hipster, huckster, or street person.

Back in London after playing around the continent for a few weeks, Layne, Hicks, and I spent a day in a hotel room relaxing and getting high. It was an unseasonable heat wave in the UK and we were happy to be able to hang out in the relative coolness of the room together, no commitments or show, no trust-fund drug-dealing snobs or degenerate freaks to endure. We were free to just lie around, catch a nod, and listen to British TV shows playing quietly in the background. In between doing the odd shot of dope every now and then, we cleaned all of our rigs out in the same glass of water that, after a while, turned pink with blood. We thought nothing of cleaning our syringes in the same water. We had been sharing needles for so long that if one of us had something, we all had it by now.

Out of the hazy blue came an unexpected knock on the door. Hicks got up to see who it was and, not bothering to put anything away, Layne and I continued to nod while sitting at a table together. John opened the door just a tiny crack. Suddenly, the King and Queen of Sweden, the same couple of Swedish assholes we'd been unable to tolerate in Ghent, came bursting through the door, pushing Hicks's slight, skinny frame out of the way. The pleasant high I'd been carefully nursing all day was instantly eradicated.

"Oh my fucking God! It's SO hot out there! We've been out there for hours!" the unbearable blond said.

"Thank FUCK we finally found you guys!" she continued, fanning herself for dramatic effect. She stormed into the room as though she owned the place. Her pompous, sweaty dealer boyfriend followed behind, carrying several bags of what looked to be newly purchased women's clothing.

"Oh my fucking God! I'm so thirsty!" she squawked. She scanned the room till her eyes locked on to the tumbler of pink water sitting on the table between Layne and me. To my slow-to-unfold surprise, she charged across the room in a blur of motion, reached right past me, and grabbed the glass filled to the brim with tepid, rancid boutonniere-colored fluid, tainted with the blood of three hardcore international junkies.

It all took place so quickly, I couldn't find my voice. High as fuck, I tried and failed to form words, then began to raise my arm to stop her. Layne clocked my look of horror, then grabbed my arm and squeezed it tight in a gesture that was unmistakable: *Let her drink it.*

In a flash, she had raised the glass straight to her lips. The Queen of Sweden was clearly someone who took whatever she wanted when she wanted it. As we watched in shock, horror, and macabre delight, she slammed the entire contents of the glass in a matter of seconds.

When we finally managed to get rid of these two extreme irritants an hour later, it felt as though we'd been held hostage in our own home by a party of drunken ex-rugby-players-turned-crooked-politicians. The three of us looked at each other, exhausted by their mood-destroying unwanted company and rude, boorish behavior. We slowly began to chuckle at what had transpired, at first quietly shocked and relieved, worn down, yet quietly amused. Eventually we began to howl, falling around the room in hysterics, laughing ourselves sick, tears of comedic joy pouring out in unceasing pleasure, like survivors of a grenade attack. The astounding crescendo of this unexpected reunion with these arrogantly grandiose, know-it-all dickheads had been indelibly stamped in our brains. Playing it out over and over in our mind's eye caused round after round of spontaneous spasms of laughter. Just when I thought I was too exhausted to laugh anymore, we would look at one another and start howling again over what we had silently watched happen as the Queen of Sweden bum-rushed our private party and then what she'd so ignorantly, indulgently, and recklessly helped herself to.

The revenge was so perfect, so poetic, it was like a Greek myth. We laughed for what felt like hours until we were completely spent. It was the first thing that came to mind when I woke up the next day and again I laughed until my guts were aching. You could not have scripted a more fucked-up scene, complete with perfectly cast character actors, if you tried. If I'd ever met someone more deserving of a drink of water, I couldn't remember who.

12

STRUNG OUT AND EXHAUSTED

WE WERE, EVEN IN OUR MIDTWENTIES, STILL WILD, UNRULY CHIL-
dren, a gang of misfit toys basically rampaging across the world, enjoying the success of the concerts, the adoration of the audiences, and the
joy of making music. After years of playing shows, it was the first time I
was singing music I believed in for large crowds, and I took pride in singing as powerfully as possible every night. Whether it was an up-tempo
rock song at the top of my range or a quieter number that took some
nuance, I finally felt like a legitimate rock singer, singing songs I'd had a
part in the creation of, singing lyrics I'd written that had personal meaning to me. The fact that it was a tour in support of a great band who
were my friends and whose music I loved and whose audiences reacted
enthusiastically to our music made me that much more grateful. Experiencing it all with the Alice guys as crazed, like-minded companions made
it an unforgettable good time.

After a concert in Zurich, we had several days to travel to Helsinki.
We got on a ferry; where, I couldn't say. It was a long, slow ride to Finland, well over twenty-four hours. The three of us heroin addicts on
the tour had procured some methadone in Switzerland, and although it
didn't get you loaded, it kept you well. Anticipating a potential nightmare, we had made sure we'd brought enough to get us there and back
to wherever we played next.

The boat was impressive, with several large casinos, a dance hall,
shitloads of bars, even an auditorium filled with seats raked back from
the stage to the ceiling, just like a rock venue. They used it to film a popular TV game show for live broadcast; in what country, I hadn't a clue.

After a few hours of boredom and no private room rented in which to chill, I began to drink. I was disinterested in all of the ship's "luxuries." I drank in the bars, I drank in the disco, in the casinos, everywhere else possible. I even watched a bit of the game show as they filmed it in front of an audience filled with rowdy, drunken idiots. Many of the passengers rode back and forth on the ferry just to get smashed and raise hell. They'd purchase round-trip tickets, party all the way over, then get right back on the returning boat just to do it again. I watched a drunken disabled girl drink dry a beer bottle full of urine someone had snuck onto her table, a drunken man fist-fighting his drunken son, a man filling his hat full of puke, and a parade of further sickening, B-movie house-of-horror scenes.

I suddenly came to—how much later, I didn't know—in a tiny, unfamiliar room to the piercing shriek of an intermittent alarm coming through a speaker hidden somewhere in the place. Then, through the same speaker came first a message in one unknown language, then another, and finally in English.

"Alert! If you are still on the ferry, it is time to disembark. This is your final message!"

I got up, my head pounding with a godforsaken, bell-ringing hangover. I fought my way through a maze of hallways until I ran into a uniformed member of the crew who pointed me in the direction of the foot-traffic exit and said, "Hurry!"

I walked off the boat into the blinding sunlight of the far northern spring and saw my entire band and crew standing in the distance. As I slowly approached the guys, I could see that they were clearly none too happy, pissed off, I assumed, because they'd been forced to wait for me.

"We've been out here for two hours waiting on your ass," said my road manager.

"Why didn't someone come get me?" I asked.

"Because we had to hide you in a cabin last night, and then we couldn't remember where it was. The ferry cops were trying to catch you and put you in the boat's jail."

"Ferry cops? Boat jail? What the fuck?" I asked with incredulous confusion. "What for? What'd I do?"

I braced myself for an embarrassing, unpleasant reply.

"You punched a couple guys out on the dance floor of the disco."

I couldn't believe what I was hearing—(a) I was never a dancer, and (b) I had zero recollection of dancing or fighting or any of it.

"Yeah, man, we got you out just in time. They actually have cops on this boat and they were looking all over for you. You'd be in jail here in Finland right now if they'd caught you."

Glad to have escaped the ignominious fate of being busted for belligerently harassing dancers, I only hoped none of the Alice guys were privy to this knowledge. If they were, I'd never hear the end of it.

We played in a smallish club called the Tavastia in Helsinki that night, and after our set I cruised the crowded bar looking for female companionship. I caught sight of a hot black-haired girl dressed in fishnet stockings and short shorts and made my way toward her. She opened a beer and handed it to me with a devilish smile; we started making out minutes after we made eye contact, openly, in plain view of a gang of people, at least some of whom I presumed had just seen me singing onstage. I never gave a fuck; I'd foolishly do anything I felt like within full sight of the public or anyone else.

After Alice in Chains were finished and the place began to clear out, my new friend told me she had to split if she was going to catch the last tram home.

"Don't worry about that, you're staying with me in my hotel." She wasn't so sure but I did my best to convince her. "Don't you want to fuck? You can take the tram home in the morning."

She smiled and reached down to squeeze my cock through my jeans and said, "Okay, let's go fuck."

"Wait a minute, I'm not even sure where we're staying yet. Let me go find my guy and figure it out."

"You better be staying—I just missed my last ride home!" she said, sounding concerned all of a sudden.

"Don't worry about it, baby, just a second!"

I went inside and searched the place until I ran into my road manager.

"Where's our hotel? Do you have my key?"

He looked at me as though I were an idiot.

"Hotel? What are you talking about, dumbass? We're leaving in five minutes, we're going to the airport."

"Fuck, man! Can I stay and catch another flight? I've got the hottest chick outside waiting to fuck me!"

"No fucking way, dude, you are coming with us. Now."

As we piled into a passenger van, my final memory of Helsinki was of the girl, standing on the now dark and empty street, screaming, "You fucking asshole! You fucking liar! How am I supposed to get home now, you prick?!" I asked my road manager if he had any local dough I could give her for a cab but he had none. We drove away with her still standing in the street, flipping me off until we'd turned a corner and she disappeared from sight.

—

IN OSLO A COUPLE DAYS later, Layne caught sight from the stage of some large, obnoxious man forcing his way through the crowd, physically throwing girls around on a mission to get to the front of the stage. Once he'd arrived there, leaving a few injured people in his wake, he began to yell at Layne in Norwegian. I watched from the side of the stage as Layne stopped the show and, through the microphone, invited the man onstage so he could share his very important news with the entire audience. Layne reached down his hand and pulled the lumberjack-sized prick out of the crowd and up onto the stage. The minute the Neanderthal got onstage, he raised his arms in the air and began to parade around like a buffoonish version of Muhammad Ali. I went on high alert, in case some violence was about to go down and Layne might need my assistance. When the huge lug turned toward Layne, he was met with a vicious straight right to the face that knocked him clean off his temporary podium, back into the packed audience. Layne Staley, victorious by knockout. No assistance necessary.

The crowd screamed their hearty, grateful approval. The security guys in the venue dragged the staggering, bloody-faced former bad guy off the floor and out of the venue.

The next day, however, the Oslo police department showed up at our hotel and took Layne down to the station to arrest him, confiscate his passport, and charge him with assault. Kevan Wilkins, Alice's quietly unassuming but badass British tour manager, went down to the station to try to sort it out.

Wilkins had come up in a rough neighborhood in Birmingham. We'd been told by somebody close to him that as a young man he'd been an amateur boxer, a good one, and it was easy to believe. He had begun his career in the music business as a bodyguard for Marc Almond. During the height of Soft Cell's popularity, Kevan had supposedly accompanied Almond into a myriad of dark, dangerous underground kink-filled scenes, private BDSM clubs. Wilkins's job had been to stay close and keep Almond safe while he leveraged his massive fame for all the heavy sex situations he could get into. We could never get Wilkins to reveal the details, but he stoically implied that it was pretty shadowy, down and dirty.

Wilkins had the aura of a man who'd seen all there was to see of this world and was the last person you'd want to fuck with. After Layne had been grilled for hours, Kevan was finally able to secure his release and his passport. The tour moved on. We wrapped after a couple more shows and I finally got on a plane for home, strung out and utterly exhausted.

13

ENJOYING THE IDIOT

BACK HOME IN SEATTLE, MY ADDICTION BECAME THE BE-ALL AND end-all of my day. I became an animal led around and around the cage by heroin as the prize, like cheese to a rat. I found myself living the same day over and over: copping, using, finding ways to get dough to get more. I was broke all the time, pouring every cent I had on hand into the bag. I also continued to try and maintain the sad, pathetic charade of sobriety for my girlfriend, but she had been long wise to my bullshit. As I sought escape in the needle, she sought escape from me.

—

IN THE SPRING OF '93, we went out on our own headline tour of the States. It was probably just the third we had played since our disastrous first tour for Epic. In the meantime, we'd played quite a few opening runs and one memorable short tour with Dean Wareham's band Luna opening for us. Dean had been the singer of Galaxie 500, the band that had directly inspired me to begin my alternate gig playing quiet music. Drunk or high most of the time, I made myself a daily nuisance by asking him at their soundchecks to play a Jonathan Richman song he'd covered on the first Galaxie 500 record, a version I loved. He grew tired of that very quickly and it never elicited a smile from him. I enjoyed their music very much and would be surprised when he deigned to interact with me, but then it would only be for him to make some droll, witty remark that always felt as if it were meant to go over my head. He'd directly influenced the direction I went in as a solo artist, something he never knew.

While at the 40 Watt Club in Athens, Georgia, I had introduced him to an employee there who I'd had an intermittent sexual relationship with for a few years. Sparks flew between the two of them and I was glad he got laid and felt good I'd had a hand in it, but he remained just as icy to me afterward as before. Not that he'd needed it, but so much for helping a dude out. From the very beginning straight through to the end, he carried himself with the self-respect of a serious person, and viewed me, as usual, as a buffoonish cartoon character. I couldn't help but think that he was an artist who felt it slightly beneath him, a tiresome chore probably, to open the show and be forced to play before us shameless hillbillies. Honestly, I could hardly blame him. It would have embarrassed me, too, had I myself not been the source of the embarrassment.

My favorite memories from that tour both happened on the same night. The first was when two incredibly gorgeous young Asian strippers made it their instantly obtained goal to fuck me together to celebrate one of their birthdays at the infamous Phoenix Hotel in San Francisco. When the sun came up that morning I realized I was actually on the balcony outside my room fully naked with the two nude young women. Even though I'd been drinking less than usual that night, I had no idea how we'd ended up outside, but I had always had a slight exhibitionist streak in certain situations so it was not a surprise I might end up publicly fucking. I became aware of the ridiculous nature of the spectacle when our soundman, coming back after a night of drinking, said, "Hey, bud, you might wanna move your party back inside" as he walked by. The second great memory of that tour came earlier that night at the show somewhere in the East Bay, Oakland, I think. I had been swinging the mic around onstage by the end of the cord a la Roger Daltrey of the Who when it came off its tether and flew across the entire length of stage where Stanley Demeski, Luna's slightly older, seemingly unathletic drummer, formerly of the much-loved New Jersey band the Feelies, standing sidestage, snatched it nonchalantly one-handed straight out of the air. A magical grab worthy of Willie Mays. A beautiful hall-of-fame catch. He was a lovable character and, like their entire band, a world-class musician. Once I had a functioning microphone in hand again, I took a moment to acknowledge his achievement to the audience, which many had witnessed, and the applause was deafening.

Now we were out again. Our openers this time were the Portland, Oregon, trio Pond and a band from Illinois called the Poster Children.

From the get-go, it was obvious the Poster Children were unhappy to be on this tour, the two brothers in the band standoffish and the female bass player in tears every other day for some reason. Only the drummer, John Herndon, a friendly, young, ultra-talented kid—someone I always heard Van Conner refer to as "Spider"—would ever hang out with us. The rest of the band were a drag to be around. We were not their cup of tea, neither as musicians nor people, and the feeling was mutual.

Only the second day of the run, I overheard their bass player, Rose, talking shit about me: "That idiot thinks he's Jim Morrison!"

That was one comparison I had grown to hate. While a more mature person would not have given it two seconds' consideration, it rankled me. Idiot, I could live with, even agree with. Morrison, I could not. True, one of the very first songs we had played as a band at our earliest practices had been a sped-up, punkish version of the Doors classic "The End," patterned after the Dickies' version of "Nights in White Satin." And on *Clairvoyance*, the Trees' terrible first full-length record, I'd been fucking around in the vocal booth and ad-libbed an over-the-top bit of obviously fake Morrison spoken-word jackoffery to amuse Steve Fisk, who'd recorded it. But Jim Morrison was far from the vocalist I sought to emulate. It was Jeffrey Lee Pierce, John Cale, the Leaving Trains' Falling James, Chris Newman of Portland's Napalm Beach, and Ian Curtis of Joy Division who I worshipped and wished to sing like, not Morrison. As our visibility increased and the Morrison comparison became the norm, I grew to regret the bad joke I'd allowed to be released. Nearly every article about us in any magazine would dig up his grave to compare us, not just claiming I sounded like him but also that I looked, acted, and drank like him as well. I was bummed out every time I came across the weak, lazy, lame "tribute." After I heard Rose utter that comment, I made it a point each day to be extra kind and thoughtful around her.

"How are you, Rose? So nice to see you today. What a treat it was to hear you play last night. Hope you have a great show tonight!"

Knowing she dissed me only made me more attentive, as thoughtful as I could be, forcing her to interact with the fakest, nicest version of myself possible, as all the while I was thinking, *Uh-oh! Look who's here! Get ready to enjoy the idiot, lady, 'cause he's comin' to see ya!* I made it my personal mission not to let a day go by that she could escape talking to me, my own mild version of Chinese water torture.

Pond, on the other hand, were the kind of guys who were fun to be around: unpretentious, good old Northwest boys. Their music was catchy and energetic with lots of good songs and a couple really spectacular ones. We established a comradery of sorts, both of us underdogs in the shadow of the great Northwestern invasion of popular bands, but for different reasons. Pond were one of Sub Pop's newer bands, the Trees nine-year veterans of the same smallish rooms we played nightly. Though it was a newer experience for the Pond guys, both bands were frustrated to be saddled with the unfortunate distinction of being "another band from Washington/Oregon."

It was easier procuring heroin in the States, but as my habit grew, it got trickier staying well. My drug buddy John Hicks's official title was drum tech, but his paramount responsibility was scoring on the street when I couldn't get away to do it myself. I also had a connection in Seattle, a dealer named Tommy Hansen who had played guitar for one of Seattle's '80s hard rock/metal bands, Crisis Party. Tommy would FedEx heroin to me a couple times a week. It was such a grind for us to keep up our habits via street scoring in an ever-changing landscape or the cold-sweat-inducing bitch of waiting for FedEx. You'd sit there, dopesick but forcing yourself not to ask at the front desk if they had something for you, instead waiting for them to alert you so you could at least weakly protest that you were not expecting a package and had no idea where it came from if this was the unlucky time the cops were waiting when you went to the hotel lobby to retrieve your clandestine relief.

Dave, the drummer for Pond, was himself a fledgling addict, just beginning to dabble with heroin. He had hit both Hicks and me up for dope many times but there was no way we were sharing or selling any of our shit to this amateur. Hicks in particular found it hard to take this harmless but slightly pretentious wannabe.

"If that pussy asks me for dope one more time," he had said one day, "I'm gonna punch him out."

That was a comical statement as John was a slight and skinny Southern white boy, all of five foot six and a hundred and thirty pounds soaking wet. Yet Hicks had balls of steel. On those occasions when I was unable to hit the streets with him in order to score the medicine that kept us well, he'd walked alone into what at that time were some of the most notorious, dangerous dope spots throughout the US and Europe and would not only survive, but return with our coveted, much-needed heroin. Places like Cabrini-Green in north Chicago, Dupont Circle in DC at three a.m., San Francisco's Tenderloin long after midnight. The huge housing projects of East Coast cities—Albany, New Haven. The combat zone in Boston. West Baltimore. Every city down the coast, Maine to Miami. He was also my only source of comic relief, doing endless routines, hilarious impressions behind the backs of all the guys in the band and crew. Such was his obsession with the character of Barney Fife from *The Andy Griffith Show* that once while we had a gig in Knoxville, Tennessee, only a hundred miles from Hicks's hometown of Johnson City, he'd waited for hours outside the backstage door of a local theater with the express mission of meeting Don Knotts, who had acted the role of Barney on TV and was now performing there in a play. Hicks had stood in the sun all afternoon just to meet him face-to-face. The greeting was accomplished guerilla-style with John ambushing and introducing himself to the startled actor completely in character as Barney Fife himself. Don Knotts had laughed nervously and posed with Hicks for a Polaroid.

Barney Fife, Gomer Pyle, Ronald Reagan, and Richard Nixon were favorites, but Hicks could uncannily imitate almost anyone, including people we had just met, and all for my personal entertainment. He was a one-of-a-kind character, an undersized, fearless badass. A long-and-greasy-haired, heavily tattooed loner who looked like the kid from the wrong side of the tracks all the straight kids in junior high school had feared. I loved and relied on him greatly. He was my one indispensable luxury.

One weekend during our tour with the Poster Children and Pond, Trees had an obligation for a one-off show somewhere. After a couple days, we joined back up with the other two bands at the Trocadero in Philadelphia, the same place we'd played with Alice in Chains the night I'd given myself a life-threatening blood infection with a dirty needle.

At the gig, in the upstairs backstage area, Pond's drummer Dave went on and on about the great powdered dope he'd scored in New York City that weekend, bragging about how powerful it was. After a while, he asked us if we needed anything.

"No thanks, man," I said. "We're covered."

"What do you got?"

"It's cool, bro. Like I said, we're good."

He wouldn't give up.

"Yeah, but what do you have? East Coast dope? West Coast tar?"

Hicks, in his heavy Tennessean accent, finally spoke up.

"Dude, we have our dope, you have yours, so why don't you just shut the fuck up and do it."

"Wow, man. Sorry. I just wanted to see if you wanted to trade some with me."

"Why would you want to give up your killer East Coast dope for some shitty tar?" I asked.

"Oh, just to change it up, you know."

"Let me see it," I said.

Dave pulled out a fairly large bag of what looked to be decent dope. I traded him a tiny piece of tar for a large portion of his bag.

Our new big-time managers, Peter Mensch and Cliff Burnstein of the powerhouse management company Q Prime, had come down from New York City for the show and we were to have a short business meeting afterward. They had at one time managed the country/folk/rock artist Steve Earle during a period of his heavy addiction, and because of that, it had been an unhappy, unproductive, and troubled association. When we'd left Danny Heaps, our short-lived previous manager who had also managed Steve Earle for a time, and then signed with Q Prime, he'd called Peter Mensch on the phone.

"Congratulations on signing the Trees," he had said. "If you enjoyed working with Steve Earle, you're going to love Lanegan."

Peter had told this story in front of the rest of the band during our first meeting, for which they'd flown to Norway in wintertime to make things official and meet us in person, the deal already done. They had signed us despite the warning, albeit with a decent idea of what they were dealing with in me. Until now it had not really been an issue, and I was trying to be on my best behavior. Q Prime were a legitimate heavy-weight in the rock management game and I knew what an incredibly lucky break it was for them to take us on.

Onstage that night, we played a particularly powerful show. I felt like we had the crowd in our hands as they were especially responsive and enthusiastic. After two encores, I ran up to my dressing room, cov-ered head to foot with and clothes totally soaked in hot sweat, hoping to do a quick shot before my managers got there. When I came through the door, the first thing I saw was Pond's drummer Dave halfway on the floor, head hanging off the edge of a chair, skin totally gray, his lights completely fucking out, obviously OD'd and probably dead. I almost lost my mind.

My first impulse was one of total anger that he had done it in my pri-vate backstage area. I habitually spun around and scanned the room for Hicks, seeking his help, and quickly realized he was downstairs packing up the drums. My dope addict's instincts kicked in and I immediately began to try and bring Dave back. I threw an empty beer tray of ice water on him. No response, not even a twitch. I slapped his face as hard as I could. Still nothing. I stuffed ice down the front of his pants while screaming his name, shaking him, and finally lifting up his not small, life-less body and walking him around the room. I was so jacked on adren-aline, walking straight offstage to this twisted death scene—which, as it was happening in my personal dressing room, implicated me—I thought I might have a stroke.

Charlie, the slightly nerdish, nice-guy guitar player from Pond, walked into the room and began to freak out. This had reached what felt like a critical point.

"Call a fucking ambulance!" I yelled at him.

I continued to walk Dave's lifeless body around, carrying all his dead weight, screaming at him to come back. I knew Cliff and Peter would walk through the door at any minute and that would be the end of our brush with power management as we'd already had the one discussion regarding my heroin habit. I heard the sound of sirens in the distance through the open window. This was it, the end of my career, and the end of this dumb rookie's life.

Then I saw Dave's eye twitch. I dumped another tray of ice water over his head and as I heard Mensch knock on the door and say, "Mark?

Everything okay in there?" Dave finally half opened his eyes. I told his bandmates Charlie and Chris, the levelheaded bass player, to get him the fuck out of the room through the side door. They got him out of the building just as the ambulance showed up. Everyone denied calling them, saying it must have been a prank call.

That wasn't the first or last time I brought someone back, but it was one of the most memorable and harrowing. It was, however, the last time I traded some shitty tar for someone's "killer" dope.

14

NOT BAD, YOUNG FELLA

IN THE MIDDLE OF OUR SPRING '93 AMERICAN TOUR, WE WERE booked to perform on *The Tonight Show*. For twenty years, *The Tonight Show* had been broadcast from one of the dozens of studios in Burbank, the longest-running talk show and for years the only late-night program of its kind with its wildly popular host, Johnny Carson, the undisputed king of the genre. But Carson had retired in '92 and been replaced by the pelican-jawed former stand-up comic Jay Leno. Leno was a drag as far as I was concerned. Letterman blew Leno out of the water in every category: humor, intelligence, and quality of engagement with his guests.

To make matters worse, when we'd done the Letterman show, we'd only been required to arrive in the afternoon, run through the tune once or twice, hang out a couple more hours, then shoot the show and get the fuck out. Leno required our attendance from early morning till well into the evening, a tedious all-day affair. The night before the show, they put us up at some fancy hotel on Sunset Boulevard in West Hollywood. A town car was scheduled to arrive at eight a.m. to take us over the hill to Burbank to ensure that the shoot came off without a hitch.

Trees A&R man Bob Pfeifer was in Los Angeles at the time, staying at his place not far from the former home of disgraced and exiled film director Roman Polanski, the house where Polanski's wife, actress Sharon Tate, and several other people had been brutally butchered by members of the Manson Family in 1969. Bob called me in my room to tell me how psyched he was that the band was gonna be on *The Tonight Show*.

"This is great for the band. I want you guys to kick ass, like on *Letterman*."

Bob had heartily approved of my refusal to allow Letterman's makeup department to conceal my black eye and had been delighted by the melee at the show's close. Bob was an old punk rocker at heart and he had perceived our drunken performance as rebellious and cool.

"Okay, Bob," I said. "What should I do, punch Leno in the jaw? I'm pretty sure I could hit that target no matter how loaded I was."

"Hey, goddamnit! I didn't say anything about being loaded! Keep your shit under control, do you hear me?"

"Yes, Bob. Just kidding. I promise we will kick ass."

"Good. I'll see you tomorrow."

I ordered some room service on the record company's dime, then proceeded to cook myself up a large shot of the dope that a Hollywood dealer named Maria had delivered to my room. She was my main connection in Los Angeles for several years and was happy to bring the dope to me, which I greatly appreciated. Unlike Seattle, where you couldn't bribe a dealer to come to you, Maria would always deliver.

After midnight, I couldn't really catch a nod or fall asleep, so I did a bigger shot. This time I managed to catch a nod but came out of it around three thirty a.m. to the sound of the TV blaring. I got up and turned off the sound, but before going back to bed I decided to cook up the largest shot yet. I'd be damned if I was gonna be awake all night and then go do this all-day wank-off TV affair tomorrow.

I had always quickly developed a huge tolerance for any drug I was using. I'd had to do nearly twice the amount of anyone else I knew just to get close to the same results they enjoyed. It was never easy for me to cop a buzz of any sort, such was my mammoth-sized tolerance. Yes, I'd get blackout drunk, but only after drinking copious quantities of hard liquor nonstop for several hours. It took determination.

In my chichi West Hollywood hotel room, I prepared a huge hit. I was expecting diminishing returns as I'd already done quite a bit already, so I decided to augment my high with a couple Klonopins, a sedative anti-anxiety drug in the same general category as Valium, Xanax, or Ativan. I lay back down on the bed with my feet where my head should've gone, lying flat on my stomach, drowsily watching TV with the sound muted.

As I started to drift off, I turned over on my back and, with no pillow under my head, finally fell asleep.

I came awake with a start and shot straight up. My lungs were on fire. I'd been lying flat on my back but somehow in my sleep I'd moved and my head had been hanging off the end of the bed. I began to try to cough up whatever was in my lungs and throat, burning so intensely I was barely able to breathe. I ran to the sink and poured a glass of cold water. It felt like hot lava going down and didn't provide even the most meager bit of respite. Just the opposite—it intensified the burn. I coughed and spat and cleared my throat again and again but the fiery nightmare would not abate. It felt like the worst case of heartburn but in my throat and down into my lungs. After fifteen minutes of this hopeless routine, all I'd done was make myself so light-headed I thought I might pass out.

I realized what must have happened. As I lay there sleeping with my head hanging off the bed, some stomach acid had come up into my throat and I had breathed it into my lungs. The effect had been instantaneous and brutal, a painful burning that I could not relieve and a sudden inability to get sufficient oxygen into my lungs. I sat there for two hours just coughing, retching, trying to clear my throat of this insane burning, but there was nothing I could do to relieve the torment of this malign malady.

The phone rang: my wake-up call. I'd given myself an hour to get dressed, do a morning shot, and then head down to the lobby to join the band and crew for a ride to the *Tonight Show* studio. Fuck all that now; I'd been fighting for two hours just to get a proper breath. With tears pouring out of my eyes, and sweat pouring off my forehead into them, I could barely even see. I stuck my head under the tap in the bathroom sink, running water over my head and face. I dried my hair with a towel for ten seconds, put on my clothes, and stood on the balcony to try once more to cough this shit out of my lungs and airway. I could not believe my chest was melting down only fifteen minutes before we were to head over to perform on one of the biggest national TV shows. Forget about my usual morning cigarette and shot of dope. I weighed my options and realized I had only one. I had to go downstairs and get in the car.

When I got down to the lobby, our guitar tech Danny Baird stopped in his tracks.

"Jesus Christ, Lanegan, what have you been doing all night?" he said, assuming I'd been out on the town carousing, judging from my bright red eyes and swollen red face.

"Don't ask," I was able to squeeze out between bouts of unmitigated coughing and wheezing.

I got in a car with Van Conner and our road manager. My incessant loud, grotesque-sounding attempts to clear my throat immediately elicited stares in the rearview mirror from the driver.

"What the fuck's wrong with you, man?" Van said.

"I was sleeping with my head hanging off the bed and I must have breathed in some stomach bile or something. Fuck, man, this is insane."

I rolled down the window and spat again and again out of the car, feeling shaky, light-headed, and impaired in a way I'd never experienced before. Did I need to go to a hospital? Was I going to be permanently damaged? Was I going to fall out? Would I ever be able to sing again? My anxiety began to spiral out of control.

About a year after I had managed to quit drinking in 1983, I had begun to have these frightening episodes. Out of the clear blue, I would suddenly be gripped by the terrifying sensation that I could not breathe. Try as much as I could, it was impossible to get a deep breath. The more I tried, the harder it became to get a breath at all. Then my heart would seem to start beating crazily, and in a few seconds, I was sure death was right around the corner. Stroke, heart attack, brain hemorrhage? The first couple times, I rushed to the emergency room only to find that the medical technicians couldn't find one thing wrong with me. I saw doctor after doctor, blew hundreds of dollars and went heavy into debt: nothing. A frustrating, baffling year later, I was lying on the couch with my eyes closed and the TV on when an ad for an upcoming episode of the show *20/20* made me sit up and pay attention. "America's secret plague! Panic attacks! Tonight on *20/20*!" I'd stopped having them by then because a girlfriend had begged me to see her uncle, a doctor fresh out of Johns Hopkins medical college who was starting his own practice. No way I wanted to see yet another doctor only to hear there was nothing wrong with me, but since it was free, I went, mainly to please her. After listening to a detailed account of what had plagued me the past year—feeling like death was seconds away twenty to fifty times a day till my life was completely held hostage to my attacks—the first thing he asked me was, "Are you depressed, Mark?" I thought about it for a moment. The word *depression* had never crossed my mind, never in relation to what I'd been going through, and, in fact, never at all in my entire life. It was not something in my limited categories of feelings, nor was it a characterization I'd have ascribed to myself.

"I'm only depressed because no one can tell me what's wrong with me."

"I'd like you to try this new medication. It's an antidepressant. You'll take it each night before going to bed for two weeks, and then I want you to give me a call to tell me how you're feeling."

I agreed and took the bottle of huge arcane pills home with me. I felt the medication the first time I took it. I had always had a hardcore insomnia that plagued me hand in hand with the anxiety. Almost straightaway after taking my first pill, an unmistakable grogginess came over me. It wasn't a pleasant feeling, but it knocked me out and I slept through the night. That first dose was the only time it felt bad, however, and within a short time the attacks had ceased.

Now, on my way to an all-day drag of rehearsals and camera-angle buttfuckery for our *Tonight Show* appearance with this unceasing burning in my lungs making it impossible to take a normal painless breath, I felt that long-ago sensation of terror gestating in my mind. It was the beginning of a panic attack the likes of which I'd not experienced since the early '80s.

Once we arrived, I discovered it would be a couple hours before we were needed to start running through our song. We had been asked to play "Nearly Lost You" again, even though it was no longer our current single. I had been bummed that in our only two major television appearances in the United States, we were playing the same song twice, but with this fucked-up physical ailment that showed no signs of letting me loose, I couldn't give a damn about that. In my current state of vocal distress, "Nearly Lost You" would actually be easier to pull off than our current single, a song called "Dollar Bill" that required a bit of nuance from my performance.

I found a corner of the dressing room and lay down on the floor behind a large chair. I wrapped myself up in the heavy coat I'd worn, a corduroy stadium coat I'd bought for ten pounds from a used clothing store in Glasgow. I tried to fall asleep, hoping I would wake up and this nightmare would be over. I began trembling and then shaking, the pit of flames in my lungs refusing to die down to embers. Still coughing, still unable to catch my breath, I kept trying to clear my throat and lungs but they would not cooperate. I finally fished three Klonopins from my pocket, hoping they'd at least calm me down a bit. I chewed them up and swallowed them without water, not wanting the liquid to kick the pain into overdrive like it had that morning. At some point, I fell into a half-awake, half-asleep dream state. Every now and then, I would physically convulse as if waking from a nightmare, painfully attempt to take a deep breath, and, failing that, fall back under.

I slept uneasily on the floor for an hour or more and woke up to the gentle shaking of my shoulder by our road manager.

"Hey, man, time to wake up. Lanegan, let's go, time for rehearsal."

I slowly got up off the floor and, still wearing my heavy coat, followed him into the studio where the show was recorded. As we set up to run through the tune, someone from the show approached me.

"Are you going to wear that coat during the performance tonight?"

It was March and unseasonably cool in Los Angeles, maybe high fifties or low sixties, but it was quite warm inside the television studio.

"I don't know," I replied. "But I'm wearing it now."

I had not done a shot of heroin yet that day, but instead of feeling any withdrawals, all of my senses were focused on my lungs and throat and the continued burning within. I painfully croaked my way through several takes of the song, my throat getting increasingly rawer, while the camera operators and sound technicians took a very long time to get their shit together.

Our only other television experiences up until that point consisted of the Letterman show and a British program called *The Late Show*, a predecessor of the extremely popular *Later . . . with Jools Holland*. We had performed "Dollar Bill" alone in an audience-less studio that was so cold I had worn this exact same dingy corduroy coat during taping. Hungover and freezing on a cold February morning, we'd played that show almost exactly one month before this present fiasco in the making. Neither of those dubious spectacles had taken an eighth of the time that these people took to set up their shit and shoot. The *Tonight Show* crew were either incompetent or hypervigilant, I didn't know which, but due to my unceasing lung and throat pain, I began to get irritated at the amount of takes they required of us. Finally, when they announced we had to run through it for what was probably the tenth time, I asked one of our crew to stand at my microphone in my stead since by that point we'd been told the sound guys were cool and now it was just more camera-positioning bullshit to be done.

An hour later, the rest of the band came trudging unhappily into our private greenroom where I was again trying to sleep on the floor.

"What the fuck, man?" said Van, who was obviously as perturbed as I had been by the multitude of takes. "This is fucking bullshit!"

I pulled my long coat over my head to try and block out the loud, unwelcome sound of my bandmate's venting. I took this as a sign I'd be getting no more rest this day and got up off the floor to attempt to drink some warm chamomile tea with honey to see how that was gonna treat me. I'd not had a drop of fluids since my shockingly painful drink of water at six a.m. I cautiously took a tiny sip of the lukewarm, room-temperature tea and found it thankfully soothing.

Another hour passed and we were once more told we needed to run through it again, so we walked back out into the studio, every one of us now pissed off. After one last take, we were finally let off the hook and released back into our depressing jail cell of a dressing room to wait another four or five hours until the actual show began. I went into the private restroom and cooked up and did a shot of dope. It helped settle me down a bit, although my voice was still very rough from the acidic beating it had taken all day long.

Finally, in the late afternoon, they began taping the actual program. I watched disinterestedly on the TV in the greenroom, my lungs and throat still raw as hell from the morning's rude awakening. The only minor boon to this hurry-up-and-wait bullshit was that one of the other guests was actor James Garner, who I'd loved as a kid in the character of private detective Jim Rockford on the popular show *The Rockford Files.*

We were to be the final guests on the show that evening. As the show dragged on, it started to become apparent that after the extensive sound and camera rehearsals we had been forced to endure the entire day, there was a chance that we may get scratched, bumped off the show due to earlier segments running longer than scheduled.

As the clock ticked closer to the end of the program, suddenly one of the show's producers came into the greenroom.

"Hey, guys, good news," the producer said. "You're going to make it on the show! But instead of 'Nearly Lost You,' we would like you to play your current single, 'Dollar . . .' I'm sorry I don't recall the name of it . . ."

"'Dollar Bill,'" Van said in a clearly annoyed voice.

"Yes, 'Dollar Bill,'" the guy parroted.

I was instantly pissed off. For one, that was the song I had originally thought we should play. Second, the endless all-day camera rehearsals were now made a worthless waste of time, since none of the camera guys had any knowledge of the tune. Nor did the soundman have any idea of how it went. On top of all that, with my fucked-up voice, I now had to sing a song that was much more difficult to pull off. I was furious. We had rehearsed a different song all day long and now, at the last minute, we were asked to play another one. A sadistic curveball had been tossed at us and we had no choice other than to swing.

"After the next break, you guys are on. I'll come and get you and you'll set up during the break. When we go back to air, Jay will announce you and then you're on," said the producer.

We got ready to go out and make asses of ourselves on national television, all of us seriously unhappy with the way this was going down. I took a second to look in the mirror and get into character. It wasn't difficult to look serious, because I was . . . seriously pissed off. This entire fucking reach-around was a goddamn mistake and I couldn't have picked a more inopportune time to breathe stomach acid into my lungs than that particular morning. A couple minutes later, we were led out into the studio.

What you see on your TV screen is much different than the reality of a television program. What seems like a giant audience and huge stage when you are watching from home is actually a small group of people and an even smaller area in which the band has to operate. The two other times we'd played a TV show it had also been much quieter onstage than we were used to, the PA and monitors more like something you'd expect to hear being used at a karaoke bar or a country square dance. Tonight was no different. There was even a large, clear plastic baffle surrounding the entire drum kit, like something you'd see in a recording studio to contain the volume of the drums and prevent them from bleeding into the microphones of the other instruments.

Sound-wise, it was a joke. The entire thing nothing more than a false front, the "magic" of television.

Leno announced us and plugged our new record. We launched into "Dollar Bill," a song we'd not played all day but luckily knew by heart. As soon as I began singing, it was clear that my ravaged throat was not going to cooperate. The burn I'd experienced for hours, combined with the shit sound in the room, made it damn near impossible for me to sing. I broke out in a river of sweat, pouring off my brow and into my eyes, stinging them so badly I couldn't keep them open, forcing them closed for almost the entire performance. I struggled mightily for the three and a half minutes of music, straining to hit the notes and stay in tune. From the first second of the song to the last, I was acutely aware that I sucked, my voice a lame caricature of its normal self, my stressing and straining to stay in key plainly obvious not only to the very few people probably watching who knew the song, but to the laymen as well. Anyone could hear how shitty my voice and my singing sounded.

As soon as we finished, the show went to break again. Covered in sweat and angry with shame, I headed for the doorway out of the studio. I felt weak and worn out and meant to grab my shit and catch a cab back to the hotel.

Before I could reach the door, the producer grabbed me by the arm.

"Jay wants you on the panel to end the show."

The producer wanted me to come sit on the couch next to Leno's desk along with the guest who'd been on before us to close the show.

As I was led up to the stage, Leno looked over at me and winked like a carnival huckster.

"That was okay, right? Sell a few records, right?" he chirped.

I nodded yes in fake agreement.

They sat me down right next to James Garner of *The Rockford Files*. Garner reached out, grabbed my hand, and with a tightly gripped handshake, in a large booming voice said, "How you doing, young fella? I'm Jim. That wasn't bad, young fella. It coulda been a lot worse!"

With his kindhearted greeting, my humiliation was complete.

15

TAKE ME TO THE RIVER

AFTER ANOTHER HEADLINING CLUB TOUR OF EUROPE, OUR TOUR-
ing cycle for the record had run its course and we headed home. Back in
Seattle, Anna had endured enough of my lies and using. She moved out.
Although it made me unhappy, a part of me was relieved to be able to
use drugs freely in my apartment and no longer have to keep up the sad
pretense of being clean.

I began working on my second Sub Pop solo album again. The combination of the drugs and my obsession with finally making a great
record began to lead me down a dark, twisted tunnel through a noctur-
nal animal den. I lost myself in the minutiae of various songs, sequences,
lyrics, and mixes. After trying to finish it with several different Seattle
producers and engineers, including both Terry Date and Jack Endino, I
was at the fuck-end of a blind alley.

While trying to mix at a studio in Woodinville, Washington, called
Bear Creek, I lost my shit. At my insistence, Jack Endino had spent two
days trying to figure out why a certain song didn't have the forward
propulsion I had sworn was there in the roughs. I had him strip the
mix down to its barest bones a couple times and painstakingly build it
back up, track by track, trying to find the missing component. Loaded
throughout the sessions, I nonetheless stood at his shoulder the entire
time, talking maniacally nonstop while he patiently tried to work out
the solution to a problem only I could perceive. At the end of a couple
days he turned to me and said with exasperation, "Mark, I don't think
the track you are looking for exists." I took this to mean that he thought

I had somehow imagined it. I silently turned and began to collect all the cans holding the spools of analog tape for the entire record.

"What are you doing? Lanegan? What's going on?" Jack asked with a worried, confused, and truly curious voice.

I did not answer. I continued to stack the large, round canisters holding two years' worth of work until I had compiled a huge mountain. Picking them up, I struggled to open the back door of the control room, which led to a lovely pastoral scene outside, green fields with a large creek running through the middle of them. Jack looked worried.

"Okay, hold on, man. What the fuck are you doing? Where are you going with those?"

I walked through the field toward the water, hardly able to carry the heavy metal containers of tape. I continued stubbornly forward, staggering single-mindedly in a zigzagging path, intent on dumping these now-hated recordings into the creek, so angry and sleep deprived I only wanted to be done with it. As it finally occurred to Jack what my intention was, he ran yelling out the door after me.

"Hey, Lanegan, hold up, buddy! Mark! Stop right now, goddamnit!"

"Fuck that, Jack!" I yelled. "Fuck this piece-of-shit record. I've had it, I'm drowning this thing!"

Endino ran around in front of me, physically blocking my progress to the water.

"Hey, mister, I can't let you do that. There is a beautiful record here and I won't let you destroy it. C'mon back inside. We'll go through it again and I swear I'll get to the bottom of this and fix it."

An overwhelming exhaustion came over me. I'd been sleeping on the couch in the control room, staying there 24/7, leaving only to do periodic shots of heroin in the bathroom every few hours to stay well. I had hardly eaten in days or showered in a couple weeks. This frustrating, unsuccessful mix had beaten me down and I could conjure no more manic energy to see it through. I handed the tapes back over to Jack. As we went back inside and he put the song on once again, I lay down on the couch and fell into a black, battle-scarred sleep, hearing the tune play endlessly on repeat through the fog of my dreams.

Jack woke me up a few hours later. He had found the problem.

"Hey, man, is this what you were looking for?" he asked, and soloed up a previously unheard track of kick drum. When put into the mix, it was rhythmically intrinsic to the forward motion of the tune, indeed the component I'd known was there.

"I found it on an unnamed track," Jack said. "Jesus Christ, these tapes are a mess. Whoever's been working on this has been doing an unprofessional job of keeping track of shit."

That was beyond obvious, and that person was me. I'd had so many different local engineers and producers trying to help me finish that it had become a hodgepodge of half-finished tracks, half-assed ideas, and unfinished songs spread across acres of analog tape. I was only keeping track of shit in my head, hence my knowledge of the hidden kick drum and inability to locate it.

My addiction had become the all-encompassing feature of my life. It had to be fed before anything else could happen. I would normally do one to two grams of heroin a day at a cost of $150 to $200 depending on where or who I scored from. For the first couple years as a regular user, I saved a shot every night to have as my wake-up. After that, I'd buy enough to last me the day. My accountants had put a strict $200-a-day limit on my ATM card and I withdrew the totality of that amount daily, nearly every cent going toward my habit. I used what was left of my substantial advance from Sub Pop for paying my rent and the endless studio bills as my obsession to complete my "masterpiece" spiraled out of control. I continuously wrote, rewrote, recorded, rerecorded, mixed, remixed, sequenced, and resequenced a growing mountain of tunes for my second solo album.

My guitar player and musical partner Mike Johnson was not a drug user. In my drinking days, he and I would often stay up all night downing alcohol while playing records, laughing, smoking, and talking so loud that my girlfriend would make several appearances throughout the night. She would first ask nicely but eventually plead, beg, and finally order us to shut the fuck up so she could get some sleep before her early-morning college classes and then day of work. We were great friends and our shared affection for the music we made together and the music that inspired it was the glue our bond was made of.

Mike also had a full-time gig playing bass for my old friend J Mascis's band Dinosaur Jr. As I descended into addiction and self-centered psychosis regarding the record, things became strained between us. Finally, I booked yet another session in a studio somewhere and he simply declined to show up. Working with or even hanging out with me had long since ceased to be pleasurable for him. He wouldn't even answer the phone when I called. He was finished with me, as a musician and as a friend. I was on my own.

Although *Sweet Oblivion* hadn't been a hit, it had sold enough to warrant Epic giving Screaming Trees another try, and they exercised their option for one more record. Time was of the essence if we wanted to take advantage of our modest success. We needed to get new material together quickly. The same team that had worked on our last album was again tapped to lead this new endeavor. I insisted the recording take place in Seattle as I didn't want to get too far from my regular sources of dope. Don Fleming and John Agnello came to town and sat in on a rehearsal session to evaluate the songs we'd generated and gauge our readiness for the studio.

I'd taken an active role in the creation of *Sweet Oblivion*. Since we had established a new collaborative way of working, one that had taken us to previously unknown heights, I was now expected to do my part again. The rest of the band as well as our always over-the-top A&R man Bob Pfeifer looked to me for some creative leadership, but now I was too strung out and mentally unstable to contribute at the same level. My dope habit was no longer a secret. Although everyone from my managers at Q Prime to the band to Don Fleming himself had tried to gently talk to me about getting some help, my denial was fierce. Nobody was going to get in between me and my beloved heroin. Nobody.

When it was brought up, I argued back intensely that I was able to do anything required of me, that my personal life was no one's business but my own. Whenever someone so much as hinted at it, I immediately attacked with such ferocity that I disarmed my well-meaning adversaries before they could get their pistols out of their holsters. I had always had the innate ability to keep people at arm's length, had always had the talent to keep the seat next to me open on a crowded, standing-room-only city bus. I'd mastered a dark, dead-eyed visage, a countenance that said "stay away or get hurt." It had earned me the nickname "Shark" from my sister's basketball-star boyfriend in high school. I projected the vibe of someone not to be fucked with, and I used this tactic to its full effect whenever I felt my drug use threatened. My heroin was to be preserved at all cost. There was zero chance of anyone getting me to stop now that I had found my one true love, the only peace of mind I'd ever had.

As far as I was concerned, heroin had lifted me up from the grave. It had kept me from dying from the horrors of my severe alcoholism, against which I had been a lowly pissant attempting to stop a freight train. It had quieted the cyclone storm of my own voice in my head, constantly tearing me down, telling me what a shit heap I was. Most importantly, heroin erased the myriad collection of endless worries that had kept me awake all night most of my life. It had freed me from feeling anything: loss, heartbreak, regret, grief, resentment, as well as the burning hatred and disgust I felt not only for myself but also for other people I thought had wronged me, real or imagined. When dope enveloped me in its golden glow, all that melted away like springtime snow. The world became black and white, boiled down to just getting enough drugs each day to keep the dogs of withdrawals off my heels. I felt as though heroin had saved me from a life of misery, and I was prepared to go to any lengths to make sure I would always have it. Heroin was my number one, and anything else—everything else—was such a far-distant second place as to be virtually unseen on the radar screen of my life's importance.

The Trees and I managed to put some songs together. Even though I knew most of it was crap, we hit the studio to try to make a follow-up to *Sweet Oblivion*. I spent most of every day locked in the greenroom of the studio, shooting heroin into the veins of my feet. I had already burned through most of my reliable sources in my arms when Layne and I would go on nightlong cocaine binges, silently locked in the bathroom at one of our apartments, doing shot after endless shot of coke. With heroin, I might do three shots total in a day, but on these coke runs, we would do one right after another, all night until the bag was gone. Even though it wasn't really my thing, I was a garbage can and would do any drug put in front of me. When it came to heroin, though, I was a purist. I almost never did speedballs where I shot both drugs together, yet I became a fiend shooting coke by itself. Both Layne and I demanded absolute silence while performing this ritual. The explosion as the coke hit our brains was what we craved and the slightest outside noise would ruin it for us. The cocaine had robbed me of my veins, one by one, until now I was down to the daily torture of hitting in my feet, a painful and painstaking routine that took precision, patience, and focus. Using the smallest-gauge, thinnest needle available, I would spend hours looking until I hit where most people would not even attempt. Between my fingers and toes, in the tiny veins running down the sides of my fingers, in my armpits at an angle that made it impossible, even with a mirror, to see if I had hit the vein or the nearby artery. The angle was so tight that I was unable to discern the fluorescent, neon arterial blood if I missed, and on a couple of bad days, I accidentally shot into the artery, causing an instant nightmare when the dope ran the wrong way through my body. Once, the shot went straight down my arm and up my neck. My face and hand both inflated like balloons. I barely had time to rip all the rings from my fingers before they'd have surely cut off all blood flow as my hand bulged to twice its normal size, narrowly avoiding an emergency trip to the hospital to have my fingers amputated. On those few occasions it had happened, I'd not only received none of the benefits of the dope (no high, no getting well) but also had to spend hours holding my arm above my head until the numbness and agonizing pain subsided. But for the most part, I had a talent for finding veins. I was the guy usually asked to give somebody a shot when they were either too green or too far out to pasture to do it themselves. It was most often girls who'd need to be injected. Whenever I was with Kurt and his wife Courtney Love, she'd have me find her vein and hit her, a task made more difficult by her nonstop talking, storytelling, or complaining.

After a couple of unproductive weeks in the studio in Seattle, the decision was made by the powers that be to pull the plug, go back to the drawing board, and generate some *good* material before reconvening in New York City later in the year to try again. I took this opportunity to further indulge my obsessive drive to complete my solo album, which by this point was all I really cared about. I was glad the Trees had finally made a record that I considered worthy but my real goal now was to create an album along the lines of Van Morrison's *Astral Weeks*, Tim Buckley's *Starsailor*, or Captain Beefheart's *Trout Mask Replica*. An undeniable classic, a wholly original piece of music that could not be compared to anything other than itself. I was, of course, shooting for an unattainable paradigm, as those records were, it seemed, created with some magical alchemy I was not privy to. Made by geniuses whose mystical talents seemed to come out of the ether itself or directed by the hand of some god I'd never met. I was still toiling with blind, dogged, childlike curiosity and primitive, homemade tools, trying to discover how to make fire. I had also hogtied myself to a dope habit that increasingly took all my time, energy, and resources to maintain.

16

JEFFREY LEE PIERCE

AS A NINETEEN-YEAR-OLD, I HAD SPENT A COUPLE OF WINTER months living in my dad's storage unit. I had with me all my worldly belongings: one suitcase full of clothes, a turntable and speakers, three boxes of records. I slept on my father's old couch in a sleeping bag and read from a box of books by the light of our old living room lamp during the cold nights. I used a space heater to warm the large, quarter-full room with rugless cement floor and a metal roller door at the front.

One day, I took a Greyhound bus to Seattle in order to get tattooed. One of my arms was adorned in crude, homemade tattoos I'd started giving myself at age fourteen and I had begun getting them covered up with professional ones. After stepping off the bus, I walked to the large Tower Records store near the Space Needle, looking through the bins and stopping to mindlessly stare at album covers that caught my eye. Artwork, name of band, name of record, etc. I bought one just out of curiosity with no prior knowledge of the group or music: *Fire of Love* by the Gun Club.

After walking down to Pike Place Market and getting some generic, off-the-wall flash tattoo in the large shop there, I took the long bus ride back home. When I got to Ellensburg, I walked up to the government-funded apartment house of three older mental patients I sold weed to in order to get one of them to give me a ride to my lush digs out on the edge of town. After unlocking the padlock, rolling up the door, and stooping inside, I plugged the turntable into the power strip that also powered heat and light and put my new record on.

From the moment the needle jumped onto the first track, I was totally engaged. I had begun unwrapping my fresh tattoo but I stopped what I was doing and just stared at the record as it revolved, as though it were a living thing, the sounds from the speaker seeming to give it a life of its own. An instant chill had run up my spine the moment the man started singing, an exotic, balls-out wail like I'd never heard before, with the intensity of punk but something different, something wholly unique to me. I thought this was what Creedence Clearwater Revival would've sounded like had they played Delta blues in the style of punk rock. I was completely floored by what I was hearing. By the third song, I'd completely forgotten about taking the plastic off my new ink. This man was the most convincingly real, crazed, and intense singer I'd ever heard; you knew beyond all doubt that this motherfucker meant it. A thought ran through my head: finally, here was the music made specifically for a person like me. Serial-killer music, music for a lost, deviant, fucked-up soul like mine! For the first time ever, I thought, *I want to do this, too, be a singer like this dude, he's as fucked as I am.* And with that sudden, life-altering epiphany in a cold, weakly lit storage unit in winter began my lifelong love affair with the music of and idolization of one Jeffrey Lee Pierce.

I discovered that there was already a second record out by the Gun Club, *Miami,* and I quickly returned to Seattle in order to track that one down. I played it immediately upon my return home and found its pull on me even more irresistible than the first record. It was just as dark and unhinged as *Fire of Love* but with a smoldering, black beauty and a depth of intelligence and emotion I'd not discerned on that record. The sense of pain and loss was visceral, a deep-rooted, aching chasm that fit me like a latex medical glove. They'd even covered a Creedence tune on it, confirming my earliest sense of the faint ghost of John Fogerty haunting *Fire of Love.*

In the spring of the next year came a third record, *The Las Vegas Story,* and this trio of albums, all of which I'd been exposed to in the span of just a few months, became my bible. Living in Ellensburg, it was tough to get information about any underground band, much less one like the Gun Club. Literally nobody I knew had heard of the Gun Club until I force-fed it to them. After not hearing anything about them for a long time, I assumed they had broken up or simply disappeared.

A few years later in 1987, I was pursuing my decision to become a singer. One day, my bandmate Mark Pickerel came to band practice with a big smile on his face.

"Lanegan, check it out! A new Gun Club record!"

The young Screaming Trees drummer shared my affection for them and waved in the air a copy of *Mother Juno*, their latest release.

"And I ordered you a copy! It's great, man!"

He had ordered a couple copies weeks earlier from Ace Books and Records, where he had a part-time job, and withheld that info from me just for the purpose of breaking the news as a surprise when he actually had the record in hand.

Now that we knew the band still existed, we regularly scanned all news of shows happening in Seattle for a possible Gun Club tour coming to town, but it never materialized. Pickerel found out that the band was now based in London and rarely left Europe.

In 1989, while in Los Angeles to do some shows with the Trees, I went to the famous Whisky a Go Go on Sunset Strip to see Firehose, Mike Watt's band who we'd gotten our first break opening for. When I saw their soundman Steve before the show I'd asked him, "Whatcha been up to, man?" He said he had been out running sound for the Gun Club. I got very excited.

"Are you kidding me? They're here in the States?"

"Yeah, man. Jeffrey will be here tonight. He's staying at his mom's right down the street."

I bristled with a wild electric excitement. I could not believe the incredible providence. I made Steve promise to introduce me after the show. But while Firehose was still playing, he made eye contact with me, then nodded his head sideways. I looked over and there was Jeffrey Lee Pierce in the flesh. I didn't wait for an introduction. In an action very out of character for me, I simply walked up to him, introduced myself, and said I was a huge fan. I couldn't help myself. Here was the mythological hero whose music had given my life a sense of purpose, meaning, and validation, a hero I thought I'd never even see in person, much less meet. I could not let this once-in-a-lifetime chance go by.

"That's cool. What do you do for a living, man?" he said, looking at me through somewhat squinted eyes, as though he couldn't quite focus them on me.

"I'm a singer in a band from Seattle called Screaming Trees."

His girlfriend Romi Mori let out a little squeal of excitement.

"Oh, I've heard you guys, you're great!" she said.

We had played the UK a few times by then and Jeffrey seemed impressed that she knew who we were.

"Do you ever come to London?"

"I'm gonna be there next month."

He wrote down his number and told me to give him a call.

When we made it to London, I called the number he'd given me in Los Angeles. When he picked up, he asked where I was staying and I told him.

"Fuck. That's right around the corner. I'll come get you when I'm done running."

Running? I thought. *What the hell?*

Sure enough, thirty minutes later he showed up at our shitty hotel with rooms so tiny that the bottom quarter of my bed got soaked if I turned on the shower. He was dripping with sweat, dressed in a 1950s-style gray sweat suit. I had not expected him to be athletically minded, especially not a runner. But I was to learn he was a multifaceted, complicated man who I already knew held real genius. He would cook elaborate Mexican dinners for his beautiful Japanese girlfriend and bass player Romi and me whenever I was around, bemoaning the fact that "you can't get any good Mexican food in London. All they have is fucking Taco Bell."

On one of my first visits to Jeffrey's flat in Shepherd's Bush, I asked him about lyrics in a song I was unable to discern.

"Ah, shit!" he said. "That's from an old folk song I heard when I was a kid. I always use lines from other songs in mine; no one ever notices and it helps me to have a starting place."

And with that began a master class in songwriting from my favorite musician of all time.

"Check this out," he said, putting on his turntable a copy of Isaac Hayes's *Hot Buttered Soul*. "You hear that bass line?" he asked. "Now listen to this," he said, putting on a copy of *Mother Juno*, the Gun Club's great fourth record. The song was "Yellow Eyes." "Check it out, man. That's the same bass line only backwards!" he shouted as he burst into laughter. "That's how you write a fuckin' song!" he said, still laughing hysterically.

Jeffrey's face was such that, even when smiling or laughing, it still had the strange appearance of slightly frowning. He showed me early VHS tapes of the band where he stood onstage with a crazy bleach-blond mop of a hairdo wrapped in a headband and whipped beer bottles straight into the crowd with full velocity. Laughing again, he said, "That's the crazy shit that got me banned."

He showed me tapes of their comeback when, while living in London, *Mother Juno* had come out to pronounced critical success. He was lean and short-haired, prowling the stage like Iggy Pop, a classic front-man who demanded your attention. I ate it all up. He told me of his struggles with alcohol and I admitted the same.

Once I'd gotten to know him, he would honestly and openly discuss anything personal. I asked him about the songs on the first Gun Club record, *Fire Of Love*, that had racist lyrics. I had always felt uncomfortable with that aspect of the record and there was never another racist line throughout the next three records, records I loved with equal fervor to the first.

"In the early days of LA punk, the cops would break up the shows, beat the shit out of people, and take kids to jail. While we were leaving a club, my friend and I got hit with batons and thrown in a cop car. On the way to the station, the black cop who was driving was giving us a bunch of shit, like, 'So you guys wanna start trouble, huh? You wanna piss people off and be anti-establishment, huh? Why don't you try singing a song about niggers? See where that would get ya!' Right then I thought to myself, Fuck yes, why not? I figured people would be fucked up by the perversity of it, with those lyrics inside a blues song that I'd turned into a punk song. I just thought that I would shake shit up and do something no one had done before. I got nothing against anyone of any color, I'm half Mexican with a Japanese girlfriend! Plus, Kid's Mexican, too!" he shouted, with more hysterical laughter and the weird smile/frown on his face.

The "Kid" he was referring to was Kid Congo Powers, the legendary guitarist and paragon of cool who had the solid-gold distinction of not only being a founding member of the Gun Club, but also a member of the Cramps and Nick Cave's Bad Seeds—three of underground rock's most beloved and seminal bands—at different times during his storied career. Yeah, Kid had the greatest résumé ever of anyone in rock music.

—

BUT WHEN THE GUN CLUB came to Seattle in 1993, there was very little excitement surrounding their show. They had toured almost exclusively in Europe and the UK for years; now they were finally playing in my town and Jeffrey sat on my couch in a dark mood. The audience turnout had been poor at every show up the coast and he was anticipating the same that night.

While sitting in my living room that afternoon he bluntly said, "Give me some heroin, will ya, man?" He had known I was strung out for a long time but he'd never shown any interest in dope until that moment. I went into the closet and grabbed a clean outfit and a small piece of the sticky black tar. I then went into the kitchen and got a spoon, came out, gave it to him, and he went into the bathroom to fix. When he returned his mood was much lighter and he said, "Fuck it. I don't give a shit if anyone shows up or not."

"I'm sure there will be plenty of people totally psyched to see you tonight, Jeffrey."

"Whatever," he said and then turned on the TV. He silently stared at it for an hour or so before leaving for his soundcheck at some small, recently opened club directly under the monorail on Fourth Avenue.

I arrived early at the gig, wanting to see another old pop/punk band from Orange County, Agent Orange, who were opening. The room sounded terrible, like the small, former storefront it was, not a place made for live music. My enthusiasm for Agent Orange waned quickly due to the poor acoustics in the room. It made every note seem as though it were being played from under a wet mattress. Not pleasing in the least. The audience turnout for the Gun Club wasn't the worst I'd ever seen, but it was far from good. Maybe seventy-five people at the most stood in the room as they took to the tiny stage, about a half foot higher than the floor. The reaction was lukewarm as the band played songs from their most recent record, *Lucky Jim*.

Jeffrey had invited me to sing background vocals on a track late one night in Haarlem, a town outside Amsterdam, while I was touring there earlier that year. Having already done a full performance for a Dutch television show, a live radio broadcast, and then a full concert at legendary Amsterdam venue the Paradiso that day, I had been exhausted when I arrived at the studio past midnight. It was their last day recording and everyone was frantic to finish. The band were wrapping up overdubs and vocals and then mixing them all on the same night. Jeffrey asked me to sing a high harmony on one of the tunes but my voice was already so fucked from three shows that day, done right in the middle of a six-week tour, I was unable to get up above his substantially higher normal range. After a couple goes, I'd said, "God damn, this has been a dream opportunity, to sing with my favorite band ever. But we both know this sounds like shit, please don't use it." He sadly agreed.

"*This* is the song I really wanted you on but it was getting late and we mixed it already."

He had the engineer put on the mix of the song he'd originally planned for me to sing on. It was the title track, "Lucky Jim." I was completely blown away and inwardly angry as hell I'd not arrived in time. It was simply one of the greatest songs he'd ever written and the recording was pristine, the words completely evocative. As I realized the missed opportunity, I was crushed.

Now, hearing the band run through this tune in Seattle, I was again captivated by it, and again felt the sting of regret. Opportunities like that didn't come knocking every day.

The crowd excitement rose to a slightly higher level than the sort of typically bored, show-us-something, hipster disinterest just three times during the set, when Jeffrey had busted out the beloved punk/blues classics from the first Gun Club record. "For the Love of Ivy," "She's Like Heroin to Me," and especially "Sex Beat" brought loud cheering and singing along from the small, previously tepid crowd. It was as if I were watching Chubby Checker on an oldies tour and he finally played "The Twist." With an extensive back catalog of brilliant, beautiful, straight-to-the-head, -heart, and -genitalia songs, albums, and performances to his credit, still hardly anyone seemed to give a damn about my idol-turned-friend, except when he was playing the most obvious "hits."

17

DID YOU CALL FOR THE NIGHT PORTER?

ONE WAY I KEPT THE DREADED BEAST OF WITHDRAWALS OFF MY back was to become a willing conduit for people who wanted drugs but had no access to them. Such people were often traveling musicians coming through town on tour, or young people I met through friends or customers, just taking their first steps into the dangerous exploration of the unknown. Much like my old London connection Craig Pike, the guy I was certain I'd never end up like, I had gained a name as a person not hard to find. I was sought out now due to my reputation as a junkie and guy who knew where the drugs were. I was also called into action by some of my rich and successful friends who could not be bothered to go out in public and score. Almost no relatively small-time dealer in Seattle during those times would deliver, just the bigger fish who supplied them.

The only person we knew who delivered was Tommy Hansen. He would drive his muscle car all day, dropping off dope, but he was done working as soon as the sun went down and would head back to his place in far north Seattle, not to come out again until the following morning. I would sometimes ride along with him on his delivery route, dropping stuff off for addicts of all stripes. Some were other Seattle musicians, a few of them guys I recognized as members of semipopular local bands, others just grinding it out trying to establish some modest success and acquire gigs for themselves. Then you had the strippers, waitresses, baristas, shop clerks, and other normal people with dope habits. Some successful businesspeople, some on the downward slide, hell-bent on finding the bottom of heroin's bottomless cavern.

Sometimes Tommy would deliver some dope to me and stay to hang out for a while. We had similar tastes in music, movies, and literature. Often, toward the end of his working day, I would send him a page and he'd call back.

"Hey, Tommy, I know it's a pain in the ass but I've burned through what I got today. Is there any way you can make another delivery tonight?"

"You know that stack of books on your dining room table? Look inside the fourth book in the stack, I left some dope in there for you."

He'd anticipated this common scenario of mine and hid some to tide me over while my back was turned. But Tommy was the shining exception, certainly not the rule, in '90s Seattle. It made no difference how famous or rich you were, heroin addicts were so prevalent that any dealer would have around-the-clock business just staying home and letting people come to them had they so chosen. Not only was I willing to deliver, I had to do it in order to supplement my small stash of dope and feed my giant habit. I had also become someone who could score any time of day or night. Most dealers closed up shop pretty early in the evening, but through my connections at the Yesler Terrace housing projects near my apartment, a place some people were hesitant to go even in daytime, I could score drugs 24/7. I would buy from a guy named Val and then deliver them to your doorstep. I also sometimes used a repulsive goon of a guy with horrible-smelling, never-washed, dreaded hair that put off a nearly vomit-inducing stench that filled his studio apartment. With his terrible homemade white-supremacist prison tattoos and grotesque, shit-encased personality, we called him "Big Ugly Ben," but his official self-created nickname was "Spanky." He used to make some of his meekest customers clean his place while he held court from a bed that he lay on all day and night, bossing people around like a tyrant while ridiculing them. Big Ugly Ben was a supreme dickhead. He worked late hours out in the U District but I despised him so much I'd only go there if it was absolutely necessary. During a particularly low period in our lives, Dylan Carlson and I sometimes spent two or more hours in his place daily. He used our presence to show off to his unfortunate regular customers that he had "rock star" friends. We'd sit together on a couch and bite our lips as he treated everyone who came through the door to an extended period of humiliation, meant to exhibit to Dylan and me the power he wielded over the peons who came to him for dope. Right when we were about to lose our minds, he would slip us each a couple of balloons on the sly, gratis. It was for this free dope he gave us as payment for hanging out that we endured the sick embarrassment of it all. One night as we silently walked away from his place together with our free drugs, Dylan turned to me and said, "Fuck, we have known some winners, but that shithead takes the cake." I instantly agreed.

When I was not in such dire circumstances, I had a string of my own customers and was given cash or dope for being the messenger man, often both. Naturally, I both overcharged and took what I felt I could get away with unnoticed out of the bag long before I returned with the goods. Kurt had once jokingly referred to me as "the Night Porter" when I'd shown up with a late-night package for him. He had watched me transform from someone whose main concerns were music and women into a different beast entirely. With the same obsessive drive I'd always had but turned in another direction, I'd become someone who made himself available anytime, day or night, rain or shine, to go out, get drugs, and carry them up to your room. For a piece of the action, of course.

—

WHILE I WAS PISSING AT a urinal in a restroom after a gig we'd played in Seattle opening up for Alice in Chains, a young kid came up and introduced himself as "a good friend of your ex-girlfriend Anna." That introduction earned him a faceful of my spit and a rattling bang of his head against the tiled toilet wall. Then I grabbed him by the front of his shirt and lifted him off the ground.

"I don't give a damn who you know but it sure as fuck isn't me. You're lucky I don't break your nose, you fucking idiot. You ever come up on me like that again and I'll put you in the hospital. Do you get me?"

The quicksilver burst of ferocity this naïve boy brought on was, of course, clearly unwarranted. But that was a chance anyone took if they approached me while I was drunk, especially if they brought her up. My jealousy and bitter resentment over the painful, self-inflicted loss of my former love brought out a negative, sometimes violent reaction. My loss of Anna was still very much a raw, open wound.

18

IT'S *GENIUS*,
DON'T YOU HEAR IT?

I HAD READ SOMEWHERE THAT VAN MORRISON'S *ASTRAL WEEKS* had been made in four days and I had originally planned to do the same. Three years later, my intended magnum opus was still unfinished and I had already burned through most of my substantial advance. Not on drugs, unbelievably, but on the record itself. I was obsessed with making a classic, one-of-a-kind record, unlike anything else, something that would define an artist, a truly great, self-contained piece of art like the records I was so enamored of.

In the same way I had fanatically obsessed over *Astral Weeks*, I had read Cormac McCarthy's *Blood Meridian* several times and it became my favorite book of all time. The recording I'd been toiling and sweating over was heavily influenced by a collision of these two completely different works of art: the bleak, descriptive lyrics by *Blood Meridian* and the ephemeral music by *Astral Weeks*. The lyrical narrative of the individual songs was rooted in my day-to-day experience: pain, loss, the inner world and trials of someone strung out and struggling. Without comfort or love, searching for what, who knew? But it was something if ever found, might be located on a spiritual plane, not in the physical world. I had given John Agnello, the recording engineer on the Trees' previous record as well as the aborted follow-up, a cassette of what I thought at the time was only the half-finished record. His reaction was one of enthusiasm and excitement.

"Holy shit, Lanegan, this is great! Let me help you finish it. Come out to New York. I know a great, kind of weird studio off Times Square we can get really cheap for a couple weeks and get it done."

We booked the studio for November. Already cold and icy in the city by then, it was a minor ordeal to get down to the Lower East Side to score each day and then back to Times Square by noon or one to start working. I had to be to the studio on time, lest I unleash the beast in Agnello. He was a hilarious cut-up but when it came to recording, he was an adrenalized machine you dared not fuck with or hinder.

The routine to score on the street in those days was a fairly sophisticated affair. There would be a certain street and on it, in one of the buildings, a doorway where you would buy bindles of coke and dope. Addicts would walk around the block until the dealer's lookouts, stationed at both ends of the block, would signal to the guy assigned to the door that the coast was clear. Then it was his job to quickly line everyone up at the door. Another guy would appear in the now-open doorway to collect the money. You would give them your order, say "ten d, five c," meaning ten bindles of dope and five of coke, then give the money to the guy inside the building. Another person wearing a full-face ski mask would then distribute the drugs. If there was a sudden warning from one of the lookouts, the door would close and the guy outside would tell everyone, "Get the fuck out! It's hot!" All the junkies would go back to circling the block, waiting until they opened for business again. Sometimes it all went smoothly. Other days, it turned into a much longer, frustrating grind.

Once, I had just handed over my money when the sharp whistle came down from the end of the street to signal danger. The door closed and the line scattered before I'd gotten my dope. I nervously circled the block for what seemed like an hour, sure my dough had been lost and I had a dopesick twenty-four hours ahead of me. But when they opened up again, the doorman hustled me to the front of the line and gave me my shit first. A first-class business operation.

One freezing cold, icy day, I circled the block with my money already in my hand, both hands shoved deep in my coat pockets. I stepped on a patch of ice and, in a second, my feet were above my head. I barely had time to pull my hands out of my pockets to partially break my fall instead of taking it full on the head. My money flew out of my hands, and not only did I have to instantly spring back to my feet after this painful mishap but then had to quickly run around and scoop my money off the frozen ground before the bitter wind blew it away.

The owner of the recording studio had an apparent fetish for, of all things, cookie jars. The place was filled with a huge collection of every different kind you could imagine. Shelf upon shelf upon shelf of the fucking things. But other than that it was a good, solid-sounding room. Fueled by John Agnello's infectious and enthusiastic energy, we set about trying to actually finish this record that had long since become a millstone around my neck.

Mike Johnson was staying in the city at the time and John gave him a call to see if he'd take part in these final sessions. Mike wanted none of it and instead sent my old friend J Mascis and Kurt Fedora, another musician from J's hometown of Amherst, Massachusetts, down in his place. They set to work with Mascis overdubbing some drums and percussion and Kurt laying down bass on a few tracks. I spent much of my time either in my Times Square hotel room getting loaded or at the Lower East Side apartment of Justin Williams, my former coworker from Seattle who had turned me on to all the music that now informed the record I was making. He shared his apartment with his girlfriend Sally Barry, who was a drummer of some renown in NYC at the time.

It was a constant battle for Agnello to get me to and keep me in the studio as my mind was tightly focused on getting loaded. One morning, Sally insisted I let her wash my filthy clothes. As I sat around their apartment in my only clean pair of boxers and a tight kimono of hers to try and stay warm in what was then brutal November weather, a call came from John.

"Lanegan, if you don't get your ass down here in the next twenty minutes, I'm shutting this thing down and going home. I need you here to help me make decisions. For fuck's sake, it's your fucking record, now act like you give a shit! Twenty minutes!"

"How long until my clothes are done?" I asked Sally.

"An hour, hour and a half, why?"

"Because I have to go now. Fuck! Do you guys have any clothes that will fit me?"

They both started laughing. She was a small woman and Justin was rail thin. Wearing their clothes was an impossibility but I knew from Agnello's tone that he was dead serious. I had no choice but to go as I was. My jacket only came down to my waist and it looked as though I was wearing a woman's slip beneath it with sockless boots on my feet.

"Go!" she said. "We'll bring them down when they're done."

I walked out into the freezing street where cab after cab refused to pick me up. I went back inside.

"One of you has to grab the cab, then I'll jump in. No one is gonna stop for me. I look like a freak."

I stood behind a car as Sally hailed a cab. When she opened one door as if to enter, I jumped in the other side and barked out the address as she closed the door and waved goodbye.

J and John both laughed themselves sick when I arrived in my women's attire. To amuse himself in my absence, J had carefully perused the vast collection of jars and had found one that gave him a particular thrill.

"Hey, Lanegan, check this out," he said with a huge grin in his distinctive slow drawl. "This is perfect for your record."

He held a cookie jar shaped like a hobo leaning against a light pole, the hobo's hat its lid. When he turned the lid, it began to make a whistling noise, the song of the bum. That delighted Mascis and he entertained himself playing with it for a long time. In the meantime, Agnello was mixing "The River Rise," the song that we planned to have open the record. J, now tired of the cookie jar, started fucking around with a primitive synthesizer and came upon a sound like wind blowing through an alley.

"That's it!" he called out. "The wind plus the whistle is a winner. You gotta put it on the record, Lanegan!"

"Will you guys please shut the fuck up? I'm trying to actually work here, in case you two clowns haven't noticed," Agnello said with an edge that told me he meant business.

"But John, it's *genius*, don't you hear it?" Mascis insisted.

"Okay, if you guys won't let me work, then get the hell outta here. Lanegan, go back to whatever drag-queen bar you dragged yourself out of. And you go home," he said to J.

"Okay, hold on a minute. How much will you give me to put it on the record?" I asked Mascis, a notorious penny pincher unlikely to foot the bill for anything frivolous.

"Umm, twenty bucks?"

"Fuck that. I'll do it for fifty."

"You got a deal, mister!"

He cackled with delight while John stared at both of us with hollow-point bullets firing from under his incredulous and irritated brow.

But after further cajoling, Agnello agreed. When the record opened, the first thing you heard was a mixture of J's simulated-wind synth noise combined with the whistling hobo cookie jar. As I'd anticipated, he never paid up for it, but it did bring him great pleasure and it felt oddly appropriate to me once it was finished.

Later, Sally and Justin showed up with my clothes and I was glad to be dressed again. She ended up singing a beautiful part on a song called "Sunrise."

A couple weeks later, a jubilant John Agnello gave me a huge hug and said, "See, asshole? I told you we could do it!" After making me insane for over three years, the record was finally, completely finished. Even though I had lost my way in a million different directions during those difficult years, when it was said and done, the final result was close to the way I had originally imagined it. A record a thousand times better than my debut, a self-contained, fully realized piece of work I was proud of. Having written every song myself and gone through much angst and unnecessary headaches, for the first time I felt I'd actually pulled it off.

As soon as I returned home, I got together with Kurt and gave him a copy of *Whiskey for the Holy Ghost* on cassette. He called me a couple days later and said, "This is truly great, man. The best thing you've ever done. I'm not crazy about the title but this is a classic record. Congratulations, brother."

19

SPANKING THE MONKEY

A MONTH LATER, I GOT A PHONE CALL FROM SOMEONE I DIDN'T know. As I listened to him leaving a message, I heard him mention Sally Barry's name and that he was a film director, then I quickly picked up, not wanting to miss out on some exotic opportunity.

"Hello?"

"Hello, is this Mark Lanegan?"

"Yes, it is. Who's calling?"

"You don't know me but your friend Sally cleans my apartment for me. When I came in yesterday, she was playing a tape of your new record."

He was speaking superfast and excitedly. I wondered where this was leading.

"Let me cut to the chase: I am a screenwriter getting ready to shoot my first movie as a director and I would like to use your music in it."

"What? Like a song or something?"

"No, man, I want to use your record for the entire soundtrack. I know you're probably thinking who is this nut but I swear to you this is legit. In fact, I'd like you to come out and meet me in New York and help me arrange the songs so that they play throughout the entire movie."

"What's it about? And I'm sorry, what is your name?"

"My name is David O. Russell. The movie is called *Spanking the Monkey*, it's sort of a classic coming-of-age story. Did you happen to see that lame car commercial a while back with the kid comparing a car to the Ramones' music?"

I actually had.

163

"Well, it was terrible but the kid is a great actor and he's playing the lead. I hope to get Faye Dunaway to play his mom."

"Can you please send me a script so I have a better idea of what it's about and how my music would be used?"

"Of course, man! And like I said, I would want you to come out to Massachusetts when we start filming and be part of my team putting the music where it would belong in the film. I can even find a part for you in the film if you want. And one more thing, you might think I sound like I'm full of shit but this is just the beginning. I'm gonna make a lot of movies and, buddy, you do this for me and I promise I will take you with me for the ride. I absolutely love your stuff!"

When I hung up the phone, I stared out the window. His approach had been rapid-fire and he had given me a lot to process, especially since I'd gotten loaded right before he called. But I was intrigued and called Sally to see what the scoop was.

"Oh, Mark, I'm sorry, I was playing your record while I was working. I know you asked me not to play it for anyone but I didn't know he was home. But yeah, he's totally legit and he flipped over your record. He's written screenplays for movies but this is the first one he's written that he's also gonna direct. He's sort of high-strung but really passionate about making movies."

"Yeah, I got that impression. Well, I'm gonna read his script and see where it goes from there. Thanks, sweetheart."

Just a day later, FedEx delivered his screenplay. Having had no experience reading one, I found it slightly difficult to follow, to comprehend how it would end up looking on-screen. When I got to a certain scene in the movie, I shuddered. The kid in the lead role is taking care of his mom who has a broken leg or something and they end up having sex. I tried to picture Faye Dunaway as the mom and realized when she had played Joan Crawford, she had reminded me of my own mother. The thought of fucking either one of them sickened me to the core. I realized, of course, it was just a movie and I myself would not be required to fuck my mom, Faye Dunaway, or anyone else, but the thought of it sickened me the hell out and I was suddenly turned off by the entire thing.

I was also deep in my addiction and did not like the thought of having to leave the ten-block radius around my house. Going to the Northeast for any amount of time raised a multitude of problems in my mind.

Instead of handling the situation like an adult, like a professional musician who gave a fuck about people, opportunity, and business, I instead simply never responded to Russell. He left several messages on my phone and always with the utmost respect. But like a self-centered child, I just never answered or returned any calls.

The movie was eventually released to great acclaim. The music of the band Morphine was used and the film catapulted them to great heights. I later saw his second picture in a theater and found it quite funny and interesting. Over the years, I watched with some selfish regret as David O. Russell became one of the biggest directors in Hollywood. Not because of his success, but because he was obviously a talented artist who'd wanted to collaborate with me and I had callously blown him off, missing out on what could have been an eye-opening and life-changing experience for me. Not that it mattered to him, I'm sure. To be in that business took a tenacity and thicker skin than almost any other corner of the entertainment industry. People in the movie world had to be bull-dogs. I'm sure he already had plans B, C, and D waiting in the wings if using my tunes didn't pan out.

I was a drug addict first and foremost. My main issue had been leaving my comfort zone for an unknown place where I'd be forced to find a source of heroin when I could just stay home and be fine. I turned down many opportunities in those days for the same reason. But he was right, it was *just the first one, there will be lots more.* Words that were to haunt me for years to come.

But it was my habit of avoidance by not answering the phone when I wanted to hide from something that was soon to really haunt me. Not in regard to this, but something much deeper and closer to home, with much more devastating results.

20

PARASITE CHILD

IN EARLY NOVEMBER OF 1993, SHORTLY AFTER I'D FINISHED *Whiskey for the Holy Ghost,* Kurt asked me if I wanted to do a version of the Lead Belly song "Where Did You Sleep Last Night?" with Nirvana on the show *MTV Unplugged.* That was the song we'd recorded for our aborted blues project and I had ended up using on my first solo record. He was always looking for ways to shine light on my talents and lift me up, but his ideas often struck me as slightly embarrassing, inappropriate charity, if you will. It just felt weird to me as a relatively unknown singer to come out and do a song with the biggest band in the world during a taping of what was a very popular show. I respectfully declined.

"Okay, I'm gonna sing it, then," he said. "Just like you did it, brother, if that's cool with you."

Flattered, I had responded, "You sing it however you want, I didn't write it. I only sang it like that because your guitar playing inspired it."

He asked me to meet him for lunch on Capitol Hill and pick up some heroin for him on the way. I had enough dough to cover it and met him for lunch at a bar. By that time, it was an unusual occurrence for him to meet me out in public in daytime, but on this occasion he did and in the gray, dark midafternoon, no one seemed to take notice of us as we drank Cokes and half finished some sandwiches before he said he had to go. As I turned to walk south toward my place on First Hill, he asked me to walk with him up to the ATM.

I thought nothing of it because for years while out in public, even long before Nirvana was on the map, he had acted as though he were uncomfortable walking around with me out in the world unless I were right at his side. Whenever we were out together, he had a tendency to stay very close to me, walk right beside me. As though I were his body-guard, big brother, or boyfriend. He had always been somewhat skit-tish in public those times we'd been out and about together, and I felt a natural impulse to protect him and would have done so at all costs if it had ever been necessary. After the worldwide explosion of popularity had hit, he had sadly confided in me at one point: "You and Dylan are the only real friends I have. You guys are the only people in this world I trust anymore." I felt an ache of guilt upon hearing that. Not only did I feel sad and worried for him but I thought, *What kind of friend am I, really?*

I had watched from the wings as what I'd always predicted and had tried so hard to convince some unbelievers of had actually come true. Now he was one of the biggest, most recognizable rock stars in the world. Even though he had his angry and sometimes petulant moments, he remained to a large degree just as normal a guy as the day we'd met. He had always had an ironclad will and intense drive. He had a capac-ity for cruelty like anyone else and I had witnessed it in action before. A sensitive, nonsocial, and thoughtful, quiet guy, highly intelligent with a wicked, biting, and sometimes caustic sense of humor, he was capable of slicing someone up or leaving them standing dick-in-hand feeling the fool if he turned it their way. But he had always been highly, if not overly, cautious to treat me with more kindness and respect than anyone else I knew, even if I was only delivering dope or performing some other task he did not want to do himself. He made me feel like a favored uncle or older brother.

He was disgusted by the pedestal he'd been set atop and the ass-kissing sycophants he encountered at every turn. His natural urge was to rebel against those things he considered the ugly, weak, non-punk aspects of mainstream stardom. He had strong opinions on what was cool and what wasn't when it came to music and, with few exceptions, they lined up largely with my own. He craved isolation and yet often sought my company. He was much more comfortable getting high with one or two friends and listening to records or playing his guitar than he ever was in the raging spotlight of superstardom.

Once we got to the ATM machine, I stood watch as Kurt drew money out of several different accounts, what must have amounted to a few thousand dollars. He counted out a couple of hundred, stuck that in his pocket, and went to hand me the giant stack of twenties left over.

"Do you need me to score again?" I asked, slightly confused since I'd just delivered a couple grams to him.

"No, brother, that's for you."

"What? C'mon, man, I can't take all that. Are you crazy?"

"I love you and you need it. It's that simple. Lanegan, take it, please."

I did need it, stopped protesting, and stood with him as he caught a cab, and watched it all the way up Cherry Street, until it was out of sight. I loved him, too. His gentle concern for my well-being and willingness to be there whenever I needed him was a largely uncommon thing in my life. I was grateful for his continued presence in my world. I sensed a piercing sadness somewhere inside, though, when I thought about our years of close friendship. How it had begun from a pure appreciation of each other's music and certain shared aspects of personality to how it had now warped into a dynamic where, instead of being a positive influence on this guy I considered a genius and cherished little brother, I had become a facilitator to his undoing.

When I got home and counted out the money he'd given me, I couldn't help but feel shame. A little over three thousand dollars. Nothing to him, but a temporary life preserver for me, something to keep my head out of the sewage just a bit longer.

Whiskey for the Holy Ghost was released to much critical acclaim, way more than any Screaming Trees record ever had. Some publications even called it a "masterpiece," the exact term that had prodded and haunted me the three long years I'd struggled to complete the record. This was toxic validation, though: I had wasted thousands of dollars and hours, days, months, and years, nearly losing my mind to arrive at a finished product not far from the very first songs I'd done during the very first sessions. I had become a paranoid, over-the-top asshole making this record, and by calling it brilliant, the world was telling me I had been correct in doing so. Toxic validation, indeed.

Like with my first Sub Pop record, I again refused to put together a band, do any touring or even one single show in support of this album. I had no plans to ever play any of this solo music live and still looked at the Trees as my main gig. I once again tried to start working with them on our much overdue follow-up to *Sweet Oblivion*.

John Hicks was staying in my apartment at this time. Hicks had always been a reliable and loyal friend. He had traveled the world with me, my most trusted sidekick who was willing to do my dirty work when I was unable or unwilling to do it myself. Late one night, I got a phone call from Kurt. He was obviously so fucked up I couldn't understand three-quarters of what he was saying and it scared me. The only thing I really understood was that he wanted me to come over and to come over right away. Since he clearly was not in need of drugs, my mind went haywire with worry: What the fuck was going on? Hicks and I hopped in a cab and took the fifteen-minute ride to Kurt's lakefront estate.

After we walked up to the door and knocked without any response, I cased the perimeter of the place until I came to a window with no blinds. The scene inside the brightly lit room sent a jolt of adrenaline rocketing to my brain. Lying flat on the floor, facedown, was Kurt. He looked like he might be dead.

"Hicks!" I yelled. "Find a way into the house!"

He began quickly checking every door and window, searching for an unlocked entryway inside. I began banging hard and loudly on the huge, thick, six-foot-high window and screaming Kurt's name to no response. I began to freak out. The thought crossed my mind to go to a neighbor's house to call an ambulance, something I knew I couldn't do unless absolutely necessary due to the massive wave of unwanted negative publicity that would bring down on him.

But then I thought I saw his hand move slightly. I began banging and yelling twice as hard. John whipped around the corner, covered in sweat and out of breath.

"I'm sorry, boss, I can't find a way in."

"Check it out," I said, "he's moving in there, he's not dead!"

After more banging and yelling, we watched as, with supreme effort that looked like it took every last ounce of physical power he had, Kurt managed to flip over onto his back.

"Fuck, no!"

I immediately envisioned Kurt's dead body, strangled to death on his own vomit.

"Go get a big rock or a brick!"

If he started to puke, I was going to have to break a window and get inside. Hicks returned in a minute with a boulder I couldn't believe he was able to carry. With the rush of adrenaline coursing through his veins, he seemed to be finding strength I couldn't imagine he'd ever accessed before.

But after an hour or so of us yelling, banging, knocking, and screaming his name, Kurt slowly began to come to life. We urged him on as he tried to stand yet fell painfully back to the floor over and over again. At one point he got to his feet and, with eyes completely closed, managed to take a couple of steps toward the door before his ankle turned in a way that looked so fucked I was sure he must have broken it.

At the end of nearly two full hours, he was still crawling his way toward the door, inch by agonizing inch. Finally, with much loud verbal encouragement from the two of us in the yard, he managed to unlock it. As we burst through, I picked him up and quickly carried him to the couch while John grabbed a towel and a cooking pot full of water and ice cubes from the huge kitchen. He soaked the towel in it and held it against the back of Kurt's neck. We spent the night keeping an eye on him, checking his breathing and making sure he was warm and kept under blankets.

The next morning, he said all he could remember was that he'd done a shot of heroin, nothing out of the ordinary, had not taken any pills, drunk any alcohol, or anything else out of character for him. It had been a stressful, exhausting night for Hicks and me, but for Kurt, it looked to be something much more dangerous. Once again, I felt the heat of guilt as I was acutely aware of my willful participation in his close-to-the-edge addiction. I had been blessed with a large frame and hardy constitution. He wasn't physically built like me, with a much slighter body, and was often ill with some unknown stomach ailments, making it torture for him to eat anything. I was, at heart, just a sick fucking enabler. No, actually something much worse: a parasite who had lived off the misery of this guy I had loved for so long by being a conduit through which he received his death doses. An actively negative presence in the life of this beautiful and talented man, who instead of showing him any positive guidance, consistently chose to take the low road so that I could continue to stay high. When these thoughts jumped uninvited into my head, I was instantly filled with an all-encompassing guilt and self-loathing.

21

DAYS GONE DARK

ONE DAY IN EARLY APRIL OF '94, I WAS LYING ON MY TATTERED, cigarette-burned sofa, chain-smoking and watching stupid soap operas on TV with the sound off, when my phone rang. As was my normal routine, I let the answering machine pick it up and waited to see if whoever called would leave a message.

"Hey, man, it's Kurt. I'm back in town. What're you doing? C'mon over and listen to records with me."

I thought about it for a minute. Though I loved Kurt, I knew I wasn't calling back today—(a) I had quite a bit of cash at the moment and plenty of dope so the thought of possibly running out to score for him was a drag, and (b) I assumed Courtney would be there. I had become conditioned to steer clear of their house because every time I had been there in recent months, some kind of drama would erupt between the two of them. It unfolded like some dreary sitcom joke: Courtney would be uncomfortably friendly to me in front of Kurt till she finally triggered an outburst from him. So I blew Kurt off because I didn't feel like playing the pawn in a fucked-up chess game that particular day.

He called twice more over the next couple hours. Despite the gnawing feeling that I was the world's shittiest friend, I never picked up, just continued to lie around the place in dirty boxers and the stained robe a stripper girlfriend had left in my bedroom, imagining myself a modern-day Oscar Wilde. Listening to a Stranglers record and staring mindlessly at the silent TV screen, I was oblivious to the gathering storm headed in my direction.

Late in the afternoon, I got a call from the entertainment lawyer I shared with Kurt, Rosemary Carroll, an extremely smart, no-nonsense woman who happened to be the ex-wife of celebrated writer/musician Jim Carroll.

"Mark, if you know where Kurt is, you need to tell me now."

A couple minutes later, another message.

"If he is at your apartment and you're not telling me, we're going to have a problem."

I called her back to assure her I wasn't hiding him.

"Mark," she said, "I don't think you realize what's going on. He checked himself out of rehab yesterday, flew back to Seattle today, and now nobody can get in touch with him."

"He's probably fine, Rosemary. Don't worry, I'm sure he'll check in soon."

In fact, I had not known what was going on: a highly publicized over-dose earlier had been posed to both Dylan Carlson and me as accidental and only much later was it revealed to us as a suicide attempt. I had also not known he'd left rehab and come home on the same day he called me.

I called Kurt: no answer. I called our mutual friends but no one had heard from him. I began to wonder if something was really wrong. I chastised myself for not answering the phone earlier, but I told myself, *How could I know?* How could I know what was really going on? How could I have known Courtney wasn't even there? How, how, how . . .

The next day someone in the Nirvana camp asked if I would go with Dylan to some Capitol Hill dope houses to see if Kurt was hanging out at any of them. A private investigator Courtney had hired named Tom Grant picked us up. With money he supplied, we went from place to place, buying drugs and looking for Kurt to no avail: he couldn't be found.

After we had gone to the spot of every last dealer we could think of, Grant drove us to Kurt's house near Lake Washington. We went from room to room calling his name but there was no answer. I went outside to smoke a cigarette and stood at the bottom of a flight of stairs that led to a small room above his garage. For a moment, I thought about going up and taking a look.

Just then Dylan and Grant walked out, ready to leave. I knocked the cherry off my half-finished smoke and put the rest in my coat pocket. For a brief second, I had a terrible premonition, but I shook it off and got in the car, eager just to get home and do my share of the heroin we had bought.

A day or two later, Rosemary called me, her voice shaking with emotion, and delivered the news. Kurt's body had been found in the small room above his garage—the same room at which I had stood at the foot of earlier—the victim of an apparent suicide. A medical examiner judged his death to have taken place the same day we were at the house looking for him. I hung up the phone and burst into tears of remorse, self-hatred, and mountainous grief. I knew I would never get over his death. It would shadow me until the day I died.

The next few days went by in a blur. Everett True, a British journalist I'd drunkenly knocked off his barstool at the Reading Festival in '92, came to Seattle and stayed with me at Courtney's request the week before Kurt's memorial. The incident at Reading had marked the only time Kurt had been openly angry with me. He had looked at me with silent fury and disappointment and quietly said, "You shithead." True and I hadn't known each other before then and he turned out to be the perfect companion for me during those dark days. Mainly, we sat together in silent, stunned, shared grief. When we talked, it was of our good memories of Kurt.

On the day of the service, a girl who was also sharing my room at the time found him some suitable clothes in my closet to wear, he having busted the buttons off his only, coffee-stained white shirt. We attended the memorial together at some hall near the Space Needle. I sat through it in a daze, unable to pay attention to anything that was said. I was lost in the darkest, most depressing regret and self-loathing I'd ever experienced.

Later, at the private wake at Kurt and Courtney's house, she grabbed me in a tight embrace and began sobbing. All eyes in the room were on her. Filled with sorrow and shame myself, it took all of my resolve to not start crying as well.

Unable to endure much of this sad party, I turned to leave. Just as I was going out, sultry, pitch-black-haired Hole bass player Kristen Pfaff was coming in. We'd only met a small handful of times, but the way she looked into my eyes and smiled at me as she passed gave me an instant hard-on. Her gaze had been an unmistakable come-on and the thought of sex crossed my mind for the first time in weeks. Although I felt a certain amount of shame for thinking about fucking at the wake for my

dead friend, my cock had a mind of its own. I got in a cab and my grieving mind took shelter in the thought of her eyes the entire ride home and
long into the night.

A couple of weeks later, my friend Lori Barbero, drummer of the
Minneapolis band Babes in Toyland, called me out of the blue.

"Hey, man, someone wants to talk to you."

I could hear her hand the phone off to someone else.

"Mark?" a young female voice on the other end asked.

"Yeah?"

"Do you know who this is?"

"I don't have a clue," I replied honestly, not recognizing the voice.

"It's Kristen, from Hole. What're you doing right now?"

So, my radar had been correct in identifying the intent behind her
gaze at Kurt's wake after all.

"... um, not much. What are you doing?"

She paused for a second and then said, "I'm thinking about you, man.
I wanna hang out, I totally want to date you. What do you think about
that?"

I laughed out loud at her directness, my first authentic laugh in a long
while.

"That sounds like an excellent idea to me. Are you guys in Seattle?"

She laughed and replied, "No, we're in Minneapolis, but I'll be back
the second week of June. So we're gonna hang out, right? You're not
gonna forget about me, right?"

"That's probably not going to happen," I said, sounding to myself
like a smoker's version of Bob Newhart. She laughed. I smiled stupidly
as I hung up the phone, thinking that my luck had taken a huge upswing
for the better. I stood up, took out my recently neglected-by-everyone
dick, and spontaneously masturbated onto my dining room tabletop.

A couple of weeks later, a tearful, completely downtrodden, and
embattled-sounding Courtney called and left a bullet-to-the heart message: Kristen had OD'd and died in a bathtub the first night she was back
in Seattle. I dizzily sat down on the floor, put my head in my hands, and
stared numbly through my fingers at the wall in disbelief. Not only was
my pipe dream of some sort of relationship with this exotic girl crushed,
but horrifically, she was stone gone forever. Life was an utterly cruel,
savage beast. Everything and everyone around me was fucking cursed.

22

WILDERNESS OF HORRORS

WITH KURT GONE, I LIVED CLOSE TO THE BONE, ESTRANGED FROM family and all my nonusing friends, haunted by my willful absence on the day Kurt died, disappearing into the painful wilderness of horrors my memories created for days on end. Always broke, I had begun selling crack outside of my apartment building to street people, mostly Eritrean and Ethiopian migrants. I spent the profits on heroin. No matter how many drugs I did, I still couldn't escape myself. I couldn't sleep more than a few minutes at a time, usually sitting up in an uncomfortable wooden straight-backed, grade-school-style chair that sat near the noisy, wheezing old radiator under one of my windows, frequently awakened by the seagulls' incessant screaming outside. I was loath to ever lie down, convinced that if I did, I would never wake up. The result was mounting damage to my feet. My toes were constantly numb on the surface but painful as hell when I walked around. If I accidentally knocked them against something while wandering my apartment in a mindless haze, the pain was excruciating.

Courtney leaned on me nearly every other day. For company, for drugs, for emotional support, for a shoulder to cry on and an ear to talk into. She told me that Kurt had been obsessively listening to my record *Whiskey for the Holy Ghost* often in the weeks before he died. I was horrified. Not only had I not responded when he was calling out for my help—a fact I naturally kept to myself, to the extent that I'd lied to a *Rolling Stone* reporter, saying I'd not heard from him for weeks previous to his death—but the thought that somehow my music had lent itself to his suicidal state shattered my already-stunned psyche. Totally devastated, the sense of obligation I felt toward Courtney was turning out to be more than I could give. I felt torn between what I thought Kurt would want me to do and my natural inclination to avoid her at all costs. She was extremely quick mentally, with ferocious, twenty-steps-ahead intelligence and a biting sense of humor that reminded me at times of Kurt himself. She was also very generous, and always interesting in a whirlwind, over-the-top fashion. But life was too all-consuming, too dramatic, difficult, exhausting, and messed-up in her sphere.

As someone who largely preferred to go through the world unnoticed, the few times we were out in public together and she drew so much attention to herself and, by extension, me, I was embarrassed, even pissed off. She talked me into seeing a movie with her and then chattered loudly throughout. Not only did everyone in the theater hate our guts, they also knew exactly who was making all the noise. The smart and outspoken widow of a beloved international rock star who some blamed as the source of his unhappiness and cause of his suicide. Courtney took no shit but was a publicly unpopular figure and a constant target for it. I watched with increasing dismay every time I would see some TV show or magazine article where she was blamed or ridiculed. Worse still were the ongoing rumors of her possible involvement in a murder meant to look as suicide. Suddenly, Dylan was also vilified. Kurt had talked him into buying the shotgun he'd used to kill himself, under the guise that it was needed for home protection. Both Dylan and I had become accustomed to performing these kinds of tasks for him, simply because the imprisonment of his fame made going out into public a fucking drag he could not escape. The crackpot theories that insinuated Courtney and Dylan had conspired to murder Kurt were complete horseshit, but with her manic energy, she did sometimes take me to my absolute limit. At one point Dylan said to me, "Fuck, man, if anyone was gonna have me kill somebody, it would have been Kurt having me do Courtney." Something I knew actually made perfect sense.

Hole guitarist Eric Erlandson, a thoughtful, caring, and intelligent guy I considered a friend, gave me a stern talking-to: I was NOT to score any drugs for Courtney. I took that to heart. Eric was the one person in our circle who I looked up to as a no-nonsense, even-keeled, steadying influence. He always seemed to be the rock in the eye of the hurricane, the proverbial boy who stood on the burning deck. It wasn't like I enjoyed playing that role in Courtney's life, but I felt as though I had inherited it. As she ratcheted up the intensity of her focus on me, I found it increasingly hard to live with and nearly impossible to get out of. I resolved to extricate myself from the situation. Something told me there was a 99 percent chance that shit would meet fan in the process.

Early one morning, I heard her voice on my answering machine.

"Hey, what're you doing? I want to see you, come over."

I ignored it. An hour or so later, I got another message, this one in a somewhat more seductive voice.

"*Hey, sugar*, I want to *see* you. What are you doing?"

Again, I ignored it. She would give up and turn in another direction for solace soon. But throughout the rest of the day and well into the evening, the calls kept coming. Her tone shifted from faux-alluring to slightly harsh to finally: "You motherfucker! Where the fuck are you? Call me back, you son of a bitch!"

As it got later, I grew tired of listening to these abusive messages and unplugged the machine altogether, and just in case she was motivated to come over, I turned off the front door buzzer. My mind a bit lighter after making the decision to disengage, I lit some incense, turned off the lights, put on a VHS tape of *Seven Samurai* with the sound off, and lay back on the couch with my feet out on the coffee table to try and catch a nod. Somehow, I fell into a deep sleep.

I was awakened by a light knocking on my apartment door. Voices in the hallway. I recognized instantly the fawning voice of my dickhead apartment manager, Christian, who I hated and who hated me. He had passed out fliers to everyone on my side of the building, telling tenants to report it anytime someone yelled up to my window, something I'd instructed some customers to do if my lights were on. I'd not wanted certain fiends to have knowledge of my apartment number and thus buzz me incessantly all night. When I wanted to be left alone, I simply left the lights off. Christian was determined to get me either arrested or kicked out, preferably both.

"I can't believe you're in my building!" he gushed. "I had no idea Mark was a friend of yours!"

"Oh yes, we're very close. He was supposed to come over today. I'm worried about him."

The other voice belonged to Courtney. It was clear she had this prick eating out of her hand. I tiptoed over to the door to hear them better and, by reflex, grabbed the badly dented aluminum baseball bat next to the door. The next thing I heard blew my mind and enraged me at the same time.

"Well, seeing how you are such close friends, I can unlock the door and let you in to take a look around. Just to make sure nothing's wrong . . ."

He wasn't just sucking up to the famous person in his presence, I knew he also intended to take a look around my place and make note of any incriminating contraband. I quietly took a deep breath and suddenly broke out in a cold, sticky sweat. My mind seized on a dark thought and I silently lifted the chain lock off the door. The moment he opened it up, I would clock him with the bat, beat my sniveling apartment manager unconscious. I would be in my rights to do so if he were to enter without my permission. Wait a second . . . No, I would actually beat them both to death, Christian and Courtney both, put an immediate end to two separate but now entwined aggravations, and let the chips fall where they may.

I silently raised the bat. I could almost hear Courtney thinking on the other side of the door. I bent my knees, tensed my arms and shoulders, ready to uncoil the moment the door swung open. She took a breath. Here it comes.

"Oh well, I'm sure he's okay. We better not invade his privacy."

And just like that, they left.

I ran into her a couple weeks later. I said I had been out of town for a family emergency. And that was it. By that time, she had new connections and interests that rarely included me anymore.

23

GO FUCK A DONKEY

I HAD BECOME KNOWN AS A GUY WHO COULD PROCURE DRUGS for traveling rock bands. When the Lollapalooza tour came to Washington at the end of August, I was contacted by an old friend.

I'd first met Paul Bearer when he was the singer for a Philadelphia band called the Serial Killers. He was a one-of-a-kind dude with a crazy, funny-as-fuck intelligence who shared my fiending, black-hole, all-encompassing love of opiates and all things bizarre. More provocative stand-up comic than singer, he was a favorite of mine ever since his band had opened for us in San Diego in the late '80s or early '90s. While I sat watching their set from the back of the empty room, his onstage banter had pissed off one of the only two other audience members to the extent that she'd thrown an entire glass mug of beer at his head from five feet away. He went straight into a hilarious retaliatory routine that included blow jobs at the Greyhound bus station restroom, unplugging the Slurpee machine at 7-Eleven, and, most memorably, telling the woman to go back to Tijuana to fuck a donkey. (Years later, I'd recited almost the exact same routine from memory while being mercilessly heckled by a drunken woman during a show in Seattle. It hadn't occurred to me that the Tijuana reference didn't exactly translate when spoken in the Great Northwest, but I'd waited years to unload it, so what the hell.)

Paul was traveling with the all-female Los Angeles band L7 on the tour. A couple of the L7 girls dabbled in dope, and in the past, I'd scored for them and they for me. Nick Cave and the Bad Seeds were also on the Lollapalooza tour and Paul had asked me if I could hook something up for Nick and bass player Martyn Casey when they were in Seattle on a day off.

I'd been a huge fan of Nick Cave for years. I felt a deep connection to his music, and he and the Bad Seeds had been a central influence on the solo records I'd been toiling away at for some years now.

Once I had collected some shit for these Australian musicians, I felt a bit of anticipatory excitement about meeting them, even if just in my capacity as a middleman for small drug deals. When they showed up in a cab at my building, we went upstairs, politely did the deal, exchanging the dope for dough, and started preparing hits. As I sat at my dining room table trying to locate a vein, Cave looked at my fucked-up arms, crisscrossed like a road map of Germany with huge, deep, red-and-black abscessed tracks.

"Damn," he said, "I guess you can't just pop into the can for a quick hit."

I was a pariah in my apartment building and was especially despised by the young Goth couple whose door was directly opposite mine. The nonstop daily parade of unwashed street people and Eritrean crack addicts in and out of my apartment had them perpetually pissed off. As Nick, Martyn, and I were leaving to go get some dinner, the couple just happened to be unlocking their door and entering their apartment. As we stepped out, they caught a glimpse of Cave standing there in his three-piece suit, his iconic jet-black pompadour perfectly in place, and almost broke their necks doing a double take. Nick calmly noticed them freaking out.

"Good evening," he said coolly.

That was a small win for me. My neighbors never looked at me the same again.

24

BACK TO THE NEEDLE

LAYNE HAD GONE TO MINNESOTA TO ATTEND A REHAB PROGRAM and I wished him well. I supported any of my friends who tried to get clean as I was often trying to kick on my own. Whenever anyone found out I was trying to kick, however, my efforts were greeted with raised eyebrows and rolled eyes from pals and using buddies alike. Neither Kurt nor Layne believed I would ever get clean due to my maniacal hunger for drugs and the lengths I'd go to get them. Both had said as much at different times in conversation with me. They both imagined they would kick for good someday, but that my chances of ever getting clean were next to nil.

I had met a fifty-something cab driver named Leon, an old-school black dude who had given me a ride one day. When we started talking, he let it be known that he got a large carry of methadone weekly from the VA that he'd sell to me if I was interested. I was, of course, very interested. I bought his seven-day dose from him every week. It became my backup plan for whenever I was unable to score. I would take a large bottle with me on the road whenever I toured, leaving it in the bus refrigerator with a sign written in bold black marker taped to it: DO NOT TOUCH! I would also try to kick at home from time to time, bringing myself down using the methadone so brutally fast that I dragged myself through some pain. I'd make it two or three days off everything, then go right back to the needle.

I got buzzed from the front door one afternoon. To my surprise, it was Layne. He'd put on a lot of weight and I'd never seen him look so healthy. He'd come directly from the airport to my apartment after finishing rehab, jonesing to get high.

"Hey, bro, you got anything on you?" he asked, knowing that I most likely did.

"Are you sure you wanna do that, man? You're finally clean, for real. Why do you want to start all over again?"

"All I thought about the whole time was getting out and getting high. I never wanted to quit. I only did it to make everyone happy and shut them up."

He cooked himself up a shot in my kitchen. I heard him puke into my sink the instant he hit the vein. He walked unsteadily out into my living room with a goofy smile, sat down on my couch, and nodded for hours. When he came out of it, I made him promise to not tell anyone he'd fallen off the wagon so soon at my place. I didn't want Jerry and the other Alice guys blaming me for his relapse.

For years, he'd had a passionate on-and-off relationship with a girl named Demri, a friend of my ex-girlfriend Anna. It had been marked by dizzying highs and dark, depressing lows. A fellow addict, she was said to be somewhat indiscriminate when it came to sex, much like myself. *Who knows*, I thought before I really knew him, *maybe it's an open relationship*. But once we'd become friends, it became clear that her behavior caused Layne some pain.

I had gotten a glimpse into her straightforward approach before I'd even met him. Like Layne and I did, she and I encountered each other for the first time outside a Capitol Hill dope house. As I was leaving, she was going in.

"Hey there, aren't you Anna's boyfriend? I'm Demri."

I was instantly attracted to this sexy, smiling creature. The first thought that rolled through my head was *DAMN!* She had an alluring outward sexuality, a beautiful face, and the most extraordinary, devilish eyes.

"Yeah, I am. Please don't tell her you saw me here, though, that would cause problems."

I felt like such a jackass whenever I was compelled to ask a stranger to keep my secrets, but most addicts were keeping secrets from someone themselves. There was some semblance of a code of secrecy among certain junkies.

"No problems here, handsome. What are you doing right now?" she asked with a coy smile.

"No plans, just heading home."

"Why don't you come home with me? We can get high and fuck."

That came out of the blue. Her brazen, direct approach put me on my heels for a second but struck me like a kick to the balls . . . a shockingly pleasurable one.

"Uhh, I don't think that would be a very good idea. Thanks, but I can't."

She grabbed my hand and said, "Aww, c'mon. I'll never tell anyone. You're cute, I like you, nobody's at my place. C'mon, you won't be sorry."

I was sorely tempted but I had a feeling I would somehow end up very sorry. Your private business could spread quickly through the small, incestuous music scene. I had heard she was Layne's girlfriend from my own girlfriend and had almost instantly found the reputation that preceded her to be pretty fucking spot-on. It was the type of situation I found nearly impossible to pass up, but her connection to Anna and to this guy I'd not met but already deeply respected as an artist and whose singing I loved made me think twice.

For once, I was smart enough to not take the bait. With more than a little regret, I again declined and walked home alone. But for quite a while afterward, it continued to play heavy on my mind. And in my fantasies.

25

NIGHT OUT WITH JERRY

ONE NIGHT, I WENT OUT ALONE TO A LOCAL DIVE ROCK-AND-ROLL bar, the Off Ramp, to see a Judas Priest cover band. Located on a street parallel to the I-5 freeway, hence its name, it was a shithole I rarely ever set foot inside. I was friends with an acquaintance of the British singer Jim Jones of the London band Thee Hypnotics and had visited him and his girlfriend once or twice in the run-down apartment they rented above the place, but other than that, I generally avoided the building. I'd seen Priest as a teenager and still, after seeing hundreds of great shows over the years, it remained the greatest concert I'd ever attended and I'd heard this band turned out an amazing imitation.

After more than a few drinks while sitting at the bar and waiting for the band to hit, I noticed two guys come stumbling through the door, obviously quite wasted themselves: Jerry Cantrell, guitarist/singer/song-writer of Alice in Chains, and local hero and nice guy Tommy Niemeyer, guitarist of the influential and beloved thrash/punk band the Accüsed. Jerry immediately came over and ordered drinks for the three of us. After watching about thirty minutes of the headliner and putting away half as many drinks, we wobbled unsteadily out the door, looking for a place to do some of the coke Jerry always had his pockets full of. My place was the closest, most obvious destination so we hailed a cab and headed up First Hill.

Always in hot water with my apartment manager Christian, whose window was directly next to the front steps, I warned the two of them to remain silent until we got upstairs. Once inside, Jerry dumped a huge bag of coke on a plate and starting cutting lines. I got a bottle of booze from the kitchen and we began one of those all-night coke-and-alcohol mind-melting sessions of intense yet instantly forgettable conversation, the kind you always regretted once the sun came up and your melon was pounding like Rod Carew had taken batting practice on your head all night, endlessly connecting his wooden bat with your skull, stroking single after single to the opposite field. After an hour or two, Tommy had clearly reached and then stepped way over and past his limit.

"Guys," he said, "I gotta go. I have to do some stuff for my mom today and I can't bail on her."

I really loved hanging out with Tommy, who was funny as hell and one of the sweetest guys ever. I hated to see him leave, but since I'd not one loving or happy childhood memory of my mother, I let him go without a fight. Good on ol' Tommy for caring for his mom; it was an impulse I would never know. As he left, I suddenly remembered I had a commitment myself that morning, one I absolutely could not miss. Bob Pfeifer was in town and I had a breakfast meeting with him that there was no way I could get out of. If the Trees were going to remain on Epic, some things were going to have to change, and Bob was hell-bent on giving me a dressing down. It wasn't something I looked forward to, but knew it would be the end of us if I didn't attend and take it on the chin.

"Fuck, Jerry! I just remembered I have breakfast with Pfeifer at nine thirty! What time is it? Jesus Christ, thank God I remembered."

"Oh fuck that, dude. You're coming out on the boat with me today. Forget Pfeifer. What's he gonna do, drop you?"

"Yeah, that's exactly what he's gonna do. Those guys have had enough of us, bro. We don't sell millions of records like you. He said, point blank, if I didn't come to breakfast, he was gonna drop us! He's serious, man." I looked at the clock in my bedroom. Four thirty a.m. If I managed to fall asleep I might get four hours or so. I could do it on that. "Jerry, hang out as long as you want, make yourself at home, but I've gotta try and get some sleep or I'm fucked. Big-time fucked."

"Okay, man. I'm gonna stay awake, come with you to breakfast, and then we'll go spend the day on my boat."

"Okay. Deal. Goodnight."

I ate a handful of Valiums and climbed into bed. I don't know how much time had passed but I was fully asleep when I felt someone gently shaking my shoulder.

"Lanegan. Lanegan," came the whispered yet persistent voice waking me up. I opened my eyes to find Cantrell shaking me awake.

"What, Jerry? What time is it?"

"It's six. I'm gonna head out to my boat now. I can't stay awake for breakfast."

"That's cool. I'll call you this week and we'll hang."

"Okay," he replied. And then, "Hey, bro, do you mind if I borrow some of your porn?"

"Sure, man, take whatever you want. I'll see you later." And with that, I fell asleep, only to be rudely awakened by the incessant banging of my old-school alarm clock at nine. I stumbled out of bed, pulled on some jeans, brushed my teeth, and opened the closet near the front door to grab my coat. I stood staring into it for a minute. Something was not right. I pulled the light string and looked in disbelief into my previously packed closet.

My closet had been crammed side to side with a quarter of a refrigerator box filled with my lifetime's collection of porn. It had every magazine, videotape, and sundry item I had collected in my twenty-plus years on the planet. It had held my nearly complete collection of Traci Lords's catalog that Gary Conner had told me to get rid of when the scandal of her underage work had broken. Gone. All gone. That box must have weighed at least a hundred pounds. In my hungover state, I realized I didn't have time to stand around pondering this mystery.

I grabbed my jacket and headed down to Pfeifer's hotel where I was treated to a hyperaggressive monologue and schooled in Music Business 101 as if I were a child over some disgusting scrambled eggs and toast. After I assured and reassured Bob that I fully understood the importance of whatever it was he had blasted me with, he gave me a hug and a way-harder-than-necessary slap on the back and I groggily began the long walk back up the hill to my place.

Weeks later, I ran into Jerry again. He claimed zero memory nor any responsibility for my missing porn collection.

26

SEASONS OF MADNESS

EVEN THOUGH ALICE IN CHAINS WANTED TO GET HIM INTO A studio to record music that he seemed to have little interest in, Layne had started playing with Pearl Jam's guitarist, the big-hearted and talented Mike McCready. The two of them, along with an older bass player Mike had befriended in rehab named John Baker Saunders and my drummer from the Trees, Barrett Martin, had started a band they named Mad Season. One afternoon, Layne called me up and asked me to meet him at the studio where they were working. When I arrived, none of the other band members were there. Layne promptly kicked producer Brett Eliason, my one-time tour manager and soundman, out of the control room.

"Let's write a song. You write a line, then I'll write one, and we'll just do it like that."

"Okay," I agreed.

He played the music in the background and we began. He wrote a line, handed me the paper, then I'd write one and hand it back to him. Whatever one of us wrote informed the other of what the next line would be. It was a cool and interesting exercise. Neither of us had ever written this way.

When the lyrics were done, he hit record on the tape machine and we got it in one go. All in all, it took us forty-five minutes to write and record a song we called "Long Gone Day." He recorded me singing on one other song and I was impressed that he knew how to run the tape machine himself. In all my years of making records, I still had zero knowledge of anything technical involved in the process. I finished my part on the second tune and then I went home. The entire time I spent working on the record was a little more than an hour.

When it came out later that year, Mad Season's *Above* became a big-selling album with a bona fide hit single, "River of Deceit." We were to do two concerts locally in Seattle as Mad Season. I remember feeling sheepish around McCready. Mike had successfully gone to rehab and kicked the drinking problem he and I had shared at my disastrous Roskilde appearance in '92 while I was more addicted than ever.

Around six months after its release, I started getting large, totally unexpected royalty checks in the mail. To my shock, the guys had given me full royalty points on the record. Since it went gold, that meant a shitload of cash was coming my way. I couldn't believe it. I did stuff on people's records all the time and you were usually just doing it for friends, not expecting anything in return. What these guys had given me for less than two hours' time (time that was spent having fun, not working) was unheard of in my world, an extremely classy and generous move. I was eternally grateful.

I found out where the checks were coming from at Sony and made sure that they kept being sent directly to me, not my accountant. That was an exceedingly stupid and foolish move, but such was my desperation for money at the time; I couldn't bear to let the tax man have a cut. It was a decision that would come back to seriously bite me in the ass.

—

THE REST OF THAT YEAR, I sporadically got together with my Screaming Trees bandmates and we began the painful process of trying to write another record. It was going to take a group of fully developed great-sounding demos before Epic would support us working again since we'd wasted time and money the last two times they'd taken a chance and booked us into a studio. Slowly, day by day, we hammered away until we had a small, raw collection of songs that showed some promise. But what had come almost effortlessly in '92 was now once again toil. I was responsible for much of the trouble due to my giant heroin habit and the demands it made on my time and energy.

When not developing songs with the band, I continued making and selling crack. Whenever I was not working, I was spending most of my free time smoking crack and shooting heroin around the clock with

Layne in his apartment. He had a roommate for a while, a really nice, normal dude named Johnny who I had at first suspected had been hired by someone to keep an eye on Layne. It became obvious after a while that Johnny was just a guy who cared for Layne, a friend and non-drug-user. Whenever we got loaded while he was home, it was in the privacy of Layne's bedroom. Johnny seemed increasingly beat down by the futility and darkness that began to pervade the place, less happy to see me and less lighthearted every time I'd stop by. Johnny moved out after six or seven months. Unsupervised, the pair of us sank deeper into the shit. Layne called one night and frantically asked me to come over right away.

When I got there, I did our secret personal sequence of knocks on the door and heard him shout from down the hall, "Come in, goddamnit!" That in itself shocked me because he would never, *never* leave the door unlocked. I came in, locked the door, and cautiously called his name.

"Down here, man! In the bathroom!"

"Why was the door unlocked, bro?" I asked while approaching the toilet.

"So I can get out of here in a fucking hurry if I have to!" he hissed.

I entered the bathroom to the strange sight of him lying on his stomach on the floor, head behind the shitter, staring intently at a tiny hole in the wall.

"What's going on, brother? Why would you have to get out of here?" I quietly asked, not sure I really wanted to know the answer.

"Quiet, man! They're back there! Wait a minute and be quiet, they'll come out again," he forcefully whispered.

"Who are *they*?" I whispered back.

"The fucking spiders, man. I was asleep and when I woke up they were coming out of my arm!"

I had known some truly mentally ill people in my life. I'd spent Christmas Eve in a psych ward with a childhood friend who had been in and out of the mental hospital for years with paranoid schizophrenia. I didn't like the look or sound of this at all.

"Hey, Layne, why don't you get up off the floor and let's go sit on the couch for a minute and talk."

"Shhhh! Quiet, man. They can hear you!"

Jesus fuck, I thought, *he's fucking lost it.* I stood there wracking my brain as to what my next steps should be. Whatever they were, they would have to be done with utmost care. I thought about calling Jerry Cantrell but quickly changed my mind. The Alice guys—Jerry, Sean Kinney, and bass player Mike Inez, along with producer Toby Wright—had recently enlisted me to try and get Layne out of his apartment and down to a recording studio where they wanted to start making music. He would begin by saying, "Tell them I'll be there at nine" and I would relay the message. Nine would turn into eleven thirty, then two a.m., and finally if I asked again he would simply reject the idea out of hand, completely and with a total finality. This routine had gone on for a few days. They would probably be as helpless or more than me in this situation. At least I held a tiny bit of sway.

"Layne, man, listen to me. I don't see any spiders back there. Just get up for a minute and let's go talk quietly in the living room."

After several long, long moments of silence, he suddenly slid backwards on his stomach from behind the toilet bowl, got to his feet, and grabbed me by the arm, leading me into the other room. Lifting his sleeve, he showed me the ugly abscess on his arm.

"I caught them crawling out of there, and saw one peeking out of the hole behind the toilet. I have to kill them before they take the whole place over," he said in a choked and extremely quiet voice.

He went to put a rock into his crack pipe—a glass tube with cigarette-lighter-blackened steel-wool Chore Boy stuffed into the end.

"Hold on a second, bro," I said, "let's not hit the pipe right now. We need to talk about this rationally."

It was pure crack craziness that I was witnessing, a frightening level of psychosis. He was convinced there were spiders coming out of his arms, hiding behind his toilet, and taking over his house. I coaxed him to do a shot of dope instead, in hopes it would even out his mind. Then I talked him into coming over to my place with me, promising I would hire exterminators to go in and clean his place out if he wished. I was pained beyond words to see him this way, the sweetest, funniest, most magical and intelligent dude I knew, out of his tree. Such was my love for the guy, he had become like the half of me I'd always lacked.

After a couple of days, he was back to normal but occasionally he'd say something that made it clear these imaginary spiders were still somewhere in the back of his mind. I kept him at my house for a week until one day he looked at me and said, "I lost my fucking mind, didn't I?"

I looked at him and the familiar mischievous twinkle normally in his eyes was back. I started laughing.

"Thank God you realized that. I was afraid we were going to have to hit the nuthouse!"

"I'm sorry, man." He smiled. "Fuck, that was weird."

"Yeah. It was, but you ain't got nothin' to be sorry about, brother, I'm just glad you're back," I responded with great relief.

27

MISS AUSTRALIA 1971

IN JANUARY OF '95, THE TREES WENT TO AUSTRALIA TO TAKE PART in the Big Day Out festival, something akin to Lollapalooza in the States. It was a huge traveling circus that hit every major city in Australia: tons of bands from several different countries playing on a bunch of different stages at every show. Somehow, we got booked on the main stage.

At the very beginning of the very first show, a huge outdoor affair in Melbourne, I got hit in the eye with something hard. It swelled shut instantly. Enraged, I looked around the stage with my good eye until I found the projectile, a thick, heavy one-dollar Australian coin. While the band continued to play, oblivious to my rage, I started talking through the mic to the crowd, holding up the coin and daring the asshole who had thrown it to make himself known. On the huge, high stage with a good ten-foot security pit between it and a fence that held back the thousands of audience members, I stalked back and forth, determined to identify the fuckhead who'd hit me and get some retribution. Suddenly, I saw a huge, blond, shirtless muscle-bound giant pointing at me, then at himself, then flipping me off with both hands. His gestures, his demeanor, everything clearly said, "It was me! C'mon, shithead, let's go!"

My extreme anger boiled over. I tried to get off the stage and into the no-man's-land between it and the crowd to throw punches at this physically huge fuck taunting me from just on the other side of the fence, but the multitude of security guys in front of the stage would not let me get down. Still being egged on by the blond steroid specimen, I searched the stage for something to throw. All I could find was a large, full, unopened oblong bottle of Evian water. I had been a quarterback and I had been a closer on my baseball team, but the shape and weight of this bottle, as well as the fact that I could only see through one eye, made hurling it into a crowd packed with women, children, and innocent concertgoers a tricky proposition. If I was to catch a child or a woman in the face or, Christ, anyone other than this blond musclehead, it would be all over for me. But as the source of my rage continued to egg me on, my intense anger could not be controlled.

I walked to the edge of the stage while the band still continued to jam, at this point five minutes into a vocal-less tune. I stood ten feet from where this son of a bitch stood, still flipping me off with both hands. *Fuck it*, I thought. I threw the heavy and weirdly shaped bottle with everything I had, maybe fifty miles an hour. It caught him horizontally right across the middle of the face. The audience roared with approval.

Intending to finish him off, I ran and leapt over the outstretched hands of the equally giant security guards hell-bent on keeping me on the stage. I landed directly on the other side of the fence from my now-wounded target. The instant I hit the ground, the excruciating pain in my heel told me that I'd broken my foot. For a brief moment, I was eye to eye with my adversary. His face was covered with blood as he tried to pull himself to his feet. On the opposite side of the fence, I had my hand on top of his, trying to do the same thing. His mug looked like shit, but I'm sure mine was equally contorted with pain. Security grabbed me and threw me back onstage. I finished the set seated on the drum riser, unable to walk.

I had not yet scored that day and instead got drunk. Hole was also on the festival, and in a shuttle van headed from the stage to the artists' area, Courtney rode along with me, whispering in my ear that she and Al Jourgensen of the band Ministry had scared something up.

Later on that shitty first day of the tour, I was busted by members of Q Prime, my management team, when they walked into a backstage tent right as I was administering a shot of heroin to Courtney. To make matters worse, Q Prime had just begun representing Courtney and Hole.

"Lanegan! What in the fuck are you doing?"

"Tell me you two are not shooting heroin or by God, Peter and Cliff are going to hear about it!"

"Lanegan, for a guy who never makes us any money, you are a complete time-wasting ass! What in the serious fuck do you think you're doing?"

"Jesus Christ! I cannot believe this! Honestly! Do you have a brain in your fucking head?"

And so on. Hardly a promising start to the tour. Now forced to hobble around with a cane and play each show seated on a stool, I turned my attention to scoring heroin, not getting busted, and staying well.

There were plenty of addicts on the tour. Besides myself, my close friend and the Trees' longtime soundman Brian "Rat" Benjamin was also strung out. I'd quickly become acquainted with Al Jourgensen, Ministry's notorious singer. He, Courtney, and I were the three most obvious dope fiends on tour. From appearances, Bobby Gillespie and Throb, the stars of British band Primal Scream, my favorite band on the tour, were also getting loaded daily and hell-raising nonstop, presumably with different drugs of choice than us. It was a continuous party.

Al's road manager was an old Scottish road manager of mine from the early '90s, Michael "Curly" Jobson, a man rumored to have a dark and mysterious past. He and I had become instantly friendly, getting along famously during the time he was employed by my band until one day in Germany. I had spent the night at the apartment of a beautiful friend of mine named Petra Hammerer who was not cool with my drug use. She had said I could come over as long as I left my heroin in my hotel. I had given it to Hicks. After an enjoyable night at Petra's, my first stop was Hicks's room to get my dope and do a shot. He opened the door with a look that told me something was very, very wrong.

"Mark, I don't know how to tell you this but Curly broke in here last night and took your dope."

I hit the roof.

"What in the fuck do you mean, took my dope? Why in the fuck did you let him have it? How'd he know you had it? And where the fuck is he?"

Hicks went into a highly animated, lengthy explanation, playing both himself and Curly, bouncing between an imitation of Jobson's threatening Scottish brogue and back into his own heavy Southern accent.

"He knocked on the door and then shoved me out of the way and forced his way in. He said, 'Where is it? Where is it, John? I'll break your

nose and tear this room apart unless you give it to me now!' 'But Curly,'
I said to him, 'Mark will kill me if I give it to you!' 'I'm gonna kill you
right now if you don't!'"

I was becoming more and more agitated by the moment.

"Where is he, Hicks?" I demanded, a furious fire welling up inside.

"That's the worst part. He got on a plane to head back to England.
He took your dope and quit."

Not only had he stolen my dope but he'd also just quit in the middle
of a tour and left us to fend for ourselves? I was in shock. I called Kim,
our hapless manager who'd hooked us up with him in the first place. I
told her either she fixed it or she was fired but that this was on her.

Our soundman at the time, Rod Doak, had also been our tour manager in the past and he took over. A week later, Curly showed up out of
the blue, full of apology and excuses, ready to finish the job. I found out
the entire fiasco had been brought on by a long-distance fight between
Curly and his wife. He'd freaked out and gone home to fix it, but not
before stealing my heroin and leaving me high and dry.

Now, years later, Curly was no longer a drug-stealing dirtbag. He
was clean and dressed impeccably in a suit or nice sweater to perform
his job of looking after one of rock's most notorious addicts, Jourgensen.
Al began to grate on my nerves right away. Curly woke me up early one
morning, asking me for something to get Al well.

Brian Rat and I always made sure we were covered. That meant hitting the streets, working the local crews and any other potential sources
of dope. Every day, Brian and I hit the ATM with his card, drew out max
dough, and set out to score before anything else. Before I'd left Seattle,
I had bought a large bottle of "pain cocktail" from a guy in my neighborhood with advanced AIDS. It contained methadone, Dilaudid, liquid
morphine, and who knew what all else. All I knew was that it didn't just
keep you well, it also got you loaded. I guarded it carefully at all times. It
was my backup, not my party drug, only there to keep me well if I were
unable to score.

Al, on the other hand, was the entitled variety of junkie, always one
to want in on something he'd put zero energy into getting. He expected
to be catered to. I gave Curly a small amount of my pain cocktail and
told him it was the last time I was giving Al anything for free.

After our show in Sydney, I met two attractive, slightly older women, one blond, the other brunette, probably in their mid- to late thirties. They were funny and sexy and insisted on taking me out on the town. As we went from bar to bar, getting drunker and drunker, I became aware at some point that the brunette was the ex-wife of Chris Bailey, the legendary singer of the Saints, one of my favorite bands of all time. I couldn't help thinking as we laughed and partied in a corner booth of a dark, crowded bar that if this wildwoman were my wife, I'd hang on to her.

We continued our pub crawl down in Sydney's well-known Kings Cross, an area of the city filled with junkies, brothels, and bars, where I had scored drugs the day before. When I ran out of cigarettes, the women went into a shop to grab me some more while I leaned on my cane curbside and smoked my last one. I stood there, staring up at the sky, starting to get lost in my head, when I heard the unmistakable sound of someone speeding from around the bend and then the squeal of tires as they hit the brakes hard. I spun around. At that exact moment, an old panel truck plowed into a girl who was running across the street. The sickening crunch of impact made a hideous sound as it sent her flying out of her shoes toward where I stood. Her body landed in the gutter right next to me.

I snapped out of my reverie, recoiling in shock. I hobbled into the street. The first to reach her, I put my finger to her neck and checked for a pulse. Nothing.

My two new friends, the driver of the truck, and more passersby crowded around. As someone tried to do CPR, the truck driver began to quietly weep. When an ambulance arrived, they took the paddles to her, trying to shock her heart into starting again. I looked down at this good-looking young woman. Knowing I'd seen her last second on earth, I felt overcome with a sad weariness. The party was over.

The women gave me a ride to my hotel and only the blond stayed. As I said goodnight to the dark-haired woman, I selfishly wished that, if I was only to have the company of one of them for the night, it would have been her. But I knew I was more than lucky to have anyone at all.

—

THE END OF THE TOUR brought us to Perth, far Western Australia, with one day off before the last show. Staying a few miles outside the city, I knew I was gonna have to hit the streets to score. On my way out of the hotel, I gave Al a courtesy call and asked him if he needed me to get him something. His curt "Nope, I'm good, man" told me he'd already lined something up for himself and had no intention of sharing any with me.

Brian Rat and I took a cab into town to a punk rock house someone had tipped us off to as a place to score. When we got there, it turned into a shitfest lasting hours as we kept being promised "It's almost here" and "Fuck, man, I'm sorry, but we have some other shit on the way." After several hours of this bullshit runaround, I was getting pretty dopesick and puked into the toilet within earshot of the tenants and their friends who knew I was a musician and who were coming to the show the next day. Finally, some guy showed up with some dope that I instantly knew was fake.

We grabbed our coats and on the way out, a girl grabbed my arm and said, "Come on, I know where to score." She took us to a house where we were finally able to get our daily allowance of heroin, always the exact amount we were able to buy with the daily limit on the ATM card. As soon as we got back to the hotel and Brian and I had finally gotten well, the phone in my room rang. I picked it up and the first and only thing I heard was Jourgensen.

"Thanks a fuck of a lot for thinking of me, asshole!" and then, *click*, he hung up.

After our humiliating day's worth of dopesick waiting, the runaround, fake dope, and, above everything else, the fact that I had specifically asked Jourgensen if he'd needed anything before starting that hellish trek, I became enraged. Brian looked at me with a slightly concerned curiosity as I jumped up and ran out the door, headed to Al's room intending to teach him a painful lesson.

I banged on his door and Mikey, his sweetheart of a long-suffering guitar player, answered. I shoved my way past him, then, obviously on fire with anger, turned to him and said, "Do you want some of this, Mikey?" He put his hands up palms forward and shook his head. I turned to find Al standing on the bed in his Speedo underwear, while lying there under the blankets at his feet was a woman who looked to be Miss Australia 1971. He had hold of the large old-school rotary phone and was brandishing the receiver as though he planned to club me with it. I crossed the room in a few long steps. I grabbed the hand that held the receiver, twisting his arm while I did it, and quickly wrapped the cord around his neck. I picked the diminutive loudmouth up against the wall with the cord as a noose.

"Don't you ever talk to me like that, you fucking pussy. You don't know me well enough for that. I asked you this morning if you needed anything so don't go throwing shit on me because it didn't work out for you. You'll wish you never met me, motherfucker!" With that, I released him and left him choking, desperate to get some air back in his lungs.

Brian and I laughed when I relayed what had taken place, neither of us a fan of Al's by that point. The next morning, a Sunday and the last day of the tour but two days before we were scheduled to fly home, the ATM ate Brian's card when he'd inserted it, to our horror. Our only source of cash gone, we were now faced with the prospect of two or more days of dopelessness before we could get home. The two of us sat on the steps of the backstage hours before showtime, dejected and wondering how we were gonna manage to score with no dough.

Suddenly, Curly walked up and, his voice filled with easily understood meaning, said, "Are you guys okay today?"

I shook my head no with a dark, disappointed look on my face.

"C'mon, boys," he said.

We got up and followed him into one of the empty tents in the artists' area. He closed the flaps and tied them shut. Then he pulled out a very large bag of the golden-brown powdered heroin we'd been using the entire tour. He poured it all out on top of a folding table and, with a credit card, pushed at least three-quarters of the pile to one side and left a small amount on the other side. He proceeded to fold a large piece of paper into a makeshift bindle and scooped the smaller of the two piles back into its original bag. Then he pushed the other huge pile into his folded paper container, closed it up, and handed it to me.

"What the fuck, Curly?" I asked, not believing he was giving me this huge pile.

He replied in his thick Scottish brogue.

"Al has to go to Japan tomorrow, he can't take it with him. And besides, little brother," he said with a smile and a wink, "I believe I might just owe you one," referring to his theft of my stash all those years before.

We both gave him hugs of joy.

"Careful now, boys," he said, "don't mess up the clothes."

At that moment, my heart was filled with love for the guy. Yet for me the best moment of the entire tour came late that night when I received a call on my hotel-room phone.

"Hello?"

"Lanegan, it's Al. I just wanted to apologize for yesterday. I was out of line and I'm sorry. You're still gonna sing on my next 1000 Homo DJs record, right? And remember, there's always a room for you at my place in Texas."

"Sure, of course, Al, I'll be there whenever you need me. All is forgiven. I'm sorry I overreacted."

"Okay, man, that makes me feel better . . . and by the way, you wouldn't happen to be holding anything would you? I hate to ask, but I'm seriously hurting."

As I looked over at Brian with a huge grin and then down at the gigantic pile of Al's dope Curly had given us, I said in my saddest-sounding voice, "Fuck, Al, I wish. We're fucked, too. Have a great time in Japan and call anytime when you're back in the States."

Predictably, I was never to hear from him again. We did run into each other by chance at a hotel lobby bar in Milan, Italy, years later. He'd packed on so much weight, it was obvious he was either clean or had traded his dope addiction for one for food. His longtime bandmate Paul spotted me while Al was giving an interview in the corner and came up to me.

"Hey, man, Al's doing really well; please don't offer him anything or fuck him up."

"Don't worry, Paul," I said. "He's safe from me. I wouldn't piss in Al's mouth if he were dying of thirst."

28

PAYBACK, THE BITCH

EVEN THOUGH I'D MADE A COUPLE OF SOLO RECORDS OVER THE course of five years, I'd never once played live. Nor did I intend to, until my manager called me on the phone one day.

"Lanegan, you've been asked to open a couple shows for Johnny Cash. You have to do it, man!"

Johnny Cash was an American hero, an original talent like no other, respected and revered worldwide. I thought, *Johnny Cash? My dad's all-time favorite singer? Johnny Cash, whose records I listened to over and over again as a child?* A few months earlier, I had been asked to submit some songs for what was to become Cash's first release for American Records, producer Rick Rubin's label. That album was to spark a late-life resurgence for him. Even though he was already a universally beloved superstar, it cemented his place in the very upper echelons of music history.

At the time the request for the songs had come in, I'd recently seen a rerun of one of Reverend Billy Graham's televised sermons to a huge stadium-sized crowd during which Johnny Cash had spoken about his commitment to Christ and his personal relationship with Jesus. I started thinking, *My tunes are way too dark to give to this man of God, he'll never use any of them.* So I had submitted a few of my songs I deemed devoid enough of death and darkness that he might consider using one of them. Of course, then the record came out, filled with murder ballads and original tunes by masters of the dark arts of the songsmith, Glenn Danzig and Trent Reznor. I realized my serious miscalculation and thought, *That's what you get for thinking, dumbass.*

I knew I had to do the shows. I'd already quickly regretted turning down an offer to open for R. L. Burnside, an honest-to-god blues legend whose records I'd loved. If I were to do that now, I'd regret it for the rest of my life. I quickly put together a band of friends, guys I'd known forever and who had played on my records: J Mascis, Mike Johnson, Barrett Martin, and Danny Peters. During rehearsals for the shows, I realized I was doing them for two reasons. One, I had grown up on *At Folsom Prison* and had especially loved the record *Orange Blossom Special* as a kid. The second reason was my father. I bought him a plane ticket, from Alaska to Seattle. He'd lived in virtual isolation in Alaska for the past ten years or so, fighting a battle with alcohol and what seemed to me lifelong depression. He'd never even seen me sing before. Seeing Cash live would be the thrill of his lifetime.

The guys in my band were all pros and as the dates neared, my only fight was with my own nerves. I had intended to never play any of these quiet confessional songs in front of an audience. With my punk rock mentality, I approached each show as something akin to going into war. Playing in front of a country music audience seemed especially daunting because it was a genre that, more than any other, depended on a certain warmth and friendliness between artist and audience. That was a skill I was completely stymied by, never having spoken to a crowd unless I'd been compelled to by verbal abuse or something thrown at me. Nonetheless, after hitting a backstage bathroom to do a shot of dope that I'd brought with me already cooked up and in a rig, I got onstage in Seattle. Despite some minor heckling that I quickly responded to with a couple of expletives probably unexpected by the mainly older crowd, I got through it.

At the halfway point of my set, I had noticed Johnny Cash standing sidestage. He'd remained there throughout my entire performance. Afterward, he introduced himself with his trademark.

"Hello, I'm Johnny Cash," he said and shook my hand. "Great voice, son. Thanks for singing tonight, I needed to hear that. Good for the soul."

I was secretly thrilled by our interaction and watched his entire show with his trio from the wings. His son, John Carter Cash, joined them for a few songs. He was still playing all the old hits and both my father and I were both highly entertained by his performance. At the outdoor show the next afternoon in Portland, June Carter Cash, Johnny's famous wife, joined him onstage for a rousing version of "Jackson," much to the crowd's ecstatic delight.

My dad was with me backstage and I offered to introduce him to Johnny. He declined.

"Just being here and seeing him play and hearing your music is enough for me, son. Thanks so much for bringing me here. I'm proud of you, Mark."

Those were words I had rarely heard from anyone in my life, except from my dad. He'd always been a hopeful champion and staunch supporter of mine, no matter what I was doing. As long as I was not in county or prison, he considered my life a success.

Once, a few years earlier, I'd received a letter in the mail from him. It contained just one item: a photo scissored from a cover of the *Seattle Times* newspaper. It was of some inmates of the local jail carrying their mattresses down a city street under armed guard. The caption had said "Inmates Move to New Jail." The very first guy in the photo bore an uncanny resemblance to me. My father had written on it with a ballpoint pen, an arrow pointing to him and the question "Is this you?" I knew he most likely did think it was me and felt slightly sad because it very easily could have been me, carrying my bedding down the hill to the new jail, to my father's great disappointment. I'd not bothered to write anything in return; I didn't have time for that shit. I had too much petty drug business to attend to.

—

HICKS HAD LONG AGO MOVED back to Tennessee to clean up and Dylan had moved into my apartment. I had been sharing it with Steve "Thee Slayer Hippy" Hanford, erstwhile drummer and producer of legendary Portland, Oregon, punk band Poison Idea. Slayer was an old friend of mine who had moved north to supposedly begin work with me on what was to have been my third and final record for Sub Pop, thus fulfilling my contract with them. Instead, we spent our days making, selling, and smoking crack and shooting dope.

To my delight, incredible luck, and dark pleasure, Slayer landed a job with none other than my still heavily disliked nemesis Bruce Pavitt, whose betrayal regarding the cover photo on my Sub Pop debut had never been far from the forefront of my mind. Bruce had had a falling out with Poneman at some point and had sold out his half of the business to Jon and now lived the life of Riley, presumably just enjoying his millions and his early retirement. When I found out Bruce had hired Slayer to, of all things, rearrange his gigantic record collection, in my drug-addled mind possibly worth a million bucks or more itself, I instantly saw the opportunity to pay the prick back for fucking me over all those years before. I carefully questioned Slayer about the contents of the collection. Thirty mint-condition copies of the first Nirvana single? Check. Twenty copies of this, fifteen copies of that? Check. Every record in the collection worth big bucks.

Each day inside Bruce's house, Slayer was left to arrange the records in total unsupervised solitude, and he came and went with his own key. I would give him a list of the most expensive records and how many copies to return with that night. It was a huge windfall for three dope fiends with no stream of income besides my sporadic royalty checks, selling crack to street people, and whatever we foraged from the occasional breaking-and-entering incident or boosting-and-returning scam— small-time junkie shit.

Dylan's part in the equation was to travel with me to all the high-end record shops and unload this stolen booty while I waited outside. I smiled with evil satisfaction, thinking, *Fuck you, Bruce,* every time we returned with our pockets stuffed full of dough, which we immediately spent on drugs. We lived like kings off his stolen records.

It took a couple of months before the job was done to Pavitt's satisfaction. By that time, and unbeknownst to him, Slayer had walked out of his house with thousands of dollars' worth of rare and pristine records. Even though on occasion Slayer drove Dylan and me crazy with his sometimes too-talkative, passive-aggressive tendencies, I had to hand it to him: he had provided me with the perfect road map and vehicle for paying Bruce back. I was more than pleased to return some of the fucking he'd so cavalierly given me all those years ago, a fucking I'd patiently waited years to be able to reciprocate.

⁓

I ALSO CONTINUED MY USUAL daily routine of scoring heroin for people. We picked up a rich customer in his fifties, an executive at Boeing we'd met through Slayer's cousin, a cute young blond woman who worked as an escort. She'd met the exec through her job, then handed him over to us. She was also an addict, and we became close as she began to spend a lot of time at my place.

The Boeing bigwig would honk his horn outside the apartment every morning and Dylan and I would go get in the car with him and take a ride. I would sell him several pieces of our rock, then we'd go to a dope house where I'd get him a couple of grams of heroin, and then finally to another place where Dylan would score him some meth. This guy was both a junkyard and a goldmine. We overcharged him and freely helped ourselves to what we could get away with out of his bag and he'd pay us an extra $100 a day for doing it.

After a few months, one morning he just didn't show up. Not long after that, Slayer left the apartment with some bogus errand he said he had to run. When he didn't come home that night and the Boeing exec again failed to show the next day, it didn't take a Nikola Tesla to figure out what had happened. Slayer and his cousin had gone behind our backs and stolen our cash cow.

I was furious. I got two of my Eritrean associates, Mikey and Dawitt, to put out a search for him among their other street-dwelling countrymen and I put out a $100 crack bounty for anyone who could tell me where to find Slayer. I planned to mercilessly beat him bloody for his betrayal. He was nowhere to be found. Not much later, word got back to me that, sadly, his cousin had OD'd and died.

It would be years before Slayer was to show his face in my presence again, in tears outside of a Trees show in Portland, begging my forgiveness. We repaired our years-long fucked-up love-hate relationship shortly before he went to prison in Oregon for a six-year stretch, busted after desperately holding up a Portland pharmacy at knifepoint. Even though we would remain inextricably linked by our longtime association and shared history forever, I found it hard to totally forgive him. No matter how many years passed.

Then one night, Dylan failed to come home. Weeks later, I found out he'd been arrested on a burglary charge and was in county awaiting trial. That left me with only my ever-growing cadre of Eritreans, Ethiopians, and street people I dealt with daily for company.

29

THE LOTTERY

AFTER DYLAN WAS BUSTED AND SLAYER MADE HIMSELF SCARCE, I was living alone. I began a relationship and scam with a homeless crack addict who, even after living hard on the streets, still had a head-turning, inherent beauty. She called herself Shadow and that was the only name I ever knew her by.

I was introduced to her by Dawitt and Mikey, a scandalous pair of crackheads who had traveled together from war-torn Eritrea in the Horn of Africa to escape conscription into the army. First to Khartoum in Sudan, where they survived by selling stolen newspapers on the street. Eventually they made their way to Saudi Arabia, where they were jailed as vagrants. Somehow they were found by some American Christian association that secured their freedom and brought them to Chicago. Mikey, the shorter, older, always-smiling, and sweet-natured of the two had supposedly won the lotto not once but twice and had lost it all both times to divorce. With the last of his second winnings, he had purchased two tickets on the Greyhound bus and they came out west to Seattle, God knows why.

Dawitt was a different story. He and I were great pals for a long time. Whenever I heard a car alarm going off outside, I knew he was in the neighborhood. He car-prowled and smoked crack all day, most of which he bought from me. Either that or he would trade some stolen shit to me for a rock or two. He had begged me to sell him some heroin one night and I did. He cooked it up and shot it in my apartment and instantly went into a seizure, falling on the floor, shaking and foaming at the mouth. I tried to pull him out of it but when it had stretched to three, then four and five minutes and he hadn't stopped seizing, I thought he might die. Panicked and jacked on fear, just the two of us there, I picked up the one-hundred-and-sixty-pound, six-foot-tall African and carried him over my shoulder, his shaking more pronounced every step I took. Down the long hallway to the four flights of stairs at the back of my building and then an entire city block to the Harborview emergency entrance. I laid him on the ground, rang the bell, and quickly crossed the street, walking back toward my building as fast as possible. Not an easy feat to pull off. After that, he hated me with a seething bitterness and would only come to me for crack as an absolute last resort. His intense burning distaste was suddenly so obvious, I couldn't understand it. He had turned on me like a snake overnight. I asked Mikey what the fuck his problem was, hadn't I saved his life after all? Mikey informed me that Dawitt would hate me forever because I had "shamed" him and as a man he could never forgive that. I guess he would have preferred to die on my apartment floor than to be carried all the way to the fucking hospital on the back of another man. From that point on, as far as he was concerned, it was war. He spent a good deal of time and energy trying his best to do whatever he could to fuck me up and take me down.

The only good thing Dawitt had done for me after his declaration of war was introduce me to Shadow. She was a dark-skinned African American who had the same skin affliction Michael Jackson had, with large patches of light, almost-white skin across her body and face. For a couple hits of crack, she would clean my filthy apartment and give me an incredible blow job. I liked having her around. She had a great off-the-wall sense of humor and giant cast-iron balls. She was not to be fucked with. If you made a deal with her, by God, you'd best stick to it. Life was dangerous and hard for a homeless woman in the '90s Northwest, a place rife with sadistic johns and a hunting ground for more than one active serial killer at all times. She had to be tough as fuck just to survive.

"Hey, Whitey Ford, I got a plan for you. I think you're gonna like it," she announced one night after smoking with me in my pad all day. Whitey Ford was Shadow's name for me. No one in my hood called me by my name. I sometimes wondered if anyone even knew what it was.

"You know that mattress in your dining room? I could get so many johns off the street up here for some good fifty-dollar head. We could split the dough and smoke all night." She paused for a second and then, "Or I can just get 'em up here, and after I got their money in my hand, you come on out of the bedroom there carrying that baseball bat of yours or the pistol I seen in the box in your closet and you just tell 'em 'GET THE FUCK OUT BEFORE I FUCKING KILL YOU!' What'ya think?"

I thought about it for a minute.

"We gotta take all their money, not just fifty bucks. Whatever they're carrying. If anyone has the balls to go to the cops, we'll say you are my girlfriend and they offered it all to you before I came out and caught them trying to fuck my woman."

"Hahahaha! I like the way you think, white boy! Let's do it!"

And so we began a routine that caught so many ugly, fat old men with their dick in their hand. It was easier than my punchboard scam as a kid. She did all the work; I was just the frightening, unexpected cherry on top. Not one guy ever put up a fight or went to the cops, or at least no cop ever showed up. We pulled this successful rip-off daily for quite a while. I always made sure to get my apartment keys back from her whenever we were done for the day, even on the occasions she spent the night. I was very fond of her but had no illusions as to what the true nature of our relationship really was, and the last thing I needed was for her to get my keys duplicated and give her free rein to my shit when I was out. Then one day, she just disappeared. Whether she'd been busted or had simply left the life to get clean, I never saw her again, to not a small amount of sadness.

—

I GOT BUZZED BY SOMEONE at the front door. I took the stairs since the elevator was out as usual. To my unhappy surprise, there was Demri, dressed in a white hospital gown, wheeling a pole with an IV bottle, at my front door in broad daylight. I was pissed off beyond words. Should Christian happen to catch sight of this scene, it would be yet one more notch on his belt of complaints.

"What the fuck, Demri? What happened to you?"

She lowered her gown and showed me the ugly red vertical scar running down the middle of her chest.

"I got endocarditis and they gave me a pacemaker." She smiled as if she were telling me she won the lottery. "Mark, baby, do you have any dope? I'll even take cottons, whatever."

"Are you fucking kidding me? No way, get your ass back over to the hospital. You're out of your mind."

Endocarditis was a dreaded malady an IV drug user could catch from the bacteria in heroin. It destroyed your heart valves and was often deadly. That she'd contracted the infection, had to have a pacemaker installed, and still wheeled her shit over to here to try and get high, even if it were just off my cottons, blew my mind. The unforgiving power of her addiction was shocking. I callously shut the door on her midsentence during her plea for drugs, turned around, walked back upstairs to my apartment, and turned the buzzer off. Like my first meeting with her, I kept this episode to myself, not wanting to cause Layne any more heartache then he'd already taken.

Around the same time, Mike Starr also buzzed me one night. Surprised to see him, I opened the door and let him in. He was the ex–bass player for Alice in Chains. I hadn't seen him in years.

"What the fuck, Mike? How you been?"

"Jesus Christ, man, I just got busted but made bail. I'm dopesick as hell, are you holding anything?"

I had not known Starr as a junkie during the time we spent touring together, just a strange cat like the trailer-park hoodlums I'd grown up around in eastern Washington, not super intelligent but with a dubious gift for getting over on people. A low-level rip-off and conman.

"Damn. Sorry to hear that, bro. C'mon up to my place."

Once inside my apartment, I saw that, despite the cold weather, he was dressed in only a white T-shirt and a pair of white boxer shorts with a very noticeable shitstain running down the back of them. No shoes, nothing.

"Sorry, bro, I don't have any dope, just a little crack for sale if you're interested."

I lied about the dope since I could plainly see he wasn't holding a wallet or any dough, no pockets to keep them in if he did; crack was something I could share a tiny bit of, if he were so inclined.

"Oh fuck. What am I gonna do?"

He was talking to himself, not me.

"Mark, can I use your phone?"

"Sure, Mike, go on ahead."

He got on the phone and went around the corner into my kitchen for privacy but in his agitated state did not notice me standing right outside the door, listening.

"No, goddamnit! He doesn't have any!" he muttered emphatically to whoever was on the other line. "He's got crack, that's all I know. No, I don't know if he's got cash up here."

Someone had either coerced him into trying to burn me or he was just the scout for whoever came next. He hung up the phone.

"Hey, man, sorry I couldn't help you out but I got somewhere to be so you gotta split now."

"Hey, can I catch a ride with you?" he asked.

"Not riding. See ya, brother," I said, opening my infrequently used kitchen door and gently shoving him out, locking the door behind.

For the next ten minutes or so, he continued knocking intermittently, saying quietly, "Hey, Mark. Hey, bro, can I come back in?" I didn't answer him, sitting on my couch with the loaded, stolen Desert Eagle .44 Magnum pistol I had traded Dawitt fifty bucks' worth of crack for on my lap, just in case there was going to be more to this scene than met the eye. Eventually, I heard him sigh heavily and the hallway floor creaking as he walked barefoot softly away down the corridor and to the stairs. I would not see him again for another several years.

30

LUCKY

AT THE END OF '95, THE TREES HAD PUT TOGETHER ENOUGH demos that Epic agreed to give us another shot at making a record. Bob Pfeifer had taken a job as president of Disney's new "rock" record label, Hollywood Records. The guy I'd hand-delivered the cassette of "Nearly Lost You" to for the *Singles* soundtrack, Michael "Goldie" Goldstone, had taken on the task of being our new A&R man. We hired producer George Drakoulias to make this record and in the fall of that year we moved to Los Angeles to begin.

George was a singular character, in a class by himself. Extremely outgoing and fun-loving, always smiling and laughing. He was physically imposing, with an unkempt mop of black hair on his head and a bushy black beard. Had you not known him or heard him talk, you could have imagined him shouting orders on the deck of a pirate ship or chopping up meat behind a butcher's counter, but his gregarious, bigger-than-life personality fit his large frame perfectly. He was forever springing shit on us in the studio with some kind of surprise or joke, and all of us loved him from the moment we met him. Although he was a year younger than me, he was a highly successful and well-known record producer who comported himself with the self-assured grace, humor, and smarts that made me feel like he was several years my senior. He was also a patient and understanding friend and had made it clear that everyone was to leave me alone, not exert any pressure, and allow me to heal from detoxing before I was expected to participate in the recording.

I was determined to get clean in order to do my best work so I started going to a Beverly Hills clinic every other day to get a shot of Buprenex.

It was a drug that kept you from withdrawals. In theory, you would wean down and eventually off of it, painlessly. It was being touted as the new "safe" methadone. Shortly before he died, Kurt had given me an entire case of small glass vials of the stuff. I'd never used it. Instead, I'd peddled it around Seattle, selling it to junkies who wanted to kick, explaining how to use it like a low-rent house-call doctor. Now I was the patient. I disliked being driven from the infamous Oakwood apartments in Burbank where I lived all the way out to Beverly Hills, a task that most often fell to our guitar tech Danny Baird, but the treatment seemed to be working.

There was rarely anyone in the waiting room of the office shared by three doctors of different unknown specialties, but one day I walked through the door and ran into Stone Temple Pilots singer Scott Weiland. We'd met for the first time through a shared drug dealer. I'd gone to let her in one day and instead of her, he'd burst headlong through the door like a rag doll, knocking me to the floor with him on top, kissing my face and telling me how much he loved me. We'd hung out a few times getting fucked up and I had even sung on one of their songs for an album that was never released, but now that he and I were going through the same routine to get clean, he was a different animal. While loaded, he'd been kind of crazy and fun to be around, but when he wasn't high, he was not nearly as enjoyable, super serious, carrying the weight of the universe on his shoulders. Way too unhappy for me; I had my own unhappiness to battle.

On day three of the Buprenex treatments, I was dropped off at a Hollywood comedy club where daily twelve-step meetings were held. I wore a heavy coat inside the club as, despite the Buprenex, even in the warm weather of California in November I still felt the pain and chills of withdrawals. The place was nearly empty. I'd gotten there early, about thirty minutes before the start of the meeting. I sat in the farthest seat from the front, intending not to participate, just to listen and learn. I was smoking a cigarette and staring mindlessly at the floor when someone put their hand on my shoulder. A familiar voice said, "Hey, Lucky."

Only one person in my life had ever called me by that nickname. He had called me that consistently in our time together but I'd not seen him in years. I looked up and the leader of the band Social Distortion, Mike Ness, was standing there with a concerned and slightly sad smile.

"How you been, Lucky? You don't look like you're doing so hot."

Years earlier, the Trees had opened for Social D for three months around the country. We traveled in our carpet-cleaning van while they traveled in a brand-new tour bus. He'd seen me making out with an attractive girl on the second day of the tour. On day three of the tour, he had nicknamed me and it had stuck. From then on, I was Lucky. It was a good-natured and ironic nickname because Ness himself had a clutch of the hottest chicks at his disposal. Wherever we went, there was a gang of beautiful, sexy women practically fighting one another for his attention. He hooked up with the most badass, jaw-dropping beauties daily.

His band came out of soundcheck unhappy every day as he apparently led the band and conducted his business with an iron fist. "Chopping block, always a motherfucking chopping block in there," said the bass player as he exited the venue one day, pouring sweat and shaking his head in consternation. Yet Mike was always extremely kind to me, going out of his way to make me a daily espresso from the machine on their bus, sharing his private thoughts, and asking my opinion on a variety of subjects in a personal manner. Had I been watching their sets? Had I seen the bit where he pulled a comb out of his back pocket and ran it through his already perfectly greased-back, rockabilly-style haircut onstage? Was it cool or lame? (It made the huge contingent of hot girls in the audience go crazy, so . . .) Mike was so completely down-to-earth, honest, and totally sincere, it was impossible not to dig him. I enjoyed his company, looked forward to hanging out, and sincerely liked him a lot. He was naturally funny, cool as hell, and fearlessly wore his heart on his sleeve. And unlike many other musicians whose paths I crossed through the years, there was zero entitled-rock-star bullshit to his personality. What you saw was what you got.

Ness had a few years clean at the time and attended meetings in nearly every city we visited. He became aware that I had the exact same amount of time as him, but with zero meetings or program of any kind.

One day, he said, "Hey, Lucky, c'mon with me down to the store, I need some Choke-a-mocha." Choke-a-mocha was his favorite drink. He would mix Swiss Miss instant cocoa drink with Folgers instant coffee. As we walked to the store together to get the ingredients for his novel beverage of choice, he said, "I don't get it, man. How do you not drink or use without going to meetings?"

"I don't know how you can stay clean going to meetings, Mike," I replied in my usual ignorant, cocky manner. "If I had to talk about drinking and using every day, I'd get loaded for sure."

He had shaken his head incredulously at me and patted me on the back in a gesture that seemed to imply he understood my misguided backwoods thinking and felt compassion for it.

Years later, at this nearly empty meeting in Hollywood, I saw the same look in his eyes.

"I always thought I'd find you here someday, Lucky," he said gently. "Welcome home."

He sat next to me and we shot the shit until the meeting was starting.

"I got somewhere to be," he said, "I just wanted to get a feel for the place since I can't catch a meeting today. So good to see you here. Stick around, it will change your life."

He slipped me his number, and with that, he split. I was tore the fuck up but he had remained clean all those years since I'd met him. Looking back, I was acutely aware of how wise he had been then and how recklessly, willfully unintelligent I was.

On another trip into Beverly Hills for my shot, I found myself alone in the waiting room with two other people: the actor James Woods and a girl who looked young enough to be his granddaughter. I highly doubted Woods was there to see my doctor. In a loud voice verging on yelling, he endlessly harangued his unfortunate young companion with nonstop, rapid-fire sentences, telling her some story obviously meant to impress. I felt sorry for her, and then, quickly, for myself. Gesturing dramatically with his hands while turned completely sideways in his chair and looming over the girl, he talked so loud and so fast, never taking a break or letting her say a word, that I started to get a pounding headache. I nearly said, "Hey, man, shut the fuck up!" but I bit my tongue.

After having to endure his presence for half an hour, I oscillated unsteadily on the last raw edge of my nerves. When they called me back to see the doc, I was so grateful to be out of his insane, over-the-top, and obnoxious line of fire that I immediately said, "Goddamn, I'm glad to see you." When the doctor looked at me with a puzzled expression, I said, "Never mind, just happy to be out of the waiting room." I stayed off dope, and even though I was exhausted all the time and definitely didn't get through it painlessly, after years of trying on my own to get clean, eventually I was off everything.

I slept on the couch at my pad at the Oakwoods; there was something about one of the bedrooms that creeped me out. It was nothing I could put my finger on, just an eerie vibe I felt whenever I went in it. I shut the doors of both bedrooms and stayed out of them the entire time I lived there.

One morning, I was awakened by a huge, sudden, celebratory outbreak coming from the apartment directly above mine.

"He's innocent!"

"Not guilty!"

I groggily realized it was my neighbors celebrating what could only have been O. J. Simpson's acquittal. His trial had been the biggest news and topic of discussion in America for months and I had been aware that the jury was out, contemplating his guilt or innocence. Now they had obviously come back with a not-guilty decision. The large, friendly black family upstairs had always been very nice to me, various family members engaging me in pleasant conversation in the hallway, parking lot, or yard. Once, one of the sons had seen me struggling to get my key out of my pocket while trying to hold a large paper bag filled with cans of soup. He had grabbed it from me as it started to rip and patiently held it while I opened the door. Excellent neighbors, but the loud yelling and early-morning partying was a bit too much to take as I lay there, still aching on the couch, day four off everything.

—

IT SEEMED LIKE DRAKOULIAS KNEW everyone in Hollywood. He was a popular, sought-after friend, dinner guest, and all-around mover and shaker. Every other day he fielded invitations to this function or that. Being by nature decidedly nonsocial, I learned to be extremely cautious if accepting any sort of invite from him.

"Hey, Lanegan, you wanna come to dinner with me tonight?" George would offer up.

"Who else is coming, George?" I would ask.

"Nobody, bud! It's just you and me, boys' night out!"

When we arrived at some fancy eatery, I would inevitably find out there were one or two other people joining us and they would always be some sort of celebrity, popular musician, or actor, people I'd never met before. I'd sit in uncomfortable silence throughout the meal while George and his pals laughed it up.

When I'd finally started feeling better in early December, George came and got me one day.

"Let's go, Lanegan. We're going for a ride."

Sitting in his truck as we drove up the 101 freeway, north of Los Angeles, I asked him, "Where are we going, George?"

"Never mind that, you just behave yourself when we're there."

This cryptic message was unlike his usual playful banter. He seemed more serious than normal, as though on a mission of some kind. Finally, we pulled off the freeway in Van Nuys, a somewhat run-down suburb filled with auto shops, Mexican food trucks, and hookers walking up and down past the shady, decrepit motels that lined the street. We took Sepulveda Boulevard, a long, seedy street that ran north-south all the way through the San Fernando Valley, over the hills and down past LAX airport. We rounded a corner and I realized we were at Sound City, a legendary recording studio I'd been to once before to visit a friend.

George got out of the truck and I followed him inside. The secretary just smiled at him, pointed to a door across the room, and said, "They're in studio one, George." As we entered through the greenroom, there was a tall gentleman dressed in black with his back to us, arranging a bowl of food on a table. He turned around and there I was, face-to-face with Johnny Cash. He immediately saw George and hugged him and then me.

"George! It's so good to see you again, and you too, young fella! Get yourselves a chicken biscuit before the rest of the guys get in here and clean them out!" he said, holding up the bowl full of sandwiches he'd obviously been making himself for his band. We each took one, then he turned to me.

"I'm sorry I don't recall your name, son, but I remember your singing. You almost put me to shame at those shows!"

—

MY DETOX PROGRAM WAS CONSIDERED a success. So much so that my doctor wanted me to accompany him to some medical convention to parade me around as one of the shining examples of the miracle of Buprenex. On my first day of treatment, my doctor had leaned in as though telling me a secret and said he was the same doctor who was infamous for shooting heroin into his dick, as characterized in Jerry Stahl's book *Permanent Midnight*. I declined his invitation to play show pony at his convention.

However, I always wondered how he'd managed to hit in his cock. For years, the huge vein running down the length of mine had tortured and taunted me as I sat searching, sometimes for hours, to find a usable vein. On one desperate occasion when I'd attempted it, the vein had immediately blown up the second I pierced it with the needle's tip. My arms had already been covered with huge abscessed wounds and I knew that if that were to happen to my boneless cock, it would be game over, so I made up my mind to stay away from it after that.

The next night, I had attended a concert by the angelic-voiced singer Jeff Buckley with a girlfriend of mine. She'd befriended another girl while playing pool who came with us to the show. I'd gotten backstage passes from the promoter and we'd watched from the side of the stage. When Buckley walked offstage between the end of his set and encore, he'd come straight to where we were sitting, and I was smoking, on large equipment cases. He reached out with eyebrows upturned and a look that said "Please?" I took one last drag off the newly lit smoke and handed it to him. He smiled, bowed, and shook my hand, grinning again as he gratefully took a long pull off the unfiltered Lucky Strike.

Later that night when the pool-playing girl had gone down on me, she said, "Jesus! What happened to your dick? It's totally fucking bruised!"

31

IS THIS LOVE?

LYING ON MY COUCH AT THE OAKWOODS ONE AFTERNOON, I WAS talking with a friend on the phone and Selene Vigil, the singer of Seattle band Seven Year Bitch, came up in conversation.

Years earlier, Hole guitarist Eric Erlandson and I had gone to see the all-female band play in Seattle. I was instantly attracted to their singer, Selene. Onstage, she was like a cross between a sexy cat and a female Iggy Pop. While we were watching them, Erlandson spotted the actress Drew Barrymore in the audience and in a break between songs he said, "I'm gonna date that chick." I said, "I'm gonna date *that* chick," and pointed to Selene up on the stage. While the show continued, Eric indeed approached and captured Drew Barrymore in conversation and they looked to be getting along famously.

Another friend of mine introduced me to a friend of his: Selene's husband. When she got offstage and came over to her husband, I was introduced to Selene as well. Her smile and incredibly smoky voice again reminded me of a big cat and now I was twice as intrigued, but sadly that was to be our last interaction.

Newly clean and exceedingly horny, the memory of that night instantly sprang to mind.

"Goddamn, she is hot. I would love to hang out with her."

"Dude, I'm pretty sure that could be arranged. She's up in San Francisco making a record, split up with that husband a long time ago. In fact, I know for certain she's single, lonely, and you are her type."

"What, the junkie type who's been clean a week?"

"No, the great singer type. A man."

.I asked him to give her my number. To my surprise, she called me a day later. We talked nonstop for what turned into a several-hour marathon. Just like that, I was completely hooked. By the end of the call, we were both saying shit like "God, I wish you were here right now!" and "I can't fucking wait to see you." Her laughter, openness, and slightly discernible melancholic edge made me want to have her as soon as possible. The ease of our conversation, the shit I'd told her that I'd never told anyone before. Throwing my usual suspicious nature to the wind, I knew she was going to be someone good for me. We made plans to get together that weekend. She was to fly down to Los Angeles and spend it with me.

When she showed up that weekend, I found myself attracted to her in a way that had been a rarity in my world. I thought, *Is this what love is?* I had never felt such a powerful pull before. I fell hard and fast. In the vulnerable state of being clean for the first time in years, I gave myself over completely to this exotic, funny, and kind creature. I found everything about her irresistible, especially her laugh, her thoughtful sensitivity, the way she felt in my arms, and her voice. I found in Selene someone who had experienced deep sadness and loss, someone who wanted love and needed someone as much as I did.

The next weekend, I went to hang out with her in San Francisco, where she was also in the middle of making a record. Lying together on the floor of her room listening to music one night, "Green Onions" by Booker T. and the M.G.s came on. She got up and began to dance in front of me. It was one of the most sensual and touching gestures I'd ever experienced. She came to stay with me again in Los Angeles, and as we sat together in the bathtub one night she said something that cut to my very core: "What happened to you to make you so sad?"

It hit me like a hammer. I realized that, even at this moment when I felt as happy and comfortable with myself as I could ever remember being, the guilt and shame I wore like a noose around my neck was still obvious to this sensitive, intuitive woman. She saw right through me.

"I'm not sure I can honestly answer that. There's so much stuff I've buried away. If I gave it any thought, I might start crying or something."

Against my will, my mind spent a quick minute going down the long list of damage I'd done to not only innocent people I hardly knew but also those I'd known not at all but who had suffered the misfortune of crossing my path. I shut my eyes. I'd been such a negative, toxic influence—I thought of all the things I did and did not do that hurt the people I'd loved the most, especially the people I'd lost. In a rare instant of raw, open vulnerability, I started to cry. She held on to me tightly as tears streamed out of my unopenable, burning eyes.

In that moment, the rabid, disease-crazed dog I had carried for years inside of me tore its way out through every barrier I'd put up around it. I had never cried in front of anybody before. Grief over the years of pain I'd caused myself and others poured out in torrents. It was as much of myself as I'd ever shown anyone. Though I was gravely flawed with damage that ran as deep as the Mariana Trench, she accepted me without a moment's hesitation. It made me think that, for the first time ever, maybe I had at last found the person who would understand, show me how to be human, and not judge me for all of my fucked-up, self-serving misdeeds. It was something I'd never thought possible. Maybe this was who I'd always been waiting for.

32

FAMILY REUNION

AS IT NEARED CHRISTMASTIME, MY SISTER ASKED ME TO COME out to eastern Washington state where my mother lived to see her. Not fucking likely.

A few years earlier, my girlfriend Anna had insisted on meeting my parents. I had called my mother and she agreed to let us come over the Cascades and spend a night at her farm in the vast valley of apple orchards and grape fields south of the city of Yakima. Minutes after we walked in from the three-hour drive, Anna saw a copy of my first solo record sitting inside an open closet door.

"Oh, I see you have Mark's record. Isn't it great?"

"Yeah, his sister sent it to me but it's so goddamned depressing I couldn't listen to it." And then to me, "Why does it have to be so goddamned depressing?"

"Hey, Mom, good to see you. Would you happen to have twenty bucks for gas?"

"No. But you can follow me to the station and I'll put ten dollars' worth in your car."

She was sure I wanted her measly $20 for drugs. We had stayed less than fifteen minutes. I drove in silence for five minutes on the way to the gas station behind my mother's pickup truck, then asked Anna, "Do you get it now?"

"Yes," she quietly replied.

My sister couldn't travel because her darkly damaged husband had charges pending against him and could not leave the state. Pablo had been accused in an attack on a disabled man in a group home where he worked the night shift as an orderly. When the details of the accusation had been brought to my attention, it made me ill. I had begged her to leave him immediately but she had been trained through years of subtly escalated abuse to ride it out. If she chose to stay with this depraved man *and* expected me to travel to, of all places, my mother's in the middle of winter, it was a no-go.

What tipped the scales was when she told me my father, who had by now lived for several years in solitude in Alaska, was going to be renting a motel room nearby. It would be my first chance to see him in years. I had a long conversation with Selene, in which she urged me to endure my mother in order to see my sister and father. We spoke, too, of our rapidly expanding plans together.

"When we're done making these records, you can move into my place," I promised her. She was just getting out of a failed relationship and had no place to live.

"Are you sure? I want to be with you, but I need you to be sure."

"Of course, I'm sure," I replied. "I love you."

So, at my sister's request, against my wishes, against every instinct, I agreed to go north for the holidays. I got on a plane back to Washington for the first time since I'd gotten clean a mere six weeks earlier.

Mike McCready, who I'd gone to a couple twelve-step meetings with in Los Angeles and who had played some guitar on the record the Trees were making, had offered to have a cleaning crew go into my apartment to remove any drugs or paraphernalia that might have been left behind. I thanked him for the gesture and declined. I wasn't even going to Seattle, just catching a connector at Sea-Tac for the short flight to Yakima. I packed my wallet, keys, and anything else attached to my apartment in my checked bag, just in case I suddenly got a crazy idea and decided to make an unplanned stop there.

On the flight, my mind drifted back to a week or so earlier, when I'd finally felt well enough to get physically active. Our studio was one block off Sunset Boulevard so, shirtless and shoeless, I took the studio bicycle and rode up and down the crowded street with no hands on the handlebars, just feeling the joy of being alive. As I passed one of the storefronts full of cheesy tourist-trap items, I heard Otis Redding's "I've Got Dreams to Remember" blasting out of the store from the stereo inside. It was a song I'd always loved, a song that always made me sad.

A thought crossed my mind from out of nowhere: *If this is living, why be alive?* In that moment, I veered wildly from joy to extreme darkness as if someone had flicked a switch. This thought that had come from out of the blue, brought on by a song I loved, gave me a sudden chill. I rode back to the studio to put my clothes back on.

Without warning, about an hour outside Seattle, I was gripped by an anguished, inexplicable fear.

Who are you fucking kidding? said a voice from deep inside my head. *You can't stay clean.*

But I must, there's so much left to do.

Fuck that. You will never make it.

I was caught in an intense, surprise anxiety attack. Only when I mentally gave in to the idea that I was getting off the plane in Seattle and going to score, did its heart-pounding, cold-sweat-inducing shortness of breath abate.

Without so much as a sweater or a jacket in the cold Northwest December weather, without my apartment keys or even a fucking quarter in my pocket, I walked off the plane and got into a cab, headed for First Hill, Terry and Jefferson. When I arrived, I wrote down my info on the driver's business card with a stub of pencil I had in my pants pocket so he could be paid later. The cabbie wasn't buying my bullshit. He crumpled it up, threw it back at me, and attempted to spit on me. Understandable.

For years, I had fought almost daily with the abundance of cab drivers in my neighborhood, known as "bloodrunners." They sat in a long line outside the hospitals, waiting to rush bags of emergency blood to hospitals all around the city. I had an ongoing battle with them for years and many refused to give me rides. I always had very specific routes to take that I knew were quickest and was constantly at odds with the drivers who wanted to go their own way. Once, a driver had taken exception to the pocketful of change I had attempted to pay him with. "I'm not accepting these nickels and dimes!" "Well, you'd better if you want to get paid," I'd said, "this is the exact amount of the fare and the last time I checked it was legal fucking tender in this country!" That scene ended up with me throwing the entire handful through his open window with as much strength as I had, pelting him in the face and torso with a machine-gun blast of coins. So this kind of confrontational taxi-driver shit was old hat.

I had skirted town owing my connection Val at the projects money so that wasn't an option. It was getting late in the day and if I was going to score, it could only be by paging Tommy Hansen, hoping he would call back and then drive into the city to front me something. I bummed a quarter off a passerby and paged Tommy by memory. He called me back on the pay phone, I explained my predicament, and in a half hour he showed up with some dope. Thank God. Now to get into my apartment.

With my keys on a plane to Yakima and my place on the fourth floor, there was only one way in. I waited impatiently until a resident came to the front door, then grabbed the handle as it was closing and followed them in. I looked furtively up and down the long hallway outside my place. Seeing it vacant, I quickly kicked open the door that came from the hallway into my kitchen, a door I never used. Once inside, I realized I'd not paid the electric bill for two months.

As the last light of day was fading, I frantically searched the pad for a lighter, candles, flashlight, spoons, and old rigs: the tools I was going to need to get high. I did my first shot in six weeks by candlelight and all the anxiety that had plagued me on the flight drifted away with the familiar blanketlike warmth of my true love.

When I awoke, it was to the gray half-light of morning flooding the room like a dam had broken and hit the sewage treatment plant on its path of destruction. The reality of coming to on this same piece-of-shit couch where I'd spent so much time getting loaded as well as being sick made me ache with regret. I should easily have recognized it could just have been a one-time slip. I had the option and free will to climb back on the wagon. But that truth never occurred to me. Instead, I was overcome with a typically morose, unshakable feeling that I had blown my first, last, and only chance to get the demon of drugs off of my back. My only choices were to either do what already seemed impossible after only one night of getting loaded—start again and attempt to stay clean—or just to give in to my true dark nature and get high to the bitter end, however near that might be. I instantly decided on the latter.

I called my accountant Laurie who put some of my dwindled-to-damn-near-nothing money in my account so I could withdraw the dough and buy a plane ticket to eastern Washington. After I carefully cleaned any evidence of drugs, I told my landlord Christian that someone had broken in to my place. I left him to deal with fixing the doorframe and replacing the door. I collected my money, bought some dope and a bag of rigs, and headed back out to the airport to make my dreaded Christmas appearance.

I called my sister from the pay phone near the gate and told her to send someone to pick me up. To my disappointment, it was Mother who came driving up. As a young child, I quit wondering why she had such open contempt for me. All I knew was that she did. Every word, comment, or look at me made it so transparently obvious, it almost made me laugh.

"So you finally kicked the drugs, I hear. Is that true?"

Her addiction to belittling and trying to squash my personality and individuality had ceased to have any power twenty years earlier.

"Yes, it's true. I wouldn't set foot into this messed-up situation if it wasn't. I can't believe you are letting him stay at your house, much less let him be around the kids."

I referred to my two-and-a-half-year-old and six-month-old nephews, the unfortunate sons of my sister. I couldn't believe I was related to my brother-in-law, even if it was just by marriage. The whole thing disgusted me beyond words. As usual, my mother's response was to minimize anything ugly she didn't want to look at while diminishing any concern of mine.

"Oh for chrissakes, he's not even been charged with anything, we don't know if he's guilty!"

"I sure as fuck do."

My mother pulled her pickup off to the side of the highway and offered to let me out if that was the type of language I was going to use.

"Knock it off, Mom, just take me to your house so we can get on with this charade."

It all came rushing back as we drove through these wind-whipped agricultural lands I had grown up to despise. There had been two giant holes on the inside of the front door of my childhood home. One from when my mother threw a weighty, solid-metal statuette at my head as I ran out the door to escape her rage, the second a year or two later, from a heavy marble bookend.

From the time I was seven years old, she had forced me to go house to house in our neighborhood asking for work. "You're going to have to work to get any money around here. I'm certainly not giving you an allowance. That's for spoiled kids and you are already spoiled enough." I would occasionally be hired to mow someone's large, unkempt lawn for two dollars.

When I was eight, I slipped and fell off a bridge into a frozen-over canal. Crashing through the ice, I broke my femur bone. My friend, who had been unable to pull me up the steep sides of the canal, had run a couple of miles through the fields in thigh-deep snow to get help. I had bobbed, fighting to keep my head above the ice and freezing water for an hour with a leg that refused to help while my dog ran barking hysterically up and down the banks. A neighbor had waded up to his neck into the ice-water and hooked a rope around my torso, under my arms. He had then agonizingly pulled me out of the water and up the side of the bank with a snowmobile. They drilled a large metal screw through my knee, put me into a full body cast, and sent me home in it after almost two months in the hospital. While I was lying helplessly immobile on the bed they'd set up for me in the middle of our living room, practically mummified in the cast that ran from my chest all the way down one leg and halfway down the other, my mother had dumped an entire large cardboard box of hardbound textbooks over my head one day in another fit of rage. Months later, I was newly freed of the cast and on crutches when, not so sure how I could navigate it, she'd impatiently tried to shove me down an escalator in a department store. Another woman had seen it and intervened.

She had friends with a vast amount of acreage filled with fields of tomatoes. She made me join the migrant Mexican farm workers, picking tomatoes in the baking summer sun. Forced out into the fields, half the time I picked a tomato, it would explode in my hand, the rotten backside out of view until it was too late. The acidic juice eventually burned the skin on my hands. By the end of the day, they were covered in an ugly painful rash since I didn't have the gloves the men who did this for a living wore. I was paid maybe five or ten dollars for a day's work, my mother refusing to allow her friends to pay me more than a pittance.

While I picked tomatoes all day, she played cards and drank beer inside the air-conditioned house. In private, she would only rage at us, but while drinking, her verbal abuse took on a different tone. Instead of the harsh recriminations she repeated daily, she took evil, smiling delight in drunkenly ridiculing us kids. Whenever she ran into someone she knew in public, her kids immediately became objects of ridicule, as though everyone found her "jokes" hilarious. While driving under the influence of alcohol, she'd crank the car radio and attempt to sing along with it. Never knowing the words, she'd be halfway behind each line, tunelessly singing the lyrics after she heard them. When she once heard me quietly singing along to something on *American Top 40*, she had laughed and said, "Jesus, don't they teach you kids to sing in school?" My entire childhood, my mother, who, unbelievably, worked as a college lecturer of early childhood education, had been a wholly detestable, damaged witch. I was now a grown man and the last person I was taking any shit from was her.

We came to their property, an apple orchard of several acres. Shortly after I'd quit drinking as a teenager, my mother and stepfather had given me a job there. I had toiled on my hands and knees in the frozen snow of an iced-over winter past. The roots had come back up through the soil and surrounded the trees, "suckers" as they were known. With a tool something like a pair of bolt cutters, I dug beneath the snow and the frozen ground and then battled to cut these thick ropes of wood until my hands were cramped and bloodily blistered beneath my gloves, my pants wet and stiff from kneeling in the snow all day, my feet frozen to numbness inside my boots. And all for the shittiest wage. Outside the one-time gift of ten bucks' worth of gas, my mother had not given me one single free dime my entire life and was loath to pay me anything close to a fair wage when I worked for them.

When we arrived at my mother and stepfather's ranch-style house in the middle of the orchard, the first thing I did was lock myself in a spare bedroom. As fast as I could, I did a large shot of heroin I'd already cooked up and carried with me in a full outfit on the plane to fortify, anesthetize, and sustain me through this dismal sideshow exhibition. My sister seemed relieved at my appearance. Her husband Pablo could not look me in the eye. He had been an older teammate on my high school football team. He had been so popular that he was voted homecoming prince one year. He had met my older sister after high school and they had married. A popular, extremely outgoing, and, on the surface, very nice, charming guy, generally liked by everyone, myself included, his deep unseen darkness not to be revealed until much later.

I had very little to say to him, disgusted that I was even here in my mother's kitchen. His lawyer had made a deal with the place where he'd been working when he'd committed the assault that he'd not be charged for the time being under the condition he not leave the state. The company he'd worked for wanted desperately to avoid a trial, afraid they'd lose their license to operate and be forced to close. It was a rigged, dirty deal.

Here I was, staying in a houseful of people I could not stand, guilted by the gesture of my father having traveled all the way here. Not that he'd be able to join in any kind of celebration at my mother's; she was too vindictive to put the past aside and allow him that. He was sitting alone in a motel nearby so his kids and grandsons could visit him for short intervals. I blamed the entire mess on my brother-in-law Pablo. I held him responsible for this homecoming that felt like a jail sentence.

MONTHS EARLIER, MY SISTER HAD shared with me some dark shit she'd discovered. She had been looking for something in the house and came across an ugly stash. Pablo had been clandestinely filling numerous notebooks and journals with bizarre sex-crime fantasies in which my sister was the star, the victim, and always ended up dead. Despite my own personal legal and consensual kinks, this clearly set off alarm bells. My sister's obvious fear put me on edge.

I had begged her to call the cops. With two babies to care for, she felt compelled to continue living with him, handcuffed by circumstance yet fearing for her life on a daily basis. Through my connections at a local pawn shop owned by a friend of mine, I knew I had at least one totally badass character in my corner and in a position to help. A huge, muscular, funny, and cool Seattle police officer named John Powers was a fan and a friend, an ace in the hole should I ever find myself in a real jam. I talked to him about my sister's situation and he agreed Pablo's hobby was troublesome. The notebooks filled with these scenarios where my sister was gang-raped and murdered could legally be considered plans he intended to carry out, not just simple fantasy stories. If I could get my hands on them and turn the evidence over to him, he'd do his best to make sure Pablo got what he had coming.

I had made plans to meet my sister one day to get them from her. After taking the ferry over to her island home, to my amazement she said she had destroyed them. She had a talk with someone in the prosecutor's office that Powers had hooked her up with and they said they would put her and the kids in witness protection, but such was her fear of being tracked down and killed by Pablo's unbalanced mother that she decided to stick it out.

His private writing habits had me convinced for certain this fuck had done what he'd been accused of: the physical assault of a heavily disabled man, a man with cognitive mental problems that made it difficult for him to communicate. If anything was going to save Pablo's ass, it was that the victim couldn't verbally make his case in an understandable way. Like many perpetrators of violent crimes, Pablo had hidden it for years with his gregarious, ultra-friendly exterior. Not only had Pablo's mother vehemently blamed my sister for his crime, incredibly, sadly, predictably, our own mother had done the same. I felt genuine grief and sadness for my sister's plight but also a seething, powerless anger toward her fearful, spiritless lack of dominion to escape and my own straightjacketed inability to help.

In the midst of my own personal addiction hell, she had become so afraid of Pablo that at one point, she had begged me to come stay in her house to make sure nothing happened. Each afternoon for the better part of a week, I would walk down the hill, get on a ferry, and travel to their house. I would sit wide awake all night in their living room, stepping outside every hour or so to hit the pipe, just so my sister felt safe enough to sleep. Finally, she found some blood on her bathroom floor where I'd sloppily fixed in the middle of the night and thought better of having me around her kids. I knew I had to disengage before my homicidal impulse spun totally out of control. After Layne Staley spent hours one night patiently yet emphatically taking me step-by-step over every reason why murdering Pablo was a terrible idea, I had finally turned my back on the entire grotesque circus.

This Christmas get-together was an obvious mistake. The "happiest" times were the couple of evenings I'd spent with my father, watching TV together in a sad, single-story roadside motel. I had to find a way out. I attended an evening AA meeting totally loaded just to receive a 30-day chip for being clean in order to falsely prove to my poor, loving, hopeful father I was no longer using. Then I announced that I had to return to Seattle the next day for a business meeting. I was, of course, taking the short, inexpensive flight to re-up on my stock of heroin and use the rest of a royalty check to buy some gifts for the family. Already shooting a gram a day and fully strung out again, I returned to play the part of the big shot. I came in wearing a huge, outlandish shiny silver coat I'd purchased and a pair of sunglasses you might imagine Elton John sporting onstage, acting the star in order to rub my mother's face in the shit of my "success." I turned a deaf ear to her ridicule and put-downs and, usurping her coveted spot as center of attention, lavished expensive gifts on everyone except her and my brother-in-law. The two of them received the exact same pair of the cheapest, ugliest, fucked-up Christmas mittens I could find, handed to them in plastic grocery bags.

I was scheduled to be there five days. On three of them, I flew to Seattle and back. Finally, while taking me to the airport yet again, my mother called me out on my obvious bullshit.

"You're not clean, you goddamn liar. Don't come back to my house!"

"Gladly. But then you'd better turn around and take me back there so I can get my stuff out of your place."

"You are no longer welcome there. I'll pack it up and send it to you," she yelled, our confrontation escalating.

"Let's face it, Mom, I've never been welcome in your fucking house. The only reason I came was to see my father!"

Slamming on the brakes about a mile from the airport, she screamed, "You get the hell out of my truck; I never want to see you again!"

I immediately exploded in furious, dangerous anger.

"You drive me to the fucking airport or I swear to fucking God, I will kill you right here in this truck and drive myself," I said at the top of my voice, one considerably more robust and powerful then hers. I meant it. All the years of taking her shit, being constantly hammered with her tirades of what a useless, unintelligent loser I was, neglected, constantly ridiculed and physically abused as a child . . . it all came rushing to the forefront of my mind and her habitual negativity and hatred was by now far outmatched by my own.

As we sat there screaming at each other, I suddenly became conscious of a third voice in the truck, that of my two-and-a-half-year-old nephew, who sat between my mother and me in the front seat of her pickup.

"No! No! No!"

As I heard his tiny voice, I realized he was punching me in the ribs with his miniature fist. I was instantly ashamed and the intensity of my anger was completely diffused. I had never felt like such a lost and lonely piece of shit. I had no idea what would happen next but I knew it wouldn't be good. Not only had I quickly relapsed after what had felt like scaling K2 to get clean, but it took a baby child to stop me from physically attacking my own mother. Still, I had to get in the last word.

"You demented hag. I spent my childhood having nightmares starring you every night, only to have to live them for real in daylight hours. This is why both your real children have always and will always detest you," I said in a much quieter, calm, and steady voice. "You have never once in my entire life shown me an ounce of authentic love or kindness. I could give a fuck that you don't give a damn about me, but you've always gone out of your way to make it your express mission to be sure I would never forget that I'm a fucking nobody and shit on your shoes. I've never known why and I no longer care. Fuck you, enjoy the rest of your pathetic, shitty life. Don't bother sending me my stuff. You can shove it up your ass."

With that, I got out of her truck. She spun her tires on the icy pavement and fishtailed out of sight.

I had long been aware that nothing was more unattractive to a woman than a grown man with mother issues, so I knew I would never share any of these events or secret residual childhood trauma with anyone. I would push it to the very back of my mind where it had always restlessly slept, and keep rolling.

Overflowing with bitterness, I trudged a mile on the shoulder of the road through the snow and muddy sludge to the tiny 1950s-looking airport in Yakima, Washington, "The Palm Springs of Washington," as the sign informed you when you pulled into town.

33

I SMOKED WEED—HIV-POSITIVE

AFTER MY FINAL, EXPLOSIVE SHOWDOWN WITH MY MOTHER, I wound up back in my Seattle apartment a couple days after Christmas. I was not due back in Los Angeles to finish the long-suffered Screaming Trees record until January 10. Though I still had my place in California, as well as numerous drug connections there, I decided to stay in the Northwest.

Out of the blue, I received a call from Anna one night.

"Hey, mister. I was just thinking about you and wondered how you're doing."

"I'm doing great, finally kicked dope," I said, not mentioning that I'd just turned right around and begun using again. "I'm heading back to LA in a little while to finish a new Trees record we've been working on. How have you been?"

She instantly broke out in tears.

"Hey, hey, baby, what's wrong?" I asked, suddenly concerned something was seriously amiss.

"Goddamnit, I'm so lonely! I miss you, you bastard."

I paused for a moment. This was an unexpected shock. The final year of our relationship had been fraught with unhappiness, fighting, my secret doping, my lying, the whole nine. It had been me in tears the last time we spoke, but they were not tears of loneliness.

Six months before heading to California, I had been alone in my apartment, trying yet again to kick on my own. I was on day two of no heroin, and the tiniest bit of methadone I had drunk did virtually

231

nothing to hold back the intense pain of withdrawals. I suddenly remembered something: a stripper friend I'd had a casual relationship with for years had left a hit of weed in a bong in my kitchen cabinet. It had probably been there four or five months.

I had not smoked in several years but I started thinking, *They give weed to chemotherapy patients for pain, it's got to work for withdrawals.* Having once read a detailed account of what radiation sickness felt like, I had always thought it sounded exactly like withdrawals. I went to the kitchen, got the bong, and took the biggest hit I could hold.

Unfortunately, no one had clued me in to how potent weed had become in the years since I'd last done it. Within a couple minutes, I was in unimaginable hell. I had kicked a big heroin habit cold turkey before and that was as fucked as it got. I had also suffered a terrifying, several-hours-long horrible acid trip. This was like an uncanny combo of the worst both experiences had to offer. Not only did the weed not relieve my pain, it intensified it a thousandfold. It was late at night and I had nothing, no Valium or benzos, no more methadone, no money to score dope, no opiates whatsoever, nothing at all to slow or stop the onslaught of this rocket ship of misery. The brutal physical discomfort of my worst kicking had always been accompanied with the most punishing black hole of indescribable hopeless depression. I began a downward spiral, a million-mile-an-hour fall. I started to sob uncontrollably, my body wracked with spasm after painful spasm with each sob. It was torment beyond description.

At the peak of this acutely unpleasant episode, the phone had rung. I jumped up off the floor and picked it up in hopes it was someone in a position to relieve my agony. But unable to stop crying, I could not talk.

"Hello? Hello? Mark! What in the fuck is wrong with you?"

On the other end of the line was Anna, who I'd not heard from in months. Realizing it was my ex who I still pined for made my sobbing raise to a fever pitch. I was still not able to say a word.

"What in the fuck, man?! You're scaring me! What is happening over there? Talk to me or I'm going to call the cops!"

With every ounce of strength in me, I had managed to say, "Don't do that please!"

"Then what is wrong with you? Should I call an ambulance?"

Anna had found me passed out drunk one night and, thinking I'd OD'd on heroin, had called an ambulance to take me the one block to Harborview, where I came to immediately when they'd given me a shot of adrenaline. When they realized I was just drunk, they gave me the option of getting up and walking out or being transferred down the street to county jail. Fifteen minutes and five hundred dollars later for the one-block ride, I'd stumbled back into the apartment.

"No!" I managed to get out through my still-out-of-control crying.

"Okay, man, you've got one minute to tell me what the fuck is wrong with you or I'm calling the cops *and* an ambulance."

With all the effort I could find, I finally managed to spit out just three words.

"I . . . smoked . . . weed."

That was it. All I could say through the off-the-hook convulsive gasping. There was a momentary astonished noise, part laugh and part stifled breath of disbelief, on the other end of the line. I cried on unabated.

After several long moments of silence, her voice oozing bitter sarcasm, she said, "Right. Ha, ha. Whatever, shithead," and, *click*, she had hung up.

—

NOW, IT SEEMED, I WAS on the other side of the street. I recognized her tears as an opening through which I could slip and insinuate myself back into her life.

I had been having regular phone conversations with Selene, who was still in San Francisco. I could tell she instinctively knew there was something different now that I was getting loaded again. But Anna, who had not talked to me in months, was unable to tell.

"Where are you?" I asked.

Still crying, she said, "I'm at home. Do you want to come over?"

"I'll be right there."

I ended up spending the night. We fell into another desperate fling, one that ran head-on into Selene's return to town.

"Hey, I'm here. I've got a few things to do and then I'm coming over" was the message I got from Selene when she arrived in Seattle just as I was coming home from another night spent with Anna. I could tell that both women knew something was up with me, but I had been lying to Anna for so long that she was obviously choosing to ignore it for the moment. She had been in another unsatisfying relationship since her original break with me and was extremely unhappy. I knew it was doomed from every angle, but I was willing to let go of Selene if it meant I could hold on to Anna just a bit longer. Selene, who I'd fallen so hard for and with whom I'd felt a such a heavy connection, like nothing I'd ever felt before. I inwardly grieved and doubted this decision, not only for the loss of that connection, but also with an aching sense of grati-tude for the nonjudgmental way she'd accepted me. I was in my most natural element, between a cement slab and a boulder, both of my own fucked-up manufacturing, trying hopelessly to find a way out. Old hab-its die hard, they say. Mine were clearly going with me to the grave.

Selene showed up at my house that afternoon. I was glad to see her and greeted her warmly but could tell something was bothering her.

"What's wrong?" I asked, thinking she was on to my using.

"I don't know if I want to talk about it. I'm worried about something I heard but I'm afraid to make you mad."

"Baby, you're not gonna make me mad. What are you worried about?"

She must have heard I was getting loaded from someone. I was pre-pared to admit it as that would get me out of a relationship that I now wanted to end as painlessly as possible so I could spend as many days with Anna as I had left before she inevitably, unceremoniously, once again showed me the door.

"I was up on Broadway and ran into Jason Finn," she said.

Jason Finn was a local drummer, an ugly-spirited toad of an irritant, a prick who was always spouting some wise-ass comment in a lame bid for attention. When Danny Peters had been drumming for the Trees, he had told me one night that while we were drummerless, Finn had told him, "Stay out of my way because I'm gonna drum for the Trees." We had both laughed heartily at that, not only because Dan had clearly jumped that hurdle but because Finn was the last guy I would ever have played with. He had eventually struck it rich with a moronically named band, Presidents of the United States of America, who had a huge hit with some kind of comedy-rock tune. Not my cup of shit, but then again, I was not the record-buying public.

"Yeah. So you ran into Finn, what about it?"

"He heard I was dating you and begged me to have some coffee with him because he had something super serious he needed to tell me about you."

"So how was the coffee?"

If what he had to tell her was that I was a junkie, who the fuck didn't already know that?

"He said he knows for a fact and that it's common knowledge that you are HIV-positive. That I better be very careful if I was having sex with you."

I couldn't help but laugh out loud. She looked at me with her beautiful eyes with a kind of curious but slightly worried smile, as if to ask, "Is it true?"

My mind, with its computerlike propensity for recalling personal slights, promptly went back to a time a few years earlier when I had been leaving the Off Ramp alone. I'd innocently made eye contact with a good-looking woman I'd never seen before in my life. Without a single word, we began desperately making out like a couple of animals. We pawed at each other, dry humping and kissing in front of everyone leaving the show. She worked in some capacity in the Canadian music industry, in Seattle visiting none other than Mudhoney road manager Bob Whittaker, another chronic antagonist of mine. He had literally yanked her off of me and she had stared back at me with a wide-eyed, crazy, lustful look, struggling to escape his grasp the entire time he physically dragged her down the long street to his car. I had stood there, watching them the entire way with my open hands turned upward toward the sky, wondering what in the fuck had just happened, swiftly and violently deprived of what for a second had seemed like paradise fallen into my lap. Was she Bob's girlfriend? Relative? At any rate, he had successfully cock-blocked me and it gave yet one more reason to dislike the fuckhead.

I had unexpectedly run into her a few months later at her job as a promoter's assistant when the Trees played a show in Vancouver. At first, she pretended we'd never met. I put it down to simple embarrassment, the regret of a night when she may have had one too many drinks. Finding her alone in an office, I walked in and said hello. After I brought it up, she admitted remembering our brief micro-encounter and we formally introduced ourselves to one another. After joking around for a couple of minutes, I got down to business.

"Hey, why don't you come hang with me and have drinks at our hotel after the show?"

That suggestion received an Arctic-cold shoulder. After an uncomfortable stony silence that told me I'd not be fucking her that or any other night, she blurted out that Whittaker had told her this same lie: that I was HIV-positive.

Apparently everyone in Seattle had known I was dying of AIDS for years, yet not a single doctor had bothered to inform me of it. I finally stopped laughing and said to Selene in a deadly serious tone, "Jason Finn hates my guts and I'm sure he wants to fuck you. I've not been tested in a few years but I've not shared needles with anyone in a long time and the last ten times I was tested it was negative. So fuck Jason Finn and his fucking punk-ass bullshit. I'm gonna beat his fucking head in."

In the anger of the moment, I forgot that my intention had been to try and end this thing painlessly. Now I was fighting to keep it because I didn't care for the ramifications attached to this kind of out.

In all honesty, I had no idea if I was HIV-positive. In the late '80s and early '90s, I was at the free STD clinic every other month. I'd had them all, multiple times: crabs, chlamydia, scabies, genital warts, epididymitis that made my balls swell to the size of small peaches and caused me serious pain whenever I came. I'd had this nasty shit called molluscum that was like a cross between a genital wart and an open scabies sore but much larger, and that gave me a sudden panic when I found out it was mostly seen in HIV-positive people. Once, the Trees had been playing a show in Italy and my balls were so badly swollen from epididymitis I could barely walk. After two encores, I exited the stage through a door to the outside of the club and collapsed on the sidewalk in such pain I thought I might be headed to the hospital to get my nuts cut off. As I lay in the fetal position holding my groin, members of the hyper-enthusiastic crowd were leaving and spotted me there. They ran over and, despite my angry, anguished protests, actually picked me up and began to carry me back inside to the stage. One guy had yelled, practically spitting in my face with a thick Italian accent, "Who do you think you are? Liza Minnelli? You come to this dirty town and give us just two encores?" I couldn't believe the absurdity of the situation. Couldn't these dickheads see I was clutching my balls in agony? Did they actually expect me to just get up and sing some more? And where the fuck was a security guy or a fucking cop when you actually needed one? Eventually, a man of Pakistani descent realized I was in serious discomfort. He and some friends forced the mob to lay me back down on the ground, then they picked me up again and carried me to his car. He rushed me to the hospital where a nurse, struggling to translate for the doctor, told me what I already knew I had and "don't wear such tight pants."

I was at the clinic in Seattle so often, they began to let me freeze-burn the warts off my dick myself. They also began letting me swab the inside of my dick myself. Previous to that, some nurse's aide would brutally scrape the inside of my dickhole with a thin metal stick with some kind of rough material on the end of it, something I found to be acutely fucked. Finally the doctor there told me it just had to lightly touch the inside of my dick and let me do it myself, with considerably less discomfort involved. But each time I was there, I had also been tested for HIV and come up negative, so I had always operated on the assumption that I was not.

Finn either really believed this bullshit of his because he'd heard it someplace else or was talking out his ass to try and fuck me over and fuck my girl. Probably both. I had always dated attractive women and had learned early on that when another musician found out someone was dating me, they would often pull out all the stops to try to fuck my girl, such was my unpopularity with my peers. It had worked more than a few times. Heavy attention from someone else combined with my shitty behavior made me a shoo-in for this kind of payback from girlfriends I'd neglected, burned, or fucked over. On the flipside, I was the easiest guy to have sex with ever: all you had to do was ask. I had no morals and would indiscriminately fuck anyone's girlfriend, sister, whoever. I fucked the wives of acquaintances, friends, coworkers, and other musicians. I would rarely turn down an opportunity to have sex with anyone I considered remotely desirable: record company employees, photographers and music journalists, barmaids, bartenders, fans and promoters at clubs we played, the random pick-ups, the next-door neighbors, it just didn't matter. I had stupidly, recklessly slept with friends' revenge-seeking girlfriends, knowing they'd only chosen me because I was an indiscriminate whore and that our coupling was only designed to injure. They'd wait until the exact moment my pal was at his lowest, then lob the grenade of my complicity in this shittiest kind of betrayal at him to finish him off. I'd either get sucker-punched in the face, guilted to death, or exiled. Usually all three. Almost my entire sex life had been a self-fulfilling prophecy of negative consequences for an hour or two of pleasure. Or five minutes of pleasure, whichever the case may have been.

—

I ADMITTED TO SELENE I was strung out again. For that reason, I told her that moving in to my place was a bad idea. I also used it as an excuse to put an end to our relationship while still vehemently denying the overt rumors of my alleged HIV-positive status. Now that she saw me through the prism of my active addiction, she had zero objections. Though it had been one of the most intensely magnetic experiences of attraction I'd had in my life, I was relieved. I hated to let her go and felt I was possibly throwing away the only chance at happiness I'd had in years, but my newly restarted obsession with Anna gripped me like yet one more drug I was unable to resist.

34

GOLD FOR GARBAGE

AFTER A WEEK OR TWO, IT WAS TIME TO HEAD BACK TO CALIFORNIA to finish the Screaming Trees record that was to become *Dust*. The night before I left, Anna finally dropped the bomb on me. She tearfully admitted she had been aware of my using the entire time we'd hung out. She asked me to please not call or try to contact her when I returned because she had to move on with her life and my presence in her world made that impossible.

When I returned to Los Angeles after my ugly Christmas experience, producer George Drakoulias knew I was loaded again the minute I walked into the studio. He had waited patiently for me to get clean to participate in the creation of this record. Now he exploded in an anger I had no idea he held within him. He grabbed me by the neck of my shirt and in a second flat dragged me from the control room out into the hallway. He possessed imposing height and girth and he pinned me against the wall, his furiously contorted face inches from mine.

"You son of a bitch! Goddamnit, I told you not to leave California! You motherfucker! I should beat your ass!"

He had told me it was not a good idea to leave Los Angeles at Christmas. And yes, he could have beaten my ass. George was a large individual but with the friendliest, funniest, and most fun-loving personality of anyone I knew. That's what made this outburst so unexpectedly shocking. He was absolutely livid.

"What in the fuck am I supposed to do with you? Jesus Christ, Lanegan, I can't fucking believe you . . . I really can't."

After he'd exhausted his rage, he leaned heavily against me. With his hand, he gently patted my face, a gesture both friendly and menacing.

"Here's what's gonna happen, Lanegan. You are gonna sing your motherfucking balls off. I don't give a damn what shape you're in anymore, I swear to God you are gonna get the fucking job done. End of story."

A couple of addicts from an Orlando, Florida, band who I'd known for years were staying in my apartment while I was out of town. The guitar player was an untrustworthy, thieving junkhead, the kind of guy who'd steal your dope and then spend a half hour helping you look for it. The bass player was a sweetheart but was under the other guy's thumb, used by him as his toady. While the guitarist had been selling dope out of the place, he'd also been selling off any of my personal shit of value as well. I came home to find half my clothes, CDs, and books missing. When I questioned him, he played stupid, as though it were news to him.

"Dude, I honestly don't know what the fuck you're talking about. I swear I haven't touched anything! Maybe someone broke in and took it."

Trees had been looking for a second guitarist to help fill out the sound on the touring we planned to do after this record was done. The Floridian had put down a boring, by-the-numbers rhythm track on one of the tunes we'd recorded earlier. The lifelessness of his playing combined with his dope-fiending rip-off of my shit compelled me to tell the other Trees, "He's definitely not our guy." These two addicts hung around my neck like a pair of old shoes taken off a dead bum. I started making arrangements to kick them the fuck out of my place.

One of the last things to do on the record besides vocals were some keyboard overdubs. Benmont Tench of Tom Petty's Heartbreakers came in to do a night of piano playing. The first thing he did was move both of the studio's old '60s Mellotrons—the huge, ancient string machines heard on so many records from that period—into the main room. He arranged them facing each other, one on either side of him. Everyone watched in awe as he played a long solo on both at the same time, one with his right hand and the other with his left. A real-deal virtuoso, the likes of which we'd never seen and certainly never had play on one of our records.

George urged me to hang tight with Benmont because he had been sober for many years. He took me to a couple meetings in Hollywood but I always felt out of place at these large, loud meetings where you'd often see some famous actor or musician in the crowd. Besides, I'd already made up my mind that I was going to ride or die with dope. There was no going back now.

I had long since ceased to enjoy the ever-changing dynamic of life with my bandmates. I had reconciled with the knowledge that all of us were troubled, damaged people, myself the most criminal example, each with our own cross to bear, but I knew in the back of my head that these songs would be the last I'd ever sing for this band. Still, despite my exhaustion with the entire parade, I couldn't help but admire and appreciate the way Lee and Van Conner, Barrett Martin, and George had worked so diligently to create this last-chance record. They had allowed me the time and space to get clean in solitude and I'd repaid them by quickly relapsing, now only able to participate in an impaired fashion.

I started the tortured and torturous process of laying down the vocal tracks, still writing lyrics for the songs even as I stood in the vocal booth to record. Drakoulias worked me hard. I'd sing a verse as forcefully as I possibly could. Then on the talkback microphone from the mixing board, I would hear his voice in my headphones say simply, "No." I would then do it again, and again, sometimes taking an entire night just to get a couple of verses he deemed good enough. My voice was definitely not its strongest while on drugs, but it wasn't as though I was completely powerless in the singing department. I had made other records and toured for years while strung out. But George was a strict taskmaster and I willingly did whatever he asked of me, knowing how long and hard he'd fought to help me get clean the previous year and how angry and disappointed he'd been at my fall.

In a recording studio one block off Hollywood Boulevard, I was put through the paces daily, strung out and straining to finish this final handful of songs. The physical and emotional drain of the demands of my drug habit combined with the hours of singing under the critical ears of Drakoulias took a toll. The lyrics I was writing now were probably the most world-weary, hopeless, and death-focused I'd written, even if I was the only one aware of their meaning. After singing for hours and then spending hours more comping vocal tracks—a process that involved going line by line through numerous vocal takes to find a word here, a line there, and putting the best of these performances together to form one cohesive vocal track to then be used on the record . . . the magic of studio mixing—I would hear the final patched-together takes and be crestfallen when I realized my singing sounded like shit to me. I would inevitably then beg George to let me sing it again, which would start the painful carousel turning once more. In the end it was I, not George, who could not live with the results. What I had originally perceived as his disapproval had, in fact, been my own self-inflicted wounded psyche that agonizingly prolonged the sessions.

I grew to think of *Dust* as not an attempt for commercial success but as only the second unique effort in our catalog of scores of records, all the early ones almost identical in sound and song type. It ended up being a very different kind of album than its predecessor, something I considered more a piece of art than any of our previous albums. Everyone involved had suffered and felt pain in its frustrating creation, and I was proud of it. Yet I knew its chances for failure with the general music-listening public were near to 100 percent. I grimly anticipated its release as the beginning of the death throes the band must ultimately endure. And waited for the day Screaming Trees were to end ignominiously, silent and beaten, sometime in the near future.

—

MY GUITARIST ROOMMATE HAD BEEN busted for selling dope outside my apartment and when he got out of jail I was preparing to leave LA. For some furtive, unknown reason, he tried to talk me into staying just a couple more days but never really had any real excuse for wanting me to stick around. We were anything but close, the rent had been paid up until the end of the month, and that meant he had three more weeks before he'd have to pay it himself or get out. One day while he was gone, his bass player gave me a warning.

"I think old boy might be setting you up to get busted. I think he talked the cops into thinking that since this place is in your name, you're the dope dealer, not him. I think that's why they let him out so soon. He sure as hell didn't have money for bail. I'd get out if I were you."

I'd had the same feeling myself, that something shady was up with this always obviously shady dude. Leaving all the shit behind that he had not already stolen, I took a cab to the Burbank airport and left California behind for the familiar confines and rainy doom and gloom of the Pacific Northwest.

A few months later, while playing before powerhouse labelmates Rage Against the Machine on a festival date, I ran into Selene. Still incredibly kind to me, she quietly informed me she had been dating Brad Wilk, the drummer for Rage. The news stung a little. I had always found him to be a very nice guy whenever I'd been around him. I wished her the best, silently chastising myself for taking this beautiful, kind, intuitive, and caring woman for granted and for ultimately choosing dope over any potentially good thing in life. They eventually married. For a long time after that, whenever she crossed my mind, I felt a dull emptiness inside. I considered my letting her go after our brief affair as one of the more glaring mistakes in a lifetime filled with them. The fabled "one that got away." But I was an expert at trading gold for garbage.

35

ONE HEAVY TEAR

AS SOON AS I GOT BACK TO SEATTLE, I WENT THROUGH THE MULTI-tude of messages on my answering machine, over a month's worth of boring shit I mostly erased as soon as I heard who was calling. Then I heard the voice of Jeffrey Lee Pierce, sounding manic and weird. I listened closely to the message but I could not understand one thing he was trying to say. It was a crazed, rambling monologue that made not one bit of sense.

When he'd returned to England after the Gun Club's disappointing West Coast tour, he'd begun to call me long-distance from London at least twice a week, often in tears. His girlfriend Romi Mori had left him for his own drummer. Apparently they'd been having an affair for some time and finally decided to quit the band to be together, leaving Jeffrey devastated. I had patiently listened to his agonized heartache every time he called. He was, after all, my favorite singer, the reason I'd become a singer myself, and I loved and idolized the guy.

During one phone call, he'd told me of his vision for a new band: he and some other badass-but-as-yet-unknown guitar player, drummer, and bass player would form a band like Television, Tom Verlaine and Richard Lloyd's great two-virtuoso-guitarists band from the '70s.

"Here's the best part, Lanegan—you will be the singer!"

I was silent for a moment. There was no way I was going to be the singer in a band with the guy I considered the greatest singer of all time. How could I do that? It was just wrong.

"Jeffrey, I can't possibly sing in a band with you, you're my favorite singer ever. Nobody can touch you in that department. I like your idea for a new direction, but you've got to be the singer. You have *got* to be the singer!"

I was flattered by my idol's plan to have me sing in his band, but I knew it was inherently flawed. You don't take the most original, powerful, and genius singer of my generation and relegate him to playing guitar solos. No way. But this call had been the only call in weeks where he'd shown any enthusiasm for music, much less living. Still heartbroken and betrayed, he was deeply unhappy.

Right before I'd begun my Buprenex treatments in the fall, he and I had gotten together with the intention of writing some songs at his mom's place in Hollywood, a couple of blocks from Johnny Depp's infamous Viper Room, the small club outside of which, years earlier, young actor River Phoenix had collapsed and died. I'd run a cassette recorder as Jeffrey'd shown me a part of a song and told me to finish it. In the very warm Los Angeles October weather, I was still feeling the chill of withdrawals. The cassette recorder captured our conversation.

"Hey, man, can you close that door? You know I'm kicking," I'd asked, the sliding glass door wide open.

"Yeah, I know. What else is new?" he'd answered with a truthful yet smart-ass response.

After spending the day writing with him, it was time for me to go back to my apartment. Jeffrey was leaving for Japan the next morning to hang out with friends there and, I secretly suspected, to look for women. While he'd been with Romi in London, every time we went out she'd brought a gang of beautiful Asian girls with her. The first time I'd been out with them in such a situation, I'd literally been mobbed by a group of these women, all vying for my attention. I quickly learned that they were women looking for sugar-daddy boyfriends. Their interest in me quickly waned.

When I listened at least a half dozen times to the message he'd left on my answering machine, I could tell he was not drunk or on drugs. With alarm bells of worry clanging in my head, I recognized his gibberish as something else I'd heard before: mental illness. Something had happened in the time since we'd sat together in his mom's kitchen that had damaged his psyche.

I called my ex-manager Kim White, someone I was no longer friendly with. Even though I did not want to talk to her, I knew she loved Jeffrey as much as I did; we were two of a group of people in Los Angeles who cared deeply for and appreciated Jeffrey's genius.

"Jeffrey is really sick," she said, "and nobody knows what to do. He was drinking while in Japan and suffered liver failure."

I knew it was from years of heavy alcohol abuse, hepatitis C, and his HIV-positive status. The insanity of the message he'd left on my phone, the result of the dementia caused as the poison from his damaged liver spread through his body to his brain.

Keith Morris was the former singer of both the Circle Jerks and Black Flag, two of the most famous of all LA punk bands. Kim told me he had tried to check Jeffrey into rehab but they'd turned him away, Jeffrey being too far gone to help.

"Can you come to LA right away?" she said.

I knew Keith a little bit, a very friendly, talkative, smart, and sort of eccentric dude, not a guy who gave up easily. If there was nothing they could do for him, his situation deemed hopeless, I was sure Keith had exhausted all avenues. Between my roommate's warning to avoid the cops by leaving California and the apparent death sentence Jeffrey had already been handed, I decided to stay put.

"He's going to die, Mark," Kim said.

"We are, too, someday, Kim," I replied. That ended our conversation.

Almost exactly a week later, my phone rang. I picked it up as soon as I heard Jeffrey's voice on the machine.

"Dude!" I spoke quickly and giddily into the phone. "Where are you? How are you? I've been hearing some crazy shit!"

"I'm staying at my dad's in Salt Lake City. I'm fine."

Indeed, he did sound as sane as the day I'd met him, none of the crazed, nonsensical, manic speech from his earlier message. He sounded perfectly normal again.

"What kind of crazy shit have you heard?" he asked.

"Well . . . everyone is saying you're about to die, for starters."

He burst into a fit of long, loud laughter.

"They always fucking say that, man! Don't believe a word those assholes say, it's all for show, total bullshit!"

We talked and laughed for an hour until he said he had to go but would call again soon. We said our so-longs. I hung up and went back to my mindless task of cooking up crack.

Exactly one week later, Kim White called again.

"Mark, we've lost Jeffrey."

"What? I just fucking talked to him. He was laughing and said he was fine!"

"I'm sorry. He's gone."

No, not Jeffrey. Denial hit me hard. No, not my only legitimate hero. Not the artist who'd selflessly taught me his personal methods of song-writing and had actively encouraged me to use the same, the only friend who showed up to see me sing every single time I played London. Not the genius whose crazed, forcefully real music and distinctly unique and powerful voice had been the spark that lit the fuse that had changed me, pointed me in the direction of my authentic life. Not the lover who'd had his heart broken in such a harsh, humiliating way that he wept in anguish as I sat there night in and night out, listening to him helplessly. Not the wildman who filled the room with maniacal laughter while telling a fucked-up story of one of his numerous misdeeds. Not the big brother who had taken me in and right away made himself an open book that he'd happily let me devour, the only relationship of that kind I'd ever had. Not Jeffrey, please. I thought I would choke on my heart.

"They found him dead at his dad's house yesterday. They think it was a brain hemorrhage."

I told her I would not be able to come to Los Angeles for his wake and tribute parties. Then I hung up the phone and stared out the window. I knew he was not well, but he was only thirty-six years old. After a few seconds, I felt the largest, lone tear I'd ever produced run burning from one of my eyes down my face. As I reached up to wipe it away, it fell off the end of my chin, splashing down onto the hardwood of my apartment floor, leaving a small pool, proof of my salty devastation. I did not want to fall into clinical despair. I did everything I could to get a grip. But after the dam cracked, I cried off and on for hours.

Every time Jeffrey crossed my mind for days to come, I had to consciously fight the urge to start crying again. I already had hardly any friends. Lately, they had been dropping like flies. I couldn't handle losing yet another friend, any one of my few friends, but especially not this one. I had worshipped his music. I had idolized him. It felt so unreal, I literally could not believe that he was gone. This felt like a loss I might never recover from. Like I'd finally been broken for good.

36

WU TANG TO WAYLON

TWO DAYS AFTER THE RELEASE OF WHAT WAS TO BE SCREAMING Trees' last record, *Dust*, we played our first show on the 1996 Lollapalooza tour. We were the second band on the main stage each day, most often playing while people were still slowly trickling into the venues, mainly just large dirt fields off the beaten path from major American cities. Headlining were wildly popular band Metallica, who we shared management with, hence our inclusion on the tour. Since they could fill much bigger venues on their own, Lollapalooza was mainly relegated to second- and third-market cities as they could make a mint headlining the major markets by themselves. Our band had hired a young kid to play second guitar, an acquaintance of Van Conner's named Josh Homme. I had not even been at the rehearsal when they first played with him, but when I heard he had been the guitarist in the band Kyuss, I wholeheartedly endorsed their decision without ever having met him. I was a big fan of the Kyuss records and knew we were getting a steal.

None of us old-timers enjoyed each other's company any longer. I spent almost every second on the tour bus alone in the back lounge, smoking crack and shooting the occasional shot of dope. Josh had a youngster's passing interest in snorting cocaine and liked the occasional drink but my brand of "partying" was something he had little experience with. Through sheer boredom and curiosity, he began to hang in the back with me, not doing drugs, just watching me do them and talking. He impressed me right off the bat. Not only was he a far superior guitarist to Lee, he was highly intelligent and, even at his young age, already a seasoned veteran. I found him to be the kind of thoughtful,

steadying influence the band never had before, as well as a natural comedian with a hilarious, quick sense of humor. Despite our difference in age
and experience, we had much in common. Josh quickly found the rest
of the guys to be dullards who weren't interested in working to their full
potential. They loathed being in my presence, rightly blamed me for the
difficulties writing and recording our long-delayed follow up to *Sweet
Oblivion*, and were by now just going through the motions. Josh intimated that until the offer to play with us had come, he had planned to
quit music altogether and the reason he'd been in Seattle was to attend
college. Despite my glaring addictions, his take on things was that I was
the only one who cared enough to try to do my best when it came to my
job, singing. I, in turn, quickly accepted him as an equal, the only guy I
considered as such by then and we became close friends and conspira-
torial allies.

We were both embarrassed to get onstage every day, Lee Conner's
routine just a shtick at that point. Yet we both still did our best to play
as well as we could and perform like professionals. Josh could have
played the simplistic guitar parts in his sleep and I jokingly asked him
how he managed to stay awake while doing it. I turned him on to some
classic underground rock he'd not heard before and he eagerly sought
out stuff I'd tell him about. He wanted to be original, he wanted to be
great. After playing so long with guys who seemed to not give two fucks
about originality or greatness, I found his attitude more than refreshing.
It was clear to me from the get-go that he had more talent and creativity
in him than the rest of the band combined. He confided in me that he
found the heavy dysfunction he witnessed daily and the band's lack of
musical proficiency amusing and confounding. I said, "You and me both,
brother." His presence was my saving grace from that moment until the
eventual end of the band. I thanked God I finally had someone to relate
to and confide in.

As monotonous and boring as the tour was, still there were some
great performances. Josh and I watched the Ramones every day. Every
day, they killed it. The thrill of being on the same tour as these punk rock
gods made it almost worthwhile.

One day early in the tour, Josh and I were hanging out with Johnny
Ramone, the groundbreaking guitar player behind their genius sound.
He came across as a harmless, curmudgeonly older uncle who rarely,

if ever, smiled amid his litany of complaints. As we stood listening to him gripe about this and that, from around the back of a trailer behind him came Joey Ramone. He snuck around the corner and, grinning ear to ear like a giant schoolkid, put his finger to his lips. With one eye on Johnny and one on Joey, we watched Joey pull out from behind his back a giant Super Soaker–type water rifle. He aimed it at the back of Johnny's head and let loose a huge stream of water. As it made contact, Johnny's hair swooshed forward. He turned around and screamed, "You motherfucker, I'll kill you!" and took off running after Joey, now laughing uncontrollably as he sprinted off into the distance.

Because most of these shows were in backwater areas of the US, I encountered quite a bit of difficulty in maintaining my heroin habit, often finding nowhere to score in several cities. As my methadone supply steadily dwindled, I stepped up my efforts to find dope. In every city where I had the time, I was out in the streets looking to score and still often coming up empty. One of Soundgarden's crew guys was also strung out. He'd come to me one day for some dope, begging, promising, swearing that he had some lined up for the next day, that he would get me back with interest. Against my better judgment, I split the last of what I had at the time with him. Knowing better than to rely on the word of a junkie, I hit the streets that night in Rockford, Illinois.

Josh always referred to my late-night street-prowling excursions as "the Walk." Bored and looking for some excitement, this time he decided he wanted to come along. His appetite for adventure began to wane as, corner after corner, street after street, the whole city was dead. There was nothing happening here.

Finally, we came across a sketchy-looking couple filling up their vehicle at a gas station. I approached the man and woman and asked them if they knew where to score. They looked over my shoulder at clean-cut young Josh and said, "He ain't no cop, is he?"

I laughed and said, "Fuck no! That's my little brother. Except he ain't so little no more!"

"I can take you to a place they might have something, but it'll cost you twenty bucks."

I quickly agreed to the deal and Josh and I got into the backseat of their run-down van, an empty baby seat between us. Josh looked at me with a raised eyebrow as if to say, "You best by fuck know what you're doing." I smiled and nodded like *Don't worry, I got this*. We pulled up to a beat-up-looking two-story flophouse. The couple dropped us off and sped away. We were now in the hood and I secretly rejoiced; this was what I'd been looking for all night.

There was an old black dude sitting on a barstool in the doorway.

"Ten bucks," he said. Then, while giving Josh a close look of stink-eyed inspection, he said, "Apiece."

I pulled out a twenty and gave it to him. We were admitted into a room with a bar a quarter-filled with some skanky women and a couple of dudes. One of the women quickly approached us.

"Hey, boys, buy me a drink?"

"Sorry," I said, "we don't have time for that, but I'll give you twenty bucks if you can take us somewhere to score."

"Whatchoo looking for?" she asked somewhat suspiciously.

"Dog food, heroin."

"Well, I don't fuck with no hare-on, but I know where you can get some rock." That was fine by me—I didn't care what I got as long as it would change my mood. "C'mon upstairs with me."

We began climbing up the couple flights of stairs behind her. At the end of a long hallway, she took my twenty bucks.

"Hang on a second," she said, "let me check it out."

As we waited outside, Josh whispered in my ear.

"Dude, these motherfuckers better not rob us."

"Fuck no, bro. Don't worry, it's all good."

After a minute or two the door opened, our guide stuck her head out and said, "How much you want?"

I told her I only had enough for a twenty-dollar piece. In any strange and potentially hostile environments, I knew better than to indicate I had more than twenty bucks on me until I had sussed out the situation and tried the wares. Anything else was an invitation to get burned. Or worse.

"C'mon in."

As soon as we got through the door, three dudes jumped to their feet.

"Bitch! What the fuck you doing bringing the cops up in here?"

"Hold on, man! We ain't fucking cops, I'm just looking for a twenty-dollar piece, bro!" I said in as firm and believable a tone as I could muster.

"Oh hell no! Maybe you ain't, motherfucker, but he sure as fuck is!"

He was pointing at Josh. At that moment I realized my folly in bring-ing a tall, young, strong-looking kid along. Now that I considered it, he did look somewhat like a rookie cop fresh out of the academy. I then saw Josh, who was standing slightly in front and to the left of me, slip-ping his left hand into his back pocket, reaching for the switchblade he always carried there. If the knife came out, this wasn't going to end well. I softly put my hand on his right shoulder. He was so electrified and put on guard by this confrontational scene that I felt him instantly tense up as though I'd touched him with a cattle prod.

"Sorry, guys, my mistake. We're leaving."

"Yeah, get the fuck outta here, you fucking narc! And take your motherfucking cop with you! Don't you ever come back up in here or I'll kill you, nigger!"

We slowly backed out of the room, then picked up the pace as we quickly descended the staircase and burst out into the street. Josh was livid.

"Goddamn it, Scratch! What the fuck did you take me into?"

Old Scratch was the lifelong nickname my close friends referred to me as, an arcane nom de plume of Lucifer himself.

"I'm sorry, bro, I didn't think about your look. I always get away with this shit because no one has ever thought I was a cop. Obviously, they think you are. Fuck it, let's get back to the hotel."

Trudging up the street, I realized that we had no idea where we were or how to return to the hotel. We were *deep* in the hood. Now every other doorway we passed held a couple people standing there who would whisper to one another as we walked by. A catcall from across the street—"White boys in the hood!"—didn't put Josh at ease. Frankly, even though I now saw opportunity after opportunity to score, I wanted the fuck out of there, too.

We came upon some tract homes and I saw some dudes across the way who looked to be obvious dealers. Suddenly, I was not yet totally willing to give up the ghost in my quest for drugs. I told Josh, "Wait here, just one second, bro." He glared menacingly at me but stayed put between a couple buildings as I prepared to approach these guys. I had not taken two steps when I heard the unmistakable sound of someone cocking a shotgun and a deep voice behind me.

"Get lost, cop."

I had left Josh directly in front of a darkened doorway neither of us had seen. Once again, he'd been mistaken for a fucking cop.

We finally made our way out of the shit and onto a main road. Hoping to catch a cab, I looked behind me at every car coming up the street while Josh walked silently next to me, obviously furious that I'd put him into such compromising, potentially deadly situations. I heard yet another car racing by. When I turned to look, the barrel of a gun came out the window, pointed directly at me. I was too shocked to move. In slow motion, I watched some stranger's trigger finger squeezing—was this it?

I was shot full in the face with a huge stream of water much like Johnny Ramone had been, the front of my clothes soaked through and through. After the momentary shock of thinking we were about to be hit with real ammunition, Josh and I laughed ourselves to tears at my expense, but he was still angry. We caught a cab back to the hotel, but after I'd given four or five different sources dough to point me toward drugs, I was broke. Josh grudgingly paid the fare, and as the cab pulled away, he said to me, "If you ever do that to me again, I'll kill you."

From his tone of voice and demeanor, I did not doubt for a second that he meant it. I paused for a moment. Realizing I had indeed recklessly endangered my new young partner in crime, I nodded my head in agreement.

"Fair enough."

———

I LAY DOWN IN MY wet clothes and fell asleep, exhausted. Our road manager woke me around eleven a.m.: time to go down to the fairgrounds where the concert was held and get ready to do our usual early-afternoon slot. As soon as I arrived, I sought out the Soundgarden bus and specifically bassist Ben Shepherd. Ben was one of my only really close friends who was not a drug user; instead he was naturally crazed. A balls-out, 150 percent, fully committed antisocial music fiend. He was the most real-life "punk rock" of anyone I'd ever met. Without looking or acting anything like the stereotypical punk rocker, Ben lived his life with the most strictly-adhered-to sense of what was cool and what was lame. If you were lame, you'd best stay the fuck out of his face. Ben was big, tough as nails, and had zero qualms about taking anyone on and fucking them up. He was a gifted and extremely serious musician. He was like the Captain Beefheart or Ornette Coleman of Seattle musicians, an extraordinary and original thinker and player. He was one of my favorite people and closest friends, loyal and generous almost to a fault. Once you were friends with Ben, you had a friend for life, one who always had your back. I knocked on the door of their bus and asked for him and in a couple minutes he came to the door. "Hey, man, where's Randy?" Randy was Ben's tech and I wanted the dope he owed me.

"Oh fuck, man, Randy went to the hospital today. He was really sick, puking and shitting at the same time."

I, of course, knew what his malady was. I was furious that he'd lied, then punked out and gone to a fucking hospital because he was dopesick. Minutes later, I got onstage in my still-wet-from-the-night-before clothes, starting to feel the uncomfortable beginnings of my own withdrawals that would shortly hit me full force. As I stood uneasily, furious, sick, and wet, singing these songs I had grown to detest, I began to lose it. Suddenly unable to stand the sensation of wet clothes on my skin, I sat down on the drum riser midsong and pulled off my boots. One after the other, I threw them as far into the crowd as I could, to the delight of the sparse audience. I pulled off my shirt, balled it up, and threw it. I pulled out my empty chained trucker's wallet and whipped it into the crowd, followed quickly by my jeans. I finished the show in a pair of wet boxer shorts, finally free of the irritating clothes.

Later that day, Cheap Trick, originally from Rockford, played on the main stage. As a teenager, I'd gone to see them at the Yakima Speedway racetrack near my hometown. Some friends and I had rented a motel room to party in before and after the show. Hours before the concert, I had walked down a deserted stretch of street from our motel, looking for a store. I looked up and saw some guys coming toward me in a car, yelling and gesturing in my direction. The small central Washington city of Yakima, population around 100,000, had one of the highest crime rates per capita in the entire nation at the time and could be a dangerous place. I thought for a moment that I was about to be targeted for some kind of attack but then realized they were pointing and yelling at some other guy who was jogging up the otherwise empty sidewalk toward me. As he got closer, I realized in a flash of teenaged excitement that the jogger was Rick Nielsen, the legendary guitarist and songwriter of Cheap

Trick. As he ran by me, I said, "Hey, Rick!" He'd put up his hand and high-fived me as he went by. I was beyond thrilled. Of course, when I breathlessly returned to our room and poured out my story, none of my friends believed me.

There were some unforgettable moments on the tour. I watched from the side of the stage, fully engaged, as the Wu Tang Clan took over the stage and captivated the crowd during their short run of shows with the tour. There seemed to be fifteen or twenty of them onstage at once. When their devastating shows were done, the stage was completely covered with the empty forty-ouncers they'd consumed in a half hour of stage time. James Hetfield of Metallica went out of his way to introduce himself and in a genuinely friendly and down-to-earth manner engage me in conversation the few times we ran into each other, something he would go on to do whenever we by chance met in subsequent years. Marky Ramone and C. J. Ramone, their newest bassist, an ex-Marine filled with enthusiastic goodwill, were also two guys who went out of their way to be friendly, converse, and hang out.

Two songs into our show somewhere outside Syracuse, New York, I was hit straight in the forehead with a tennis ball. I shook it off and kept playing. A song later, I was nailed by an entire sub sandwich that caught me horizontally straight in my chest with a huge thud, loud enough that it reverberated through my microphone. Luckily, it was tightly wrapped in cellophane so I'd not been covered with a disgusting mess, but in my already shitty mood, I just dropped the microphone to the stage and walked the fuck off, directly to the back lounge of our bus, show over.

We stayed in DC the night before a show in the countryside somewhere in Virginia, and I spent the entire night in the infamous Dupont Circle, smoking crack with a large group of pipe-hitting black dudes. When the sun came up, one of the guys and I went walking to a crack house to score some more. Halfway there, I felt a strange feeling in the middle of my chest. Suddenly, it felt like my heart was missing every other beat. I leaned down, out of breath with my hands on my knees, waiting for the heart attack I was sure was coming. When my heartbeat finally steadied itself, I continued on and scored more crack.

Later that day, we played in yet another dirt field that passed for a concert ground. After our show, my heart was again acting strange. I lay on the floor of the back lounge of the bus in a freezing-cold sweat, waiting to die. Again, to my surprise and relief, it didn't happen.

—

AT SOME POINT DURING OUR set in Indianapolis, Lee Conner inexplicably took his microphone off of its stand and began whipping it around on the end of its cord. It had suddenly come loose, flown across the stage, and struck me like a fifty-pound barbell directly in the spine. The pain was excruciating but my anger was even larger. I furiously walked off the stage to seek some pain relief I had stashed on the bus. After fixing a shot, I prowled, brooding and lost in furious misery, through the huge lot the busses were parked in for the night. I was considering beating Lee's head in, quitting the band, flying home, and, lastly, dying. I honestly didn't know how much more of this self-inflicted torture and humiliation I could take.

As I paced up and down between the long row of tour busses, someone came up behind me, gently put their arm around my shoulder, and spoke in a heavy Texan's drawl.

"Son, you look like you ain't having too good a day. I know how that feels, I've had a few of those myself."

I looked to my side and, to my shock, the man who had his arm around me was country music legend Waylon Jennings. He had been on the tour for a short run of the shows. He gave me a sad-eyed smile, as though he really did understand my angst, felt sorry for me, and understood exactly how I felt. I looked over his shoulder and there was a producer friend of mine from Houston, Randall Jamail, with a huge sheepish grin. He had obviously seen how unhappy I was and asked Waylon to say something to me, knowing I was a huge fan and that it would be a thrill. I remained in awe of Waylon's kindness toward me from that day forward. He had been everywhere and seen all there was to see yet took the time to make a simple, beautiful gesture that a sad, hardcore addict would carry with him in gratitude for his entire life.

Later that same day, Josh burst into the back lounge right as I exhaled a huge cloud of crack smoke. He fanned it out of his face and sat down. He was slightly worked up and excitedly had something to tell me.

"Dude! I just saw the most incredible girl. Jesus Christ, I can't believe it! What a fucking smile!"

"Who is she?"

"I'm not sure but I think she might be Tim Armstrong's girlfriend or something."

Tim Armstrong was a member of the band Rancid, a group of staunch antidrug AA Nazis. An old friend of mine in Los Angeles had told me to get to know these guys because they held private meetings every day and would let me join them. I hadn't the heart to tell my friend that was an idea I was emphatically opposed to. One afternoon early on in the tour, I had been walking alone up a wide cement sidewalk in the backstage area when I came face-to-face with the entire Rancid band. On either side of the walkway was deep, wet, muddy ground. Even though there was enough room on the cement to drive a Mack truck through, they had stepped off en masse into the ankle-deep mud instead of walking by me. I instantly recognized it for what it was: they had clearly made me for an active junkie and their gesture said they'd rather walk through shit than to have to share the sidewalk with me. I had thought, *It's a good thing I don't give a fuck about your meetings. Fuck you guys,* and stored the slight away in the back of my head.

Now, hearing from Josh that one of them was with a woman he desired, I jumped right in.

"Oh yeah? Fuck that guy, you should go after her, bro. She probably hates that sour-apple son of a bitch. Those Clash rip-offs are a bunch of fucking pricks; I'm sure she can't stand that preachy fuck."

I was always one to hold on to a grudge. I went out of my way to encourage young Josh to make a move on this guy's girl simply because they had rudely gone out of their way to avoid me.

Later that day, I caught sight of the young woman in question. She was an extremely beautiful young Australian woman named Brody with an unnameable quality that hit me like a tractor beam. I instantly saw how Josh's infatuation was born. It turned out to be her first ever day in the US. She was there to see if her budding romance with Tim was going anywhere, never realizing she was actually there to find Josh. He never stopped thinking about her or talking to me about her. Seven years later, they met again by chance, began a deep, life-changing romance, and were eventually married and raised a family together. She was, in fact, the true love of his life.

—

WHEN THE TOUR NEARED ITS end in California, we played a pair of shows in Irvine, just outside Los Angeles, close to the metropolitan area of a large city for once. I had been filled with the electricity of childlike excitement as the last few shows had included one of my favorite bands ever, Devo. Originally from Akron, Ohio, Devo were absolute originals, underground legends who had also hit the mainstream. Their records were classics. With a sound unlike anything that came before and an outrageous stage act that included synchronized moves and trademark bright-yellow janitor suits and plastic hats resembling dog food bowls, their version of the Stones classic "Satisfaction" took it apart, put it back together, and made it completely their own. As an underage high schooler, I'd taken the Greyhound to Seattle and snuck my way into their concert. I'd spent the night in a frat house with some college-aged Devo enthusiasts I'd met during the concert who had taken a liking to me and admired my moxie for having gained entrance. The singer of Devo, a short bespectacled man named Mark Mothersbaugh, was the main focal point and sang in a high, semihysterical-sounding voice. The band included him, his brother, and a second set of brothers. I absolutely loved them.

After playing our set at Irvine Meadows, I had waited patiently for Devo's show. It was as incredible and entertaining as their previous shows on the tour had been, even as great as the one I'd seen as a teenager. Afterward, I'd stayed on the side of the stage to see the next act and about halfway through had become bored and started walking down the ramp from the stage area to the dressing room area. Suddenly, Mark Mothersbaugh had come running up the ramp wearing a post-gig costume of silky-looking shorts and white T-shirt, with a Heineken in his hand. As we came face-to-face, he stuck out the flat of his hand to high-five me as he ran by, just as Rick Nielsen had when I was a teenager. As we slapped hands, in his high-pitched, excitable-sounding voice, he yelled, "Great singing, man!"

That single act lifted my spirits skyscraper-high and made the entire shitty tour worthwhile. In a weird way, I'd come full circle.

37

SECRET DEATH GAMES

SHORTLY AFTER RETURNING HOME FROM THE TEDIUM OF Lollapalooza, I got buzzed one day. I went downstairs and, to my surprise, there was a guy I'd never expected to see in Seattle: St. Louis Simon.

A year or so earlier I'd been in St. Louis, out on the street in daytime trying to score. Some street person I'd hit up showed me a house and said there were guys there that had dope but that they were dangerous and not to go walking up and knock on the door. After an hour or so of watching this place for any sign of activity, a tall, young, handsome blond guy wearing a woman's skirt had come out of the house and walked up the sidewalk directly toward me. I stopped him and asked where the dope was.

"Not at that place," he said, "those guys are fucked. Let's get a cab and I'll take you somewhere better."

We went to the house of a young couple who had a baby sleeping in a cradle, scored, and, he not being an addict, exchanged numbers and went our separate ways. I called him the next day and again he took me to the same place to re-up. I had taken a liking to this helpful, strange dude and had given him not only my phone number but also my address in Seattle and told him to look me up if he were ever in the area.

"Hey, man! What the fuck are you doing here?" I asked, wondering what had brought this kid more than halfway across the country and to my apartment.

"I hitchhiked out here, it took almost a month. I'm ass-kicked. Can I come in?"

I opened the front doors to the building and said, "Sure, man, c'mon up."

Once inside my apartment, he laid his backpack on the floor and then lay down on the floor himself, using it for a pillow.

"Hey, dude, go on in through those French doors, there's a mattress there."

He slid apart the heavy wooden doors that separated the living room from the dining room. The dining room was just a nearly empty room that held one small round table where I'd often sit in the morning looking for a vein for my first hit of the day, a couple of hard wooden chairs, a stereo and some vinyl records, a few books, my phone and answering machine . . . and the mattress where Shadow and I had ripped off so many guys who had come in thinking they were gonna get some pussy.

After Simon had slept for a few hours, he woke to the sound of me cooking up a batch of crack in the kitchen. He looked around the corner.

"Is that for you or to sell?"

"Both," I replied. "Why? You want a hit?"

"I'd love one."

I knew I had yet another homeless crackhead on my hands.

Almost the entire time since Anna had left me, there had been sometimes one, sometimes two other drug addicts staying with me rent-free. They were naturally expected to do all the shit I didn't want to do in order to earn their keep: running crack down to customers, running to the dope house for me, etc. St. Louis Simon was a perfect runner. Sending a heroin addict out to score your heroin was an invitation to get burned. They'd return with dope, but only after raiding the bag and then bringing me in a light package. Slayer Hippy had been the king of that move. Dylan and John Hicks were the only two honest junkies I ever knew, who I totally trusted to bring me back what they went out to get.

Simon was not a junkie, just a crackhead, and the crack was the one thing in my house I always kept a strict handle on. If he wanted a hit, it could only be handed out by my benevolent goodness. After a couple weeks, he admitted he had left Missouri to avoid a statutory rape charge. According to his story, he'd met a young girl on the same street where I'd first met him. She had invited him home and, in the middle of their sexual encounter, her father had walked in. He'd beaten the shit out of him and called the cops, who took him in. She'd said she was eighteen, but she was fifteen, and he was twenty-three. After his mom secured his bail, he'd immediately stuffed his backpack full of both the men's and women's clothes he wore depending on his mood, and split. My place was his intended destination from the drop.

We fell into a routine where I manufactured crack, he delivered it and brought back the dough, and we both smoked all day. Sometimes I'd realize five or six full days and nights had passed without either of us sleeping. It was a dangerous drill, but the hold crack cocaine had on me was a totally different beast than anything I'd gotten hooked on before.

I was born a garbage-can of a fiend and was fairly confident I would die one just the same. From the time I'd been a kid, as soon as I came down from whatever drug I'd just done for the first time, I instantly did it again. The first time I came to after drinking, I drank again. When I came off my first acid trip, I immediately took it again. Weed, heroin, powdered cocaine, meth, prescription opiates, everything I'd ever done, I'd turned around and compulsively done it again right away. But after two or three runs on those drugs, I'd always taken a short break and a breath at some point before starting again. With the exception of heroin (which by necessity I had to do every day to avoid the horrors of withdrawals), I could leave everything else alone for a day or even a week at a time. Not crack.

From the very first hit, crack was the executioner destined to take me down. For a very long time, Layne had tried to entice me into smoking some with him but I'd always declined, saying, "No thanks, bro, I got enough problems already." I was a perfectly functional junkie for years, but crack quickly took me to my knees. I would smoke all day, all night, every day, every night. The hold it had on me was unlike anything else in my experience. It had to come first before everything else. I could wake up dopesick, have dope on hand, and I would not get well until I had a hit of crack to smoke at the same time. It was like a hillbilly speedball. I did not like to shoot speedballs because the coke kept me from catching a nod, but that notion went directly out the window once I'd started smoking crack.

Fucking around one day, I had discovered my preferred method of consumption. I would take a foot-long piece of rubber tubing like some junkies might tie off with (I always used a sock, belt, or nothing at all). I would then cure the Chore Boy, blackening a piece of it with a lighter, burning the copper covering off the common household dish-scrubbing ball used as a screen in a crackpipe. I'd stuff the screen into the pipe, stick a huge piece of rock into the thin glass tube, and finally fit the other end of the pipe in the end of the rubber tubing. Then I'd take a previously prepared outfit full of dope and search until I got it in a vein. I'd register, drawing some blood into the syringe to make sure I was in, and then, careful not to jiggle the rig out of my by now nearly impossible-to-find veins, hold the tube out at arm's length and melt with a butane torch the biggest hit of crack rock my lungs could take. I'd hold it until I would begin to seize up, on the verge of stroking out. The ringing in my ears was as if my head were inside a church bell being slammed with a sledgehammer. Just before my eyesight went totally black, I'd jam the plunger on the rig, shooting the dope into my arm as quickly as I could. The heroin would bring me back.

It was a sick, potentially deadly practice, yet I could not help myself. I was compulsively hooked on this dangerous routine of my own invention. It was something I never shared with even my closest friends. I imagined it was like those guys who would choke themselves out while jacking off, the combination of those two sensations coupled with the thrill of going right to the cusp of oblivion was something they could not resist. How many of those guys had miscalculated their sex thing and gone past the point of no return, ended up in a morgue? I was hooked on something similar. I'd go right to the very edge every time.

This was a secret death game I was compelled to play as often as possible, but only by myself. It was not to be shared. The only way someone was gonna discover my covert activity was if the stench of my decomposing body brought the cops in someday.

38

SEE YOU IN MIAMI, MATE!

IN SEPTEMBER OF 1996, SCREAMING TREES WERE BOOKED FOR AN arena tour of the East Coast. We would be the middle band on a three-band bill with British superstars Oasis headlining. I liked their music and hoped it would a good time, an opportunity to become friendly with a couple bands whose music I enjoyed. Popular Welsh band the Manic Street Preachers were to open, and I was particularly fond of leader James Dean Bradfield's singing. But from the drop, the tour was fraught with tension, mainly between myself and Oasis's ignorant, loud-mouthed, and obnoxious lead singer, Liam Gallagher.

On the first day, Josh Homme and I were sitting at a table in catering, drinking Cokes, eating some food, and talking quietly. Minding our own business. Gallagher burst through the door with an entourage of two large sweat-suit-wearing bodyguard/toady types and some other pussy, maybe a journalist or press guy. He came straight up to where we were sitting.

"Howling Branches!" he shouted.

I continued eating a bowl of soup and said nothing.

"Howling Branches?" he demanded, wild-eyed, affecting unhinged intensity.

I realized he was addressing me and attempting a weak joke with the over-the-top intensity of a put-down. The corny play on our band name and rude intrusion mildly irritated me.

"Fuck off, you stupid fucking idiot" was my brief blasé retort, spoken as if to a bothersome mosquito.

I was sure it was the first time a member of an opening band had dared to speak what every one of them must have thought when forced to share the same air with this low-rent tyrant. Having dismissed this wannabe badass, I turned back to my soup and conversation with Josh.

"What did you say?" Gallagher yelled. "Are you mad?"

He launched into a bizarre, lurching half dance, lunging forward as though to physically attack only to back up again while gesticulating crazily. He intended for it to look intimidating. He looked fucking pathetic.

"You're fucking mad, mate!" he yelled. "I'll put you through that wall!"

I finally looked up at him and while still seated, soup spoon in hand, said, "What are you waiting for, tough guy? I'll fuck you up."

This brought on an incredibly bad reaction. He shook his head side to side, palsy-like, as if in disbelief that anyone would have the balls to speak to him that way, and turned to glare at his bodyguards as if to say, "Are you going to let him talk to me like that?" Josh stood straight up, hands tightly curled into fists in anticipation of what looked like was about to turn into an all-out brawl at any moment.

"You're gonna be sorry, mate! Very fucking sorry, you daft cunt!" Liam yelled as he pretended to struggle while allowing his bodyguards/paid pals to pull him out the door of the cafeteria.

Josh howled with laughter.

"Damn, he went white as a sheet! He was scared shitless when you stood up to him!"

"What a fucking moron," I agreed.

The next day, our tour manager Kevan Wilkins, who we had inherited from Alice in Chains, no longer touring due to Layne's aversion to travel, pulled me aside.

"Hey, buddy, watch your step around Liam. Those big guys with him are thugs he uses as bodyguards. They're gunning for you."

I took Wilkins's warning to heart, but if it was a fight Gallagher wanted, a fight he would have. I was not accustomed to taking unwarranted shit off anyone, especially not this entitled "rock star" who had introduced himself by animatedly spitting an insult into my face.

On day two, he had made it a point to stand directly on the side of the stage while we performed, straight in the sightline of everyone in the arena crowd. Arms folded, glaring, in a weak, childish attempt to rattle me. This douchebag clearly didn't have the smarts to quit while he was ahead. His public show of limp-dicked intimidation and disruption of our show was the tipping point. Now I was legitimately pissed off.

During the instrumental break in the first song, I let go of the mic. Turning to face him with a dark, expressionless look on my face, I mouthed an unmistakable "Fuck you." A second later, I mouthed "C'mon, motherfucker" and motioned for him to come out onstage, extending him an invitation to his own public ass-kicking party. If he was hell-bent on receiving a beating, I could think of no more appropriate place to administer it than in front of fifteen thousand of his fans. He declined my invite, of course, because he'd left his chaperones backstage so the crowd would think he was a rough-and-tumble lone wolf. Nothing could have been further from the truth. At no other time did I see him unaccompanied by his two huge sweat-suited goons, uncanny clones of 1970s British wrestler Giant Haystacks but for their bald domes instead of Haystacks's huge, wild bush of crazy hair.

Liam continued to stand there like a petulant child trying to look menacing at the very edge of the stage so he was clearly in plain view of everyone who'd come to see his band. Van Conner was the closest to where Liam stood, practically onstage himself. When the second song began, Van started walking in ever-widening circles, passing closer and closer to Liam with every revolution. Finally, as he passed by the fourth or fifth time, he clubbed Gallagher directly in the face with the head of his heavy Fender Precision bass with vicious intent. The force of the impact nearly knocked Gallagher to his knees. In obvious pain and furious anger, Gallagher began to dance around in a comical manner, as if he were fighting the urge to actually storm the stage and attack Van. Had he done so, our gigantic bass player would have publicly annihilated him.

This circus played out in front of the 15,000-plus audience. It made me laugh out loud, his humiliation witnessed by the entire huge crowd. And it couldn't have happened to a more deserving guy. This dickhole had stood right next to our stage, trying to mad-dog me the entire time we played our stupid fucking set, just begging for a beatdown. Of course, once I walked offstage looking for him, he was nowhere to be seen.

It would take more than one blowhard singer to intimidate the Trees. I was a veteran of violence foreign and domestic, onstage, backstage, rural countryside, big city, barroom, parking lot, pool hall, and alleyway. I'd been an active participant in bus stop, trailer park, housing project, public sidewalk, private party, crack house, dope house, and jailhouse violence that stretched back fifteen years or more. I had always had trouble getting along with Lee Conner, and my once close friendship with Van had burned itself out in his resentment over my role in destroying the band's momentum via my addiction and my indignation over his rightly placed blame, yet we had been conditioned through a lifetime of unending conflict to take every threat as a serious one. We had learned to always strike first whenever an insult had been thrown or a threat insinuated, and to always have each other's backs. We had shut people's mouths onstage and off while this dude Liam was still shitting in his diapers. Win, lose, or draw; good, bad, or indifferent—the Trees never backed down from anybody, particularly not from some bad actor who exuded fake violence and crybaby fear.

This clown had accidentally stumbled into the high life, courtesy of his talented older brother, Noel Gallagher. Noel was the one-man hit factory and true genius behind Oasis, writing all of their great, classic tunes. He had been friendly and respectful, treating both our band and crew with common courtesy. The limelight of popularity Liam basked in had evidently uncaged a monster, one without teeth or claws, but a small, irritating monster nonetheless. Success looked to have unleashed his inherent narcissism, his look-at-me-ism, his transparent deep-rooted insecurity. But what the fuck did I know? He had probably been a lowlife cocksucker his entire life. Maybe he'd been a bedwetter, shit his pants at school, or been cut from football squad as a youngster and never gotten over it. I couldn't believe someone hadn't beaten, knifed, or shot him to death by now, such was the reckless, witless, and despotic nature of his insufferable facade. Where I was from, a person wouldn't last a week behaving as he did. One day, they'd simply disappear, their mangled body discovered years later, haphazardly tossed into a shallow grave somewhere deep in the woods.

I reasoned that he was still alive because the unbearable, minor-league-dictator aspects of his buckshot-wild, painfully feeble, head-injury-victim's personality hadn't fully flourished until he had hit the big time and made enough cash to hire the two giant fucks glued to his hip, paid to shadow him every moment of every day and finish the fights he would indiscriminately start at the drop of his dunce cap. His manner was strongly reminiscent of a child ruined with indulgence, but one with an unpredictable predilection for cruelty and an ocean-sized, burning-black-hole need for attention. I could see him as a kid in short pants, on a bright sunny day, gleefully jacking his miniscule dick while frying ants under a magnifying glass.

Or maybe these woefully amateur theatrics had been generated and saved up especially for my personal benefit? All I knew was that in my thirty-one years on earth, I had never encountered anyone with a larger head or tinier balls. And he had chosen exactly the wrong guy to fuck with. He'd gone out of his way to interrupt my slumber and I was now wide-ass awake and looking for the first opportunity to throw down. I detested bullies with a smoldering hatred and refused to put up with them. Liam Gallagher was an obvious poser, a would-be playground bully. Like all bullies, he was also a total pussy. Always with the big fucking mouth as long as he was safely wrapped in the wet-nurse security blanket of the company of the two tall, rotund dudes paid to protect and, I assumed, suffer his endless stream of bullshit.

The tour took us north of the border for one date where Oasis and the Trees, along with my friend Jason Pierce's band Spiritualized, were to open a huge outdoor show playing before Neil Young and Crazy Horse at the Molson Park amphitheater outside of Toronto.

There was no way I was carrying any drugs across the US border. I'd once been arrested by the Canadian customs officials on the mere suspicion I was holding, only to be released hours later after they'd completely taken apart my car, stripped, and cavity-searched me and found me to be clean.

I spent the entire night and morning getting loaded before boarding the bus to cross over. I'd left the rest of my stuff with my clothes in a bag in the motel room of our merch guy who was staying on the US side. We were coming back that night to pick him up; I would just have to bite the bullet and spend the several hours in Canada without getting high. As we sat on the bus waiting for Van Conner, often the last guy to arrive for any lobby call, bus call, plane flight, or stage time, Kevan started to get agitated as ten minutes stretched to thirty. We were due onstage in early afternoon and the border crossing could take a few hours, depending on how thoroughly officials on both sides decided to take a look at you.

Finally, Wilkins went back into the hotel and called Van's room. No answer. He came back to the bus and asked us all if we knew where he was. Nobody had a clue as to his whereabouts. Wilkins went back inside, up to Van's room, and pounded on the door to no response once again. Now Kevan was worried. Even though Van was still a relatively young guy in his mid- to late twenties, he nonetheless lived an incredibly unhealthy lifestyle. Wilkins began to envision him possibly deceased inside his hotel room.

He got the desk manager to unlock the door. Upon entering, his worst fears seemed to be confirmed: the apparently lifeless body of our free-spirited, hilarious, and contrarily rebellious bass player was slumped over in a chair before a TV set blaring porn, pants around his ankles. Kevan yelled at him. No response. He put his finger to Van's neck. Feeling a pulse, Wilkins slapped him across the face. Van came to and immediately stood up, the half-empty bottle of scotch in his naked lap spilling the rest of its contents on the carpeted floor. The minute he reached his full height, he tumbled backwards over the chair and hit the floor himself. He'd passed out while watching porn and jacking off, and at seven a.m. he was still completely shitfaced, so drunkenly incoherent he could barely stay on his feet. A giant at six foot four and nearly three hundred pounds, it took great effort for Wilkins to get him upright, his pants on, and down to the bus.

Once Van got on the bus and we started rolling out toward the border, he came back to life, and in a big way. He stumbled around the moving tour bus with a newly cracked fifth of booze in his hand, slamming down giant mouthfuls of it, yelling in his brother Lee's face and generally raising hell. At some point he burst into my sanctuary in the back lounge, the only place on the bus that had windows that actually opened all the way up.

"Fuck, Lanegan, why is it so goddamn hot back here?" he slurred and began struggling to pull both windows all the way up, blasting a rush of cold air through the smallish room and creating an instant whirlwind. Once he'd accomplished the mission of freezing me out, he stood with his arms upraised like Rocky Balboa. Suddenly, to my shock and horror, he grabbed an empty beer bottle out of the small garbage bin on the floor and whipped it out the window directly toward a car driving by.

"Van! What in the fuck, man?" I shouted over the din of the wind tunnel he'd created.

He paid no attention and reached down to fumble through the trash for another bottle. I jumped up from my seat and wrapped my arms around him in a bear hug.

"Get off me, Lanegan!" he yelled and effortlessly threw me against the wall, falling to the ground himself as the effort of shaking me off had thrown his drunken equilibrium into a spin. I jumped up and slammed my body down on him.

"Hold on, bro! Wait a minute, Van, just hang on a second!"

He lay there not moving for a few seconds and I realized he had actually passed out. *Jesus Christ, he is FUCKED UP*, I thought, and cautiously left him snoring on the floor and went up front to let Kevan know what had been transpiring. We were for sure going to have a major problem getting through the border with him in such a compromised state.

After an hour's drive, we arrived at the US/Canadian border. After being waved through by the Americans, we were asked to pull over and get out, go inside the office, and sit while some officials went through our bus, I assumed to look for contraband. Van kept slumping against me, on the verge of passing out every minute we sat waiting. Finally, a uniformed customs officer informed us that all was cool and we got back on the bus, heading into Canada. As soon as we arrived, I hit the couch in our backstage tent.

An hour or two later, we took the stage, first on the bill. Standing in the bright sunlight of the early afternoon, before we could even begin playing, Van went up to the microphone and began rambling incoherently through the PA, still completely smashed. I looked back at Barrett and yelled, "Let's fucking do this!" Still mumbling into the mic, Van was taken by surprise and came into the song late and hitting the wrong notes. In doing so, he lost his balance and fell straight onto his back to the stage floor with a resounding thud. We played on as he lay there like an overturned turtle, unable to get up for the entire length of the song. Between songs, two of our crew guys struggled to get him on his feet while I stood there dick in hand, feeling the heat of humiliation on my face, in front of this very large crowd. I had seen a lot of fucked-up shit onstage through the years and had been guilty of some of the most embarrassing scenes myself, but this was a new tragicomic high/low.

Finally, thankfully finished with our short thirty-minute set, I went and lay back down on a couch in one of the tents backstage that served as dressing rooms and fell asleep. I was awakened by a commotion. I stuck my head through the opening of the tent and, to my shock, was greeted by the sight of Van Conner chasing some guy around with a huge, real machete.

"Van!" I screamed. "What in the fuck are you doing?"

My groggy mind raced. Where in the fuck had he found the sword, and more importantly, was he going to kill this guy? At that exact moment, I watched as he stumbled over a small inflatable children's wading pool full of water that was inexplicably sitting on the ground in the backstage area. He toppled face first into it, the machete flying harmlessly away as he did so. Van got wasted often, but I had never seen this advanced degree of prolonged insanity from him in my life. He rolled over on his back and lay there smiling, self-satisfied, his weight smashing down the sides of the pool, draining all the water out of it. My mind flew back to that lifetime ago when I had been walking to school as an elementary student and had first seen him, as a baby, smiling this same smile as he lay in a kiddie pool exactly like this.

Wilkins finally got him up and put him to bed in his bunk on the bus. He was down for the count, not to appear again the rest of the day. As day turned to night, I watched from the side of the stage while the power of Crazy Horse blew my mind. When Neil Young began singing "The Needle and the Damage Done," I was caught on my heels. My heart went straight up into my throat, the sad majesty of this song I'd heard a million times bringing tears to my eyes as I thought about all the friends I'd lost to the scourge of the same heroin addiction I was still fully in thrall of and beholden to.

After returning to the States, I was talking to one of the catering guys traveling with the tour I'd become friendly with, he sharing my affinity for crack.

"Did you meet Neil?" he asked me.

"No, you?"

"No, but I was there when that asshole Liam Gallagher did. He was so rude to Neil I wanted to punch him out."

This bit of news enraged me. It was one thing to be a prick to me, but how dare that son of a bitch be rude to Neil? One of the all-time greats and one of my heroes? It was the cassette tape of *After the Gold Rush* that had been my only companion and lifesaver during one of the lowest points of my life. This made my hatred grow to epic proportions and gave me all the more reason and resolve to kick Liam's fucking ass.

While walking down the corridor in the Philadelphia arena home to the 76ers before doors, I came face-to-face with Liam, flanked by his two huge bodyguards, Tweedle Dumb and Tweedle Dumber. Heeding Wilkins's warning, I stepped to the side to avoid potentially getting hospitalized by Liam's triple-extra-large employees. As they passed, Gallagher turned back and curled his lip in yet another failed attempt to intimidate, a "crazy"-eyed facial expression with all the scare factor of a Z-grade Steven Seagal.

He shouted, "I'll see you in Miami, mate!"

I stared at him with shark-dead eyes.

"You got it, man."

I was going to have to put this putrid piece of shit down, that much was clearly obvious, yet everywhere he went, his goons went as well. I was in no hurry to walk weaponless onto a battlefield, one against three, especially when two of the three were gigantic paid ballbreakers.

Once back in the dressing room, I asked Kevan what the deal was with Miami.

"Miami is the last date on the tour, buddy."

I broke out into laughter as I realized his Miami comment had been the classic grade-school threat of "I'll see you after class." *What is this, fucking kindergarten?* I thought. I was a grown fucking man with a life-long propensity for violence who'd had to literally fight my way out of life-threatening situations in the past. Who did this fucking idiot think he was dealing with?

After we played our forty-five minute set that night, I was jonesing for a hit. I decided to head to a Philly neighborhood where I'd often scored crack in the past. I got into a cab outside the arena and told the driver where I wanted to go.

"Hey, fella," he said, "that's a pretty rough neighborhood you're going to."

"It's cool, man. I'm no stranger to it."

He glanced in the rearview mirror and immediately clocked the sour expression on my face.

"If you don't mind my saying so, you look pretty angry, friend. What's the matter?"

"I'm working on a job and there's an unstable loudmouthed prick there who's been threatening me with violence. I want to take him out but he is surrounded by these huge dudes who will put me in traction if I do it. Or worse."

"Do you have a spare ten dollars?"

I pulled a wrinkled ten-dollar bill out of my pants pocket and handed it to him.

"Here," he said, handing me a roll of quarters. "Keep these in your fist and the next time you see him, break his fucking jaw. An asshole like that won't give up until his friends get you down and he's able to jump in and finish the job once you're hurt. You have *got* to hurt him first. He won't give up until you're destroyed; you've got to destroy him first."

His looking glass into future possibilities and its variety of outcomes had already occurred to me, but it was still refreshing to encounter a dude with the same worldview as myself. This arrogant, spoiled, wounded baby Gallagher was so full of himself that I could not put anything past him.

After the next concert, I got an unwelcome surprise. Cliff Burnstein, one of my managers, had shown up unannounced. After kicking everyone off the bus except me, he began to give me the sternest talking-to I'd ever received in my adult life.

"Lanegan, you have a deadly serious problem. I know it, you know it, the band knows it, the record company, everyone. At this point, it's even obvious to the people who come to watch you play."

Fucking hell. He'd come to give me a one-man intervention.

"You're dying, Mark. This drug addiction is killing you and we at Q Prime are no longer going to be party to it. You have two options. Either you go to treatment and get clean or we are sending you on an extended six-week tour of Canada."

Canada? Six weeks? Were there even enough places to play there in order to stay six weeks? A six-week tour of Canada was essentially a forced kick. I could only assume that outside of Toronto, Vancouver,

Montreal, and Ottawa, Canada was a heroin-free zone, devoid of any reliable source of dope. Neither of these choices held an ounce of appeal.

"Let me sleep on it for a night? Please, Cliff."

"Okay, but if I don't hear back by tomorrow, we're booking a Canadian tour."

I stayed up the entire night, running what I'd been offered over and over in my mind. Eventually, I decided upon a third option, an option of my own invention. We had been a Q Prime pet project that had never earned them a cent. They could afford to indulge their ultimately failed effort to break the Trees because at that time they had behind them the most clout of nearly any other management company in the rock world with a stable of some of the biggest-earning bands in the business. I would fire Q Prime, the world-class powerhouse management team who had taken care of us for years. And I would quit the band. I just wanted it over.

Since I had made up my mind I was done with the band, that also meant this dismal Oasis tour. Not wanting to create chaos on the band front for the moment, I told only Wilkins of my decision, but I insisted he first allow the bus to show up at the next arena in order for me to go inside, find Gallagher, and finish what he'd started. There was no possible way I was leaving before I'd taken out my retribution on this cancerous slug.

Probably just humoring me, Wilkins said, "Just hold on a second, buddy. Let me go inside and see what's going on. I promise that before I tell them we're quitting, I'll let you go in and take your shot at him."

I waited impatiently for twenty minutes, getting intensely worked up. I was finally going to put this fucking cunt in his place, walk the fuck away, and be done with the bullshit charade of the Trees and of rock music in general, forever.

Finally, Kevan came back on the bus.

"I don't know how to tell you this, buddy, but the tour's over. Not because of you, but because Liam quit the band and flew back to England last night. The good news is we're being paid for all the remaining shows."

He had quit and bailed before I could have a go at him. Before his promised playground battle royale in Miami. *Typical*, I thought. He hadn't sought me out to "put me through a wall," with or without his hired gorillas. That phony motherfucker had pissed his pants and gone home to mama before I had a chance to blow this whole thing up myself.

Later, an employee of Epic Records asked me how the tour had gone. He said they'd been taking bets in the office as to how long it would take for Liam and I to come into conflict.

I said, "Whoever put their money on 'immediately' won the pot."

39

ABSENCE AND HARDSHIP

IN THE FALL OF '96, TREES HEADED BACK TO EUROPE FOR A TOUR.
I taught St. Louis Simon, my runner, how to cook up a batch of crack on the kitchen stovetop and left him at my apartment to watch over and keep up my crack-selling business. He already knew my coke connection because I'd sent him there a million times to re-up. I paid my annoyed apartment manager Christian my next month's rent early and the Screaming Trees got on a plane for London in the cold autumn weather.

I had dressed for comfort for the long flight in coach: pajama bottoms and a hoodie under a coat, two full rigs in the top of each of my long sweat socks. I knew by experience that I never once got patted down in an airport in those pre-9/11 days and that the tiny points of metal on my syringes never set off the alarm while going through security. Once on the plane, I immediately went into the can and did a shot before we'd even taken off. I also had crack and a pipe on me but had no plans to risk smoking that in the bathroom; it was way too iffy. But I found it nearly impossible to go even an hour without taking a hit on any normal day so I knew it might prove challenging to resist the urge. The other guys had a good laugh when they'd caught an eyeful of my attire but I didn't give a damn. Due to their size alone, they were in for a long, uncomfortable flight.

I fell asleep before take-off, then woke up already several hours into the flight. I went to the bathroom and did another shot. Remembering the crack pipe, rock, and lighter in my hoodie pocket, I was suddenly gripped with an unstoppable urge to take a hit. There was a strong sensor and smoke alarm on the ceiling of every airplane restroom and to smoke in there was insanity. But wait a second . . . any time you flushed the shitter on a plane, it sucked everything down with incredible force. Couldn't I just hold the smoke in my lungs and blow it into the toilet as I flushed it?

That idea seemed reasonable enough to me, so somewhere over the Atlantic Ocean, I prepared to hit the pipe. I put a medium-sized piece of rock into my pipe, took a good-sized hit, and after holding it as long as I possibly could, I forcefully blew the smoke down into the toilet just as I pushed the button and flushed. To my horror, instead of being sucked down, the huge cloud of smoke went straight up to the ceiling, right up against the smoke detector. I stepped out as quickly as I could and, in the darkness of the plane, busted ass back to my seat. I slunk down low and, with my heart pounding like a jackhammer and a thick coating of ice-cold sweat covering my face, pulled the hood of my sweatshirt up over my head and feigned sleep, mind racing as I waited for the alarm to go off. After a minute or two, there was still no alarm. I realized I had lucked out this time.

I sat restlessly wide awake the rest of the flight. I wasn't going anywhere near the toilet. I had to save the other two syringes full of dope—one possibly for our layover or short second flight, the other for our arrival in France. The first flight was landing at London's Heathrow where we were to catch a connector to de Gaulle in Paris.

During our two-hour layover in London, I went directly to Heathrow's smoking area. There were three or four other people in the large room, one of them Van Conner. He sat next to me while I smoked an unfiltered Lucky Strike, my preferred brand of cigarette since I'd begun smoking at fifteen, buying them out of a machine at the truck-stop restaurant where I washed dishes during the eleven p.m. to seven a.m. shift one summer. He began clowning on my PJs again.

"You're gonna freeze your ass off when we hit Paris, Lanegan."

"I'm gonna put my pants on as soon as they come down the chute in baggage, dumbass," I curtly replied.

While he was staring sleepily off into nothingness, I pulled my crack pipe out of my pocket in the near-empty room. I shoved a piece of rock in it, took a huge hit, and when he turned around to give me some more shit, blew it directly into his face. We both instantly sprang to our feet and got stuck in the door like Laurel and Hardy as we attempted to run through together at the exact same moment, each of us wanting to escape the scene of the crime. After a quick and comedic tussle, he shoved me out the opening with his giant hands and the immense weight behind them.

As we walked quickly down the hallway side by side, he whispered, "Thanks a lot, you sick son of a bitch, now I stink like crack."

"You always stink like crack . . . dirty asscrack" was my half-witted comeback.

In the baggage area at de Gaulle, I waited for what seemed an eternity for my bag to come down. After everyone else had retrieved their shit and left, just three people still stood waiting: our road manager Kevan Wilkins, Josh Homme, and me.

I guess I am gonna freeze my ass off, I thought as it became apparent our bags weren't coming any time soon. Kevan went to the counter and was informed that my bag containing all of my clothes and toiletries, Josh's bag, and one of his guitars had failed to make the flight. *Thank God I have my dope and methadone on me* was my first thought. My second thought was *My fucking cigarettes are in my bag*. I had three cartons stashed in it but had brought one in my carry-on. My third thought: *I need some fucking clothes*.

As we joined the rest of the guys outside in the bitterly cold air, Van couldn't stop laughing as his prediction had come true.

"Yeah, really funny ain't it, Nostradamus," I said.

It was early on a Friday afternoon and we weren't due to play until the next day. As we rode into the city, Josh and I decided our first order of business was to go clothes shopping. I sure as fuck wasn't going onstage or anywhere else in my goddamn pajamas. We got the keys to our hotel rooms when we arrived, I stashed my two still-full syringes and backpack in my room, and then the two of us went out walking to find some threads. Within a block of the hotel, we came upon a place that sold all leather products. Since I didn't have nearly enough dough for dope, much less a complete new wardrobe, I decided to go full rock star and buy a pair of leather pants, knowing I'd never take them off, the only pair of pants I'd need. Josh decided he would do the same and we each got fitted for a pair, his brown and mine black.

As soon as I got back to the hotel, I stood in front of the full-length mirror on the closet door, absentmindedly admiring my new pants. I'd shorn my head of the stupid-looking extra-long hair ages ago, thrown away the flannel shirts I'd worn my entire life, given away the chained trucker wallet I'd worn for years to my Eritrean pal Mikey . . . I had basically removed everything from my appearance associated with the fashion joke "Seattle grunge movement." *Grunge* being a term I, and everyone else I knew who had been shitstained with the moronic, media-generated term, bitterly detested. I was thin but not skeletal, my hair its natural bright red, shoulder length and greased back. With my shiny black combat boots and shiny black leather trousers, I now looked the part of the rock singer more than at any time in my career.

I was also imprisoned by the largest drug habit of my life. While on the road, it far outweighed my ability to pay for it. I had, luckily, brought the bottle of methadone in my carry-on backpack. You were still allowed to bring liquids onto a plane back then and no one had ever even looked into any of my shit anyway. I found it strange and fortunate that the most plainly obvious addict seemed invisible to security people, customs officials, and cops everywhere I traveled in Europe. It was if I were a ghost. In the US, outside of the airport, it was a completely different situation. I was shaken down by the police while out on the streets on a regular basis. My cop pal John Powers had once given me some good-natured but truthful shit. Elbowing me in the ribs slightly, he'd said, "Man, you have to do something to tone down your look. You're too obvious to us. Eat a meal once in a while, take a shower, wash your clothes every now and then . . . and brush your fucking teeth at least once a month!"

There was a knock on my hotel-room door. I looked out the peephole and saw Wilkins on the other side, unlocked the door, and let him in. By the sad, beaten-down look on his face, I knew he had bad news.

"Hey, buddy, I'm sorry to tell you this but Demri has passed away. Layne would like you to call him as soon as you can."

Fuck . . . not again, I thought. This was going to destroy Layne. He had loved her so passionately that after their final break-up, one of many in their tempestuous years-long off-and-on-again relationship, he had made a conscious decision to never date another woman. If not with her, he preferred to be alone. My heart was broken for him. I called and left a message with my room number and the phone number to the hotel, and he called right back.

"Oh man . . . I can't believe it. She's gone" were his first words. Then he broke down in tears.

"Goddamnit, brother, I am so fucking sorry, I don't know what to say. I'm just incredibly sorry this is happening to you."

Even though I'd had plenty of experience with loss, I was still a piss-poor comfort to those in pain. I had never developed the necessary skills to verbally express any real words of wisdom to help anyone in that way. My first public response to the death of a friend was stoicism. Privately, I might cry like a baby.

Through his tears, Layne said, "I can't stand to be alone right now, when are you coming back?"

"I just got here today. We're not back for six weeks."

"Fuck," he said, "I wish you were coming back sooner, I need to hang out with someone. This is tearing me up."

"I'm sorry, bro . . . St. Louis is at my place, go stay there. I need some-one to keep an eye on him anyway. Kick him the fuck out of the bed-room and you take it. He can sleep on the couch or the mattress. You'd be doing me a favor, man."

Layne had been around Simon and I knew he could tolerate him. He even found him slightly amusing, shooting me a sly, side-eyed grin when he'd seen him dressed in women's clothes once when the three of us had been together. Simon's generally quiet nature made him easy to be around, and I trusted him.

"Okay, I'm going over there," he quickly said.

"Just let me know when; I should call Simon and give him a heads-up."

"Right now."

I quickly did the math. Two thirty in the afternoon in Paris meant it was five thirty a.m. in Seattle, but I knew my protégé was most likely still awake from the day before. I also knew Demri's mother lived just a block from my apartment because she had harassed me on a semi-regular basis when she'd been staying there. I wondered if Layne might drop in there to offer his condolences, or get a tiny sip of relief in sharing their pain of loss, even though they'd had a bit of a strained relationship.

After calling St. Louis to tell him that Layne was moving in for a while, I began to think about the reality of what lay ahead. Taking stock of the multitude of possible difficulties I might likely run into, I tried to mentally brace myself for what I knew was going to be a difficult tour.

Because I had come with so little cash, I was dependent on our pitifully small per diems and, at some point, my cut of merch sales to pay for the dope I would have to score on the streets every day to keep from going into withdrawals, a nightmare scenario.

Years before, I'd had to kick a large habit cold turkey in a Denver hotel room. We'd traveled there from Salt Lake City in a blizzard and barely made it. Our show scheduled for the following night was cancelled and postponed for three days due to the severity of the massive, days-long storm. Denver had always been a place where it was very easy to buy heroin on the streets, but not under these conditions. Hicks had gone out into the storm to attempt to find some dope but not surprisingly had found the streets totally empty. He had hardly any habit at the time and was fine. I was not.

By day two, I was shooting the blackest, most foul fluid I'd ever seen out of both ends at once. I lay on the bed tossing and turning in agony, my legs kicking out as I spasmed uncontrollably. After the first twelve hours, my shoulders, knees, and back were already raw from the constant contact with the sheets and mattress as I convulsed. There was zero possibility of sleep, zero possibility of any relief forthcoming. Hicks had called Kurt who had immediately FedExed some heroin to me hidden in a bag of coffee but, of course, it couldn't make it there through the intense blizzard. Everything was shut down. Short of going out into the shit and making my way to a hospital, I was on my own.

During the blissed-out Dilaudid run on tour with Alice in Chains, I'd spent an evening with a beautiful young Mexican American girl named Antoinette in Denver. For this snowed-out concert, she had come up to Colorado from Florida, where she worked playing Pocahontas at Disney World in Orlando, intending to surprise me at our show. Finding it cancelled, she had located us by chance in the midst of this huge raging storm when she'd seen a tour bus outside our hotel. John had been having drinks and taking pictures of himself with Watergate bad guy G. Gordon Liddy, who happened to be stranded in the same hotel. When Hicks brought her up from the bar where he'd run into her, I was ashamed to be seen in the throes of a full-force cold turkey kick. I was completely helpless to do anything besides suffer and moan in agony. Antoinette was incredibly kind and loving and attempted to nurse me through this anesthesia-free botched brain surgery, this wide-awake quadruple amputation, an experience that I felt must be akin to being gang-fucked nonstop by Satan's hordes for three full days and nights . . . and not in a good way. She massaged my aching legs when I could stand to be touched, even praying quietly over me as I agonizingly tossed and turned, thrashing about nonstop. She and Hicks turned my thin mattress over only to find I'd actually sweated completely through it to the other side, at which point John gave me his bed and slept on the couch. It was a physical and mental ass-beating the likes of which I had never been prepared for. I had always had methadone to see me through an emergency but not this time. The indescribably unbearable physical torture combined with a dark, unending black hole in my mind was a double whammy of the most confounding kind. I felt like I had no future, like I'd never been born.

On day four of the kick, our rescheduled Denver show was to take place. The storm had let up but there were still no dealers on the streets. Although I was still hurting badly, the worst was over so I made a conscious decision to try and stay off heroin for real. During the show that night I had to rush sidestage three or four times to puke in a garbage can barely out of sight from the audience. I drank my way through that night and all the way to and through our next show, in Lawrence, Kansas. Then we had a long drive to Florida. I opted to fly by myself instead of sitting uncomfortably on the bus for two days.

I was passed-out drunk in the back lounge of the bus when we stopped at the St. Louis airport where I was to catch my flight. I picked up my bag and stumbled outside into the five a.m. dark. When I arrived in Fort Lauderdale later that day and got to my hotel, I realized that in my alcohol-soaked, still-slightly-sick-from-the-kick, hazy state of mind, I'd grabbed our soundman Brian Rat's bag instead of my own and left mine behind. At the time, I had no idea whose shit I'd taken with me to Florida, I just knew it wasn't mine. It had been Brian's first day on the job and we'd not even had as much as a hello yet. By the time the bus carrying everyone else arrived, I had actually fallen asleep and slept soundly through the night without booze or the aid of drugs. I had actually kicked.

The next day, I went out to the bus to get my stuff and then sheepishly found Brian in his room to return his bag. He was gracious and funny and we were to become close friends after that. I took my bag back to my room and started digging through it to find some clean clothes when I came across my toiletries bag. Curious to see what was in a side pocket, I unzipped it. Inside were four months' worth of cottons. I had compulsively stashed them away after every time I'd gotten loaded. Since I hadn't run out of dope that entire time, I'd never had to go into the stash to stay well. Through the entirety of my nasty, traumatic withdrawals, my stash of cottons had been a mere couple of feet from me, totally escaping my mind.

Two things flashed through my head at once. My excruciating, nightmarish kick had been totally unnecessary as I could have easily stayed well and gotten high for at least three weeks off the cottons alone. And, now that I had this bounty of dried heroin-soaked filters in front of me, fuck stopping. I was going to get loaded immediately. The entire demented merry-go-round began to spin once more.

—

HERE IN EUROPE, YEARS LATER, in the shitty, bitter, cold-ass winter, I shuddered involuntarily as I recalled that horror show from the distant past. The thought had invaded my mind that I may very well have to face a similar situation at some point during this current icy hellride. *No fucking way*, I told myself. *Never again*. And thus began the most intensely stressful and strenuous, balls-caught-and-twisted-in-the-vise-grips-of-absence-and-hardship, fucked-up trip of my entire life.

40

ICE-COLD
EUROPEAN FUNHOUSE

I'M WAITING IN THE FREEZING RAIN AT AN UNCOVERED BUS STOP after a show in Sheffield, England. The moment I left the stage, I walked out the back door of the club, down a long, dark alleyway, and around the corner to this cold and empty spot. I was dopesick, I was cold and wet. I had tried to scare up some heroin between soundcheck and show but had come away from my search with no joy. The band had no show the next day, yet Wilkins had refused to drop me off in London en route to the next city we were playing in because it was inconveniently out of the way. So I'd stayed behind while they rolled on. I had to fix sooner than that or else it was going to be disaster.

We were scheduled to be in Europe and the UK for almost another month and things were looking grim for my prospects of staying well. I had already run out of my meager supply of methadone and there were still many more shows to be played. Wilkins was long over me. I had routinely woken him (as well as Josh Homme once and even Lee Conner) at all hours of the night and early morning to hit him up for cash. A cash advance in order to stay well. The last time I'd done it, he'd told me, "This is it, buddy, the last time. You have reached your limit. If you wake me up again, you're going to be sorry." I believed him. Kevan was a good guy but tough. After years of tour-managing Alice in Chains, getting them out of jams and shepherding their crew all over the world, he was tired. The last thing he wanted to deal with was yet another junkie, especially one in the aggravating habit of knocking on his door in the middle of the night.

As I stood there in the rain, a young couple huddling together beneath an umbrella walked up. They had seen the show and wanted to talk.

"Hey, Mark, just wanted to tell you how beautiful the show was, we love your music. What are you doing out here?"

"I'm trying to get a bus to Heathrow . . . but, hey, can I ask you guys a sensitive question? Where can a guy get some brown around here this time of night?"

"Brown? Do you mean heroin?" the girl gasped.

"Yeah, that's exactly what I'm talking about."

They quickly found a reason to flee. My desperation to obtain relief so great that with zero care about what it looked like, what I looked like, I had taken to asking innocent young concertgoers where I could score. It was time these kids grew the fuck up anyway, got with the motherfucking program, and faced the cold, hard reality of life. I had done my last, tiny hit at seven thirty that morning and it was now ten thirty at night.

Four days earlier in Manchester, I had been welcomed into the council-flat home of a dealer I'd met on the street. He was overly generous, excited to have an American rock singer in the house. It was exactly three weeks and one day until my thirty-second birthday but I looked at least ten years older, worn down from the demands of touring while battling the years-long, exhausting imprisonment of my crippling addiction. The balding man and his not unattractive blond wife, both in their midforties, had let me stay up all night in their flat shooting dope and occasionally taking a hit off the crack pipe. Shortly before midnight, the man had said, "C'mon, let's go grab some cigarettes from the shop." When we returned to the modest-sized public housing apartment, I was greeted by the sight of the wife lying on the couch, dressed in lingerie, her bare breasts exposed, pretending to be asleep. The man had walked over to her and started squeezing and rubbing her tits while I stood there uncomfortably in the middle of the room. She began to quietly moan and he said, "Nice, huh? Come on over here and get yourself a feel." It was an obvious setup, exactly the kind of situation I had lived for in my youth, but as an old man of thirty-two, sex was the last thing on my mind. I shook my head, said, "No thanks, man, I'm good," walked past them into the kitchen, put a small rock in the pipe, and hit it.

Four days later, standing in the rain and going into withdrawals, my intention was to catch a ride to Heathrow and then take the Tube into London to buy some heroin from a Portuguese dealer named Juan-Joseph I'd met on one of my many excursions to King's Cross, a notorious London neighborhood where I always scored when in the city. I would then take the train to Bristol. Thee Hypnotics bass player Craig Pike, my old connection in London, had overdosed and died a couple years before. Now I habitually haunted this busy but shady neighborhood, scoring drugs whenever I was in town.

In the several-block radius around the large hub of the train station, you could almost always find someone selling drugs if you looked hard enough. Through the years I'd formed regular connections with some street dealers I'd met at different times in the Cross: out in front of the Ladbrokes betting shop, along the side street that paralleled the station, or near the porn magazine shop on the other side of it. Some would give me their phone number so we could hook up immediately when I was in need. Juan-Joseph had actually taken me to where he lived, three long blocks from the station, so that I could go directly to his flat when I wanted to see him.

My previous regular hook-up was a young blond punk kid in his early twenties. I had spotted him on the street one day and made him for either a dealer or a panhandler and decided that even if he didn't have drugs, he'd sure as fuck know who out here did. Sure enough, when I'd approached him, he'd led me into an alley, unbuttoned his pants, and removed several balloons of heroin that he'd stuffed beneath the uncut foreskin of his dick. He'd kept them safely stashed there in case he was shaken down by the UK police, who at that time had the legal right to frisk anyone they cared to on the street, regardless of any evidence of wrongdoing. While walking together back to the bustling High Street after doing our first deal, he'd asked me where I was from and what I was doing in London. I'd told him I was a singer from Seattle playing some shows. He stopped in his tracks straightaway.

"Fuck, Yank! I love all Seattle music! Look at this!"

He pulled up his sleeve to expose his arm. The kid was a cutter, something I'd only seen a couple of times before. His forearm was covered with crude symbols and names carved into his skin with a razor or knife.

He had messily cut into his flesh "God Bless Kurt," now manifesting as a large, raised white scar.

"Damn, dude. A tattoo woulda been less painful," I said, knowing full well that had been the point.

Shortly after parting company from that first encounter, I'd passed two cops myself. They'd quickly given me the once-over two or three times, turned around, and started following me. I'd unfortunately had no choice but to quickly transfer the balloons previously held under the skin of his cock from my coat pocket to my mouth so I could swallow them if stopped, questioned, and frisked. To be caught with drugs in the UK meant not only jail time in what were said to be some of the Western world's shittiest prisons (especially for foreigners) but also most certainly a lifetime ban from the country. For this same reason, I always carried balloons and crack rocks in this fashion while out and about in America. At home in the US, I was often stopped and searched by cops. Wise to this common practice among street users and dealers, the police often asked me to open my mouth to show them if I was holding anything within. On the couple of occasions I'd had to swallow my stash with nothing more than my spit to help choke it down, I'd been compelled to search through my own shit in the days following in order to find the balloons or rocks within, they being more valuable than gold to me.

My current Portuguese-immigrant dealer wisely did not look the part. I'd met Juan-Joseph when he'd actually approached me late one night while walking his dog on the King's Cross side streets. He'd seen me cruising the area, obviously looking for drugs. He told me to follow him a few blocks off the main drag to his flat, where he sold me dope and crack, gave me a clean rig, and allowed me to fix in his place. He had a thick accent that was difficult for me to follow word to word. He didn't shoot dope himself. Instead, he was one of a very small group of people I'd met throughout my shadow life that was addicted to shooting crack. Not coke as was the norm, crack.

In order to shoot crack, he had to break it down to liquid form. He first crushed the rock into something like a powder, then added citric acid like you did with dope. Instead of cooking it up, he just added cold water and continued to crush and swirl the now-liquid with the plunger end of a syringe until it was a clear, not cloudy solution. When he tied off and did one of these shots of liquid crack, he immediately went into this crazed, fucked-up, bizarre routine. As soon as the drug hit his blood-stream, his face contorted in a way totally mirroring that of a person with cerebral palsy. He'd stand up and, in a heavily animated and spastic manner, he would do a strange dance, falling around his kitchen, pulling violently and shamelessly at his dick through his baggy brown corduroy pants. In a loud voice, he would emphatically attempt to say something to me. Whatever it was Juan-Joseph was trying to say, it took a Herculean amount of effort on his part just to spit it out as he struggled, stammered, and spasmed. Of course, through his twisted mouth and already thick accent, whatever he was loudly trying to say was impossible for me to understand.

Not great company, but soaking wet from rain in the frozen, cold, pre-midnight air waiting for the bus to Heathrow Airport, I desperately needed to see him. If I didn't make my way onto this bus, I was fucked in the worst way.

I stood waiting, shaking and shivering in the bitter November night air. An hour passed, then two hours. Still no bus. Now I began to enter a fairly advanced state of withdrawal, stomach cramping, cold sweat covering my body, mixing with and joining the cold rain running off of my face and pouring from my soaked, hatless head.

Finally, a short time after midnight, a bus going to Heathrow pulled up and let a couple people off. I reached into my pocket and pulled out a ten-pound note and started walking up the stairs.

"Hey, mister, are you scheduled to take this bus? I don't see anyone on my list to be picked up here."

List, I thought, *what the hell?*

"Yes, I should be on the list."

"Ticket?" he asked.

"I forgot to bring it, can I just give you cash?"

"No, you cannot, mate. These busses are preticketed and my work ledger tells me this bus is fully booked to Heathrow. I've got people to pick up on the way, I can't take you."

"How can I get a ticket?"

"You have to go to the local bus station during normal working hours or pay for it by credit card over the phone. Now off you go!"

Well, that was fantastic news. I hadn't the slightest clue as to where the station was. It was obviously closed anyway and I had never even owned a credit card my entire life. I walked back down the steps, then turned around and asked, "When is the next bus coming to this stop, sir?"

"Three thirty, mate, but you won't get on it either, unless you've booked it in advance."

With this distressing knowledge, I got off the bus. I considered my situation: completely empty, rain-washed streets, no extra money for the train, only enough for one from London to Bristol, no idea where either a bus or train station was, no dope in the foreseeable future, soaking wet, freezing, going into withdrawals, no phone nor anyone to call. My options were extremely limited. I absolutely *had* to wait until the next bus at three thirty. I would try this again but with a new strategy: I would play on the sympathies of the driver and hope that if the next one were not fully booked, a little bit of cash and a little bit of pity would net me a ride.

As I stood in the increasingly biting cold air and rain, getting sicker by the minute, I silently cursed Wilkins and the rest of the entire goddamned band and crew. How hard would it have been to go an hour or two out of their way to drop me off where I could have taken a train directly to the huge station in King's Cross? None of those assholes had an ounce of compassion for my self-created plight. They had begun to refer to me behind my back as "Mr. Burns," the old, bitter, bent-over, and creepy boss on *The Simpsons* cartoon television program, slightly reminiscent of Klaus Kinski in the title role of *Nosferatu the Vampyre*.

I was admittedly getting skinnier and older-looking by the day. I was constantly operating on no sleep, walking the local drug neighborhoods of every city and town we visited every minute of every night I was not required to be with the band. Not in order to get high, forget about that, it was in order to just stay well. Every day I was subsisting on the barest minimum of dope that I could get by on, carefully rationing every last grain. When I could afford it, I also needed crack, since I was obviously a fucking degenerate crackhead also. Every spare second was spent on my feet and wandering, haunted, sticking out like a raw cock in my by-now filthy leather pants, eternally scanning the streets of the worst neighborhoods in every city we visited for more.

I paced up and down the sidewalk behind the bus stop in the freezing rain. My hair and clothes were soaking wet, only the leather trousers not saturated with rainwater yet. Shaking, shivering, and occasionally gagging, on the verge of vomiting every second. I was constantly spitting out the thick, sick mucus that kept forming in my throat, a strong road-sign that full-on withdrawals were right around the corner. If they came on before another bus showed up, there was no possible way any driver was going to let me on, regardless of my obvious "charms." Every five minutes or so, I would try to sit for a moment on the slatted, rain-covered metal bench at the stop and attempt to relax. But it was so uncomfortable and my already-through-the-roof discomfort so high, that I would inevitably stand right back up again.

As the hours crawled by like an extra-wide tarantula, I began to shake uncontrollably. I could not stop. Just when I began thinking seriously about trying to find a hospital where I planned to desperately throw myself on the mercy of the emergency room staff, I saw the unmistakable high headlights of a bus shine against the boarded-up building at the end of the block. A bus pulled around the corner, stopping to let a few people off where I stood on the street, shaking like a victim of Parkinson's disease. After the last passenger got off, I quickly ran up the steps to where a kind-looking middle-aged female driver sat. I glanced at the clock on the dashboard: three thirty a.m.

"My Lord, lad! How long have you been in the rain? You're soaking wet!"

I tried to hide my severe discomfort and talk normally.

"A few hours, ma'am. I'm so sorry to put this on you, but I'm in an emergency situation. I got a call before midnight that my mother had been in an auto accident and is in hospital in London. They told me to come straightaway as she might not make it through the night. I know I need a ticket for this bus but it was after hours and I had no way to get one. I can pay cash. If I could just get to Heathrow, I can take the Tube into the city. I pray to God I'm not too late!"

I poured out this river of horseshit as fast as I could, thinking I might puke at any second from the effort it took just to talk at all.

With a sincere look of horror and empathy, she said, "Oh my! I'm so sorry, son! Please take the first seat behind me; this bus is mainly unbooked to Heathrow. And don't worry about payment, this is an emergency!"

I nodded my thanks and sat painfully down in the seat. I held my face against the window to feel the heat blowing up from the side of the cushion while fighting the urge to vomit.

—

BY THE TIME THE BUS arrived at Heathrow, it was daylight and I was now on the verge of serious withdrawals. I knew from experience that my body had been generating a gutful of midnight-black venom for hours now. It took every bit of strength I had to not start shitting and vomiting it up, but I knew, no matter what, my body would soon begin to successfully purge. I walked to the Tube station, trying as hard as I could to literally hold my shit together.

I got onto the train headed into King's Cross. It was morning rush hour and getting off the crowded, standing-room-only train, I fought my way through the mob in a hurry to get to their jobs, being physically knocked around from person to person like a human pinball, a raw, skinless human pinball of all exposed nerves. The last three blocks to my dealer's flat were the harshest. I had to stop frequently due to the severe contractions in my stomach up through my esophagus and the brutal cramping of all my limbs. A block from his place, I finally could not hold back any longer. I began to projectile vomit so hard that it took me to my knees, then flat out on the ground. Despite the fact that I'd not eaten any food in two days, up came copious quantities of pure-black liquid.

I could not believe I had come so far and had gotten so close just to come up short here, practically on the doorstep of the doctor. Scatman Crothers in Stanley Kubrick's film *The Shining* flashed through my brain. He'd flown all the way from Florida to Colorado, had taken a snowplow and driven in a blizzard all the way up to the Overlook Hotel to try and save the kid Danny, only to be axed as soon as he got through the door. I highly doubted any children's lives would be saved by my demise here, less than a block from the dealer's. I spasmed like a jellyfish on my side upon the hard concrete sidewalk, puking uncontrollably, tears streaming from my eyes. Through the hazy blur of my saltwater-flooded corneas, I could see a group of giggling, uniformed schoolkids walking around me where I lay incapacitated on the ground. They pointed at me and whispered to each other and then broke out into loud laughter as they passed by the pitiful scene of my public shame and sickness, displayed out before them in the crisp, cold morning air.

Okay, goddamnit! Get your fucking ass up off the ground! my mind screamed at me. What was I going to do? Just chill here kicking on a street corner for three days and nights? I had to get up the stairs I could see clearly in the distance, the stairs to my only hope, my savior's pad. With every ounce of strength I had left in my cruelly ravaged body, I staggered to my feet and began running the last half block to the apartment building, puking off to the side the entire way, trying not to get any on my already-soaked-through, disgusting clothes.

As I began climbing the staircase, I puked in the direction of a trash can, covering the top of it in black vomit. I continued painfully pulling myself up by the handrail next to the steps, foot by agonizing foot. I banged loudly on my dealer's door and heard his small dog begin barking inside. In a second, he was there, opening the door in his pajamas, obviously just awakened by my insistent knocking.

The minute he looked at me, Juan-Joseph knew what was happening. He put up his hand and in his thick Portuguese accent said, "One second." He turned around, ran into his kitchen, and returned with a small trash container, which he handed to me to puke into. I said, "Toilet!" Pulling me by my arm into his place, he shoved me through the bathroom door. I narrowly avoided destroying my only pair of pants, getting them down a half second before the powerful, unstoppable explosion of the same black liquid ejected like a shotgun blast out of my ass as, at the same instant, I puked again into the bucket I held in my hand.

When it was safe to get up for a moment, I went back into the other room. He sat me down on a chair in his small kitchen dining area where he'd already started to cook up a shot for me. I continued puking and heaving into the can. "Oh my God, oh my God," I heard him muttering to himself in English, and then something else louder in his native tongue as he scurried around his kitchen, quickly preparing a dose for me. When finished, he turned to me and pantomimed the motion of sticking the syringe into his ass, a gesture that said it was no time to search for a vein, that I should just muscle the hit, something I already knew. I got the first hit into my asscheek while he was cooking up a second, and then a third. I stabilized enough to search for a vein with the fourth. Sickness finally killed, I fell into a dark, dreamless sleep, sitting halfway up on a loveseat in his living room.

I awoke at noon to the feeling of my Portuguese friend's little white dog licking my hand where it hung down to the ground. After buying a couple more grams and doing another shot for the road, I got ready to leave and catch the train to Bristol. I asked Juan-Joseph if he was going to be around at the end of the month because my band was going to be on the *Later . . . with Jools Holland* television program and if he wanted to come I could get him a seat in the audience. I was hoping my gesture might lead to me getting some free dope. He shook his head no and told me he was going to be in Portugal visiting family then. That was a drag because not only did it mean no gifted heroin, it meant when we came back to town, I would be back out on the street just a few blocks down from where I was presently, forced to cop once again.

After playing in Bristol the next day, we caught a flight to Germany on an off day while our guitar tech and a salesman who worked for the merch company drove a van full of our equipment over to meet us for an appearance on a German television show filmed in Essen. All I had for the three days we would be traveling was what I had left over from my unscheduled stop in London. It was less than a gram. I tried hard not to think about a replay of the running gun-battle that had been Sheffield to London, only this time on German TV. I would have to ration myself almost down to nothing each of those days if I was going to make it. Hopefully there would be a train station full of drug pushers in Essen . . .

We arrived to a wintry scene of deep snow and ice. I was deflated when I saw that we were being driven to a hotel far outside the city. We checked into our rooms in the late afternoon. Upon getting inside, I prepared to cook up and do my last shot of the day, then realized if I were to do that, it would bring my meager stash down to around a half gram. *Just a fucking half gram to get through two more days?* I began to quietly freak out and prematurely grieve the upcoming avalanche of shit that was going to bury me, breaking out into a cold sweat in the process. A cold sweat that told me I was already beginning to withdraw, and we'd only just gotten there.

I inquired at the front desk as to where the train station in Essen was. "It's twenty-five miles away, I'm afraid" was the depressing report I received. As I stood staring out the lobby window into the darkness, I could see that a massive snowstorm had kicked off. I could not afford to take a cab twenty-five miles and back while still having money to purchase drugs, so I decided to stay in my room and try to sleep. If that was not successful, I would stay awake all night, waiting as long as was humanly possible before allowing myself another shot.

I turned on German TV and stared at the screen with the sound off. I thought about what was happening at home. Were Simon and Layne still keeping my meager business together? I lamented the fact that if I were only there, none of this self-inflicted torture would be happening. If I were home, I'd be selling crack and supporting my habit. And while Layne was staying with me, I'd more than likely be kept loaded due to his generosity. There had never been a time while I was in his company that he'd scored and not given me the same amount for free. But that was there and then; my present reality was far from that twisted, wistful fantasyland.

As the clock revolved, I could not help but check it every few minutes, wishing like hell that the morning would come soon. I would turn and glance at the clock and, realizing only ten minutes had gone by since my last look, my heightened anxiety increased. I had to force myself to not glance at it until an unsettling mania inevitably arose as I lay all night on the uncomfortable hotel bed obsessing over the brutal reckoning coming my way. Finally, at eight a.m., still awake and heading into deeper withdrawals, I could hold out no longer. I did my next shot, only to discover to my horror that it barely got me well. A half gram left. Late that afternoon, we would do sound and camera check for *Rockpalast*, a German concert show, then play an abbreviated set in front of a live audience that night, wait until the next day, then catch a flight with an afternoon arrival in Amsterdam, the city of our next engagement. I was never going to fucking make it, that much was abundantly clear. I was going to be into a full-on kick by tonight and there was no way on earth I would be allowed to fly on any airline in the condition I'd be in by tomorrow . . .

Before we were to leave the hotel to drive an hour to the venue where *Rockpalast* was filmed, and once more on the verge of withdrawals, I did another tiny shot to even worse results. I had reached the point of seriously diminished returns. Had my survival strategy been inherently flawed? Should I have just done a normal-size shot, emptied my tiny cache of heroin into my veins and thrown the fucking chips wildly into the unknown? It was too late because now I only had the smallest amount of dope to get by on. Come what may, I had to get to Amsterdam tonight after the show.

I asked at the front desk and discovered Amsterdam was only a two-hour drive from Essen. I wouldn't have enough money for a train and dope, so my only chance was if the equipment van was rolling out tonight. I would ride with them. In the large square in Amsterdam where I had copped in the past, the dealers were up all night. That was the only way I could possibly get by. We were scheduled to play there the next day but the proximity of the city made it a crapshoot whether the crew were going tonight or tomorrow morning. If it was the latter, I was fucked.

As band and crew gathered in the lobby to wait for a van ride to the *Rockpalast* studio/concert hall, I asked Wilkins what was the deal, were the crew driving that night?

"Yes, buddy," he answered wearily, as if to a bothersome child. He was sick of giving me updates as to our every single movement every fifteen minutes.

"I know what you're thinking and there's no room for you in the van, Mark. Unless you want to ride in the back, on top of the equipment," he said in his lilting, sing-song Birmingham Brummie brogue.

"Yeah, man. I'm going to do that. I have to, it's critical."

"Okay, buddy, that's up to you. I'll make sure you have a room in the hotel when you get there tonight." And then, in a tone that intimated he knew this was against his better judgment, "If you should happen to need some extra cash, you can get it from James the merch guy. He's traveling there tonight and you have some money coming from what we've sold already."

This news almost entirely put my mind at ease. It was now all but assured I'd be well by late that night at the very least. I could change in my hundred-dollars' worth of British pounds for Dutch guilders at the hotel desk, and I had a fallback plan if anything were to go wrong. I'd just get a cash advance from our merch salesman.

Confident I would easily slide through this nightmare of self-imposed rationing, this strict austerity program I'd set up for myself, I did my last tiny bit of dope in the dressing room toilet before our soundcheck, a full six hours before our scheduled appearance on German TV. It was too little, too late to make any noticeable improvement in my condition. I could smell the imminent, sickening cyclone of a kick coming on but was sure I could get to Amsterdam before the eye of it hit and tore my building down.

At *Rockpalast* my spirits were momentarily lifted when I found out my acquaintances L7 from Los Angeles were also on the show. Perhaps one of them had something to tide me over. That notion was kicked in the nuts when I found out they were all clean. *Goddamnit, man*, I thought, *why in the fuck aren't you clean? Everything would be so much easier . . .*

After we played the show, I had to wait around while our van was being loaded. It was almost midnight before me, our Irish guitar tech Dave, and James the merch guy who had been with us such a short time that I'd not even spoken to him before got into the vehicle and headed out slowly to Amsterdam. From a precarious perch atop a stack of haphazardly packed equipment and merchandise in the back of the van, I watched, dopesick and unhappy as James drove syrup-slow due to his overly cautious respect for the snow-covered backroads and then the slippery Autobahn. *Jesus Christ, you motherfucking pussy!* I seethed inwardly. *My fucking grandmother could drive faster than this and she's been dead for fifteen years. C'mon, shithead! Move your fucking ass!* I tried to close my eyes, to calm down and rest; none of my silent rage would get us there any faster. The only thing my volcanic inner storms would bring quicker was full-fledged withdrawals and, maybe someday after surviving that, the undertaker. I was running, raging, and drugging myself to death. A bitter, mountainous, unnamed, unrecognized, and poisonous grief melded with my rage. Rage pointed inward, and oftentimes fired wildly outward if I could find a semi-legitimate excuse to explode. Until then, I would silently kill anyone within range via silent, focused hatred. My mantra had become *Die, motherfucker, die.*

Sleep was an impossibility. I was lying across hard surfaces with several different levels, nothing straight enough to stretch out on and rest. I was cramped, uncomfortably stuffed like another piece of equipment on top of the uneven pile. That, the heavy-metal radio station, and the absence of dope kept me wide awake the entire shitty ride.

We finally pulled up to the American Hotel after two a.m. I had last stayed in this same hotel with Layne. We'd gotten loaded for a full twenty-four hours straight. My clothes were still damp from the sweat of my *Rockpalast* performance as I climbed gingerly down from the equipment mound. I stopped to rub my sore and tender legs, which started to cramp the moment I exposed my body to the freezing-cold night air. I was in a hurry to get my room key, exchange my British pounds into guilders, then walk the thirty minutes or so to the large square not far from the train station to score my medicine and get right. Not my preferred order of events but the order in which they must go if I were going to kill the fast-rising dopesickness, now at the same fever pitch it had been while I'd stood five hours in the rain at a British bus stop only four days prior.

After exchanging my money, I set out on foot on what had turned out to be a much colder night than any of the freezing nights we'd already seen on the tour. I'd not anticipated the severity of the low temperature and soon realized my clothes were not cutting it. I was freezing to death. I started to shake and then run in an exhausting, hopeless attempt to get warm. In a desperate bid for warmth, I stopped into a nearly empty late-night "coffee shop," one of Amsterdam's storied weed-smoking establishments.

After everything else, was I now being prohibited from reaching my painful, solitary goal by the fucking weather? Was this turning into a fucking replay of Denver? I was so goddamned close! Just a scant thirty-minute walk was turning out to be Shackleton's attempt to reach Antarctica. Except to my knowledge none of those guys had been stranded dopesick just out of reach of the dealer on the shore. Yes, my heroism knew no bounds and I lamented my terrible luck. I was, after all, simply a victim of poor timing and circumstance. After staying inside long enough to feel a tiny bit of life return to my extremities, with the thaw came the uncomfortable awareness that I was in fact nearly into a full-on, fucked-up kick. I'd best, by God, get my ass up to the square. Who knew? Maybe this Arctic chill had kept everyone inside tonight and I'd find the square empty anyway. That was a thought too horrifying to consider, and I shuddered at the image of myself suffering the consequences of such a scene. I had to get up there fast to find out.

After struggling the last fifteen minutes to the well-known dope spot, I spied two lowlife-looking characters, the mirror image of myself, at the base of the huge statue in the middle of the square, the place where dealers always stood waiting for customers. I approached them, and after smelling and taking a tiny taste first to make sure it was legit, I bought two-hundred-and-fifty-guilders' worth of heroin, saving thirty guilders to cab back to the hotel. It was too cold to walk now and if I needed more dope money, I'd just get some from James.

Three a.m., back at the hotel, I'm searching the hallways for a room service tray in hopes of finding a slice of lemon in an empty glass with which to cut the dope while cooking it to make it safe to shoot. The young woman at the night desk had informed me that the bar was closed and room service was also shut down until breakfast time. Nearly at the last room on the last floor, I finally came across not a slice, but an entire half of a lemon, sitting untouched on a plate next to the vacant shell of a lobster tail. *Thank God*, I thought. I took it as a sign of good luck and hurried back to my room where I retrieved the spoon and two used-too-many-times syringes from my backpack. I proceeded to cook up, psyched that I'd pulled it off.

You made it, you stupid motherfucker, I said to myself in disbelief. By all rights, this should have ended worse than Sheffield to King's Cross. Yet here I was, basking in the beautifully familiar smell of brown European powdered dope as it was heated, knowing I had crossed a mighty frozen ocean without a compass in an open dinghy against incredible odds. I quickly found a vein, more good luck. I registered and did the shot and . . . something was terribly wrong. Instead of feeling the warm, enveloping rush of the drugs as they coursed through my veins and sped to my brain, instead of the strange addictive phenomenon of smelling the heroin from inside your brain as it hit, instead of the sickness-crushing heat of the dope, I felt nothing at all.

Confused, I picked up the bindle that contained the rest of my dope. I re-smelled it: *Yes, goddamnit! This is dope! What in the fuck?* I cooked up the other hit and shot it. Again, nothing. I silently imploded. *How in the fuck did they make that fake dope?* It smelled, cooked, tasted even, exactly like the real deal. This was something I'd not encountered before but I didn't have time to sit and dwell on it. I had to get more cash and get back up to the square and fast if I were going to get something *real*. If not, I was going to hit the red line on the sickness meter very soon.

I went upstairs to James's room and knocked. Silence. No! Had he fucking gone somewhere else for the night? I knocked much louder and still not a peep. What in the fuck, man? I began to freak out, pounding on and kicking the door as hard as I could with the toes of my heavy combat-style black boots. I heard him move inside, and as the realization came that he was hiding, willfully ignoring me, I started talking to him, quietly but loud enough that I knew he'd hear me.

"Hey, man, I'm sorry if I scared you. I just need to get my cut of the merch dough. Or a cut. Give it to me and I'll get out of your hair."

And "Wilkins said it was okay, I swear to God it's all good, bro."

And "Hey, man, it's critical I get it right now so if you could just unlock the door . . ."

"Go away" came his angry, unmistakably belligerent voice from inside the room.

I exploded in disbelief, screaming through the door, "You open this motherfucking door, James, or I swear to God, you're dead, you fucking piece of shit! It's my money, motherfucker!"

My voice dropped down several notches as I suddenly became aware of the insanity of my verbal attack.

"Okay, it's okay, bro, I'm sorry, I'm sorry."

Getting no response, I then shot straight back up in wild furious volume.

"You can give it to me, man! What in the fuck are you thinking, dude? Open this motherfucking door, James, or I will fucking murder you in your sleep, you fucking cunt!" I screamed at the top of my lungs.

A door down the hallway opened and an angry-looking older woman stuck her head out the door and in an indiscernible European accent said, "Get out of here! I have called the front desk!"

"Hey, lady, fuck you, all right?" I responded with wild-eyed intensity, then flipped her off with both hands as she slammed her door as loudly as I'd been yelling.

"Either you leave me alone or I'm calling the cops" came from behind James's door.

This infuriated me beyond belief. I began trying to actually kick the door in, trying my damnedest to gain entry to actually murder this recalcitrant son of a bitch.

"Go ahead and call them, you fucking cocksucker! Let's see what they've got to say about you stealing my money, asshole! You work for me!"

"No, I work for the merchandise company, not you."

"I don't give a fuck who you work for, part of that money belongs to me, you piece of shit!"

Now the blood-pressure spike and adrenaline surge of my mania and the physical effort of trying to kick down the door, on top of every previous day, hour, minute, and second of the debilitating nightmare of this trip, pushed me over the edge into near-full withdrawals. I could no longer scream anymore because that brought me so damn close to puking. This was it. I had avoided nothing and the storm was going to annihilate me anyway, despite my heroic efforts.

Right then, two fifty-pound British notes slipped under the door in front of me. I quickly bent down and grabbed them up, lest he pull them back in.

"Take it, you animal!" I heard. "If you come back here again, I *will call the cops!*"

Clutching the money, wet and shivering, I ran down the six floors of stairs to the lobby and up to the counter, sweat streaming off my face, my shirt completely soaked through. The same young woman who'd exchanged my money earlier was still there. I slapped my money on the counter.

"Is everything okay, Mr. Lanegan? I have received reports of a disturbance on the sixth floor."

"Umm, I didn't hear or see anything. As you know I'm on the fourth floor, so . . . Do I need you to call me a cab or can I still hail one outside? It's getting late."

I tried to get my response out without gagging in front of her but it took too great an effort to hold it back. I turned around quickly and bent down, hands on knees, almost vomiting from the sickening mucus that filled my throat. *Here it comes you idiot, you're fucked!* I thought. The grueling brutality of the past two weeks' events, no, the dysfunction of my entire life, all of it had brought me to this moment of supreme lunacy, confusing self-laceration, and pain. I faced a tidal wave of dopesickness that was going to obliterate me. Of that, there was no doubt.

"There should be a cab right outside, Mr. Lanegan. Here's your guilders."

When I got back to the square, the two guys who'd burned me with the phony dope were gone. In their place was one smaller, smiling guy. He walked me around a corner and I followed him into a crack between buildings. Once in the shadowy darkness, he turned around, still smiling.

"The guilders?" he said.

"The brown?" I asked. As I reached into my pocket and brought out the dough, I felt the unmistakable sharp point of a knife against the back of my neck.

"Don't fucking move," said a deep, older-sounding male voice, speaking English with a heavy Dutch accent.

No fucking way, my mind screamed. I couldn't believe that in my desperation to get well I had fallen for the oldest trick in the book and walked directly into yet another rip-off.

I loudly protested, "Oh, c'mon man, don't rip me off! Please, dudes! If you only knew my fucked-up situation I'm sure you'd . . ."

"Take the money and check his pockets," the guy behind me said to the smiling man who had led me, lamb to the slaughter, into this setup.

He was still smiling as he grabbed the money from my hand. The guy behind me shoved me hard, face first up against the wall, while his pal rummaged through my pockets, taking the rest of my guilders. He then shoved me even harder, completely flat against the wall, to create a space in the tight crack for his pal to get around me.

"You stay here and count to a hundred. If you come out of here before that I will gut you, mister," said the man holding the weapon, poking the end of the knife so hard against my neck that I could feel a small stream of blood trickling down onto my back.

"Please, dudes, leave me *something*, I'm begging you guys," I said in a pathetic voice of shattered disbelief.

But they were already gone. I heard the smaller man let out a triumphant laugh as they ran down the cobblestone street. I walked out in time to see them running around a corner, already so far ahead that chase was futile. Besides, I could barely walk two feet without gagging on the pre-vomit snot that filled my throat. I bent over and again put my hands on my knees. I had no alternative than to go back and, hell or high water, get the rest of my merch money from that fuckhead James.

I walked back up to the square and got into one of the cabs that sat idling near the now-empty tourist area.

"American Hotel, Leidsekade," I croaked to the driver.

Without a word, the small, dark, and angry-looking man threw his transmission into drive. He hauled ass over railroad tracks and then up onto the high raised median that ran parallel to the tracks to get around a tram, then straight back onto the rails in front of it, sharing the roadway with the train now directly behind us for a harrowing roller coaster of a ten-minute drive back to the hotel. I sat right behind him, every second teetering sickly atop the edge of a bottomless abyss, at the verge of puking onto the back of his head.

"Six guilders," he hissed when we arrived.

"Hey, man, I'm really sorry that this happened, but I was just robbed at knifepoint. I thought they'd missed the ten I had left in the bottom of my pocket. I just realized that they got that, too. If I could get your info, I *promise* you I will get it back to you later today." And then, pulling out the dubious rock-star credentials, "I'm an American rock singer named Mark Lanegan. I'm playing tomorrow night at the Paradiso. *I swear to you, I will pay you back*," I strongly stressed. "Please, man, I did not mean for you to give me a charity ride."

"You are not getting any charity from me and I don't care if you're Engelbert Humperdinck, you are not leaving this car without paying me, mister."

"Are you not hearing me, man? What part of no money did you miss?"

I tried to unlock my door but he'd locked it with the master switch.

"Unlock this fucking door, man. Don't you get it? I was robbed! I'm broke! Let me the fuck out! I have an armed robbery to report to the police. I will fucking hit you with an obstruction charge, kidnapping, and accessory after the fact to armed robbery!"

I quickly lay on my back across the seat and began methodically attempting to kick out the side window with the bottoms of both my feet, a powerful double-footed attack with my heavy boots, threatening to explode the glass with each thrust of my legs.

"Hold on! Hold on!" the driver yelled, unlocking the door. He got out into the frigid, freezing, foggy night air and quickly walked around the back of the cab to hover over me.

"Get out of my car, con man!" he yelled as I climbed through the door. As I glared at him, considering whether or not I had the strength left in me to sucker-punch this fool, he said, "Okay, now go up to your room and get my six guilders."

"I told you, man! I don't fucking have it! Figure it the fuck out! I can pay you later today!" I yelled menacingly, my face two inches from his, and started walking up the stairs into the lobby.

The cabbie ran up behind me and tried to grab a handful of my coat. I clubbed his hand painfully away with my fist. My mind was racing. I'd been ripped off twice already that night, the extreme hurt in my body had me on the edge of a vomiting, pants-shitting trip to the critical care unit, and how the fuck was I going to get more cash out of that prick James? It all flooded over me at once, more than I could take. Then the driver started a loud commotion in the lobby.

"I have a theft to report! This customer of your hotel has robbed me of the fare from the ride I gave him. Please call the police."

My head began to simultaneously melt down and swell up as if it were being microwaved like a fucking bag of popcorn. I couldn't believe this fuck would still not let me slide. Instead, he was hell-bent on escalating this time-wasting scene to the utmost degree while I still had to get more money from that bitch James and locate some dope!

"Yes! Please do call! Call the cops! This man kidnapped and held me against my will. I was held up at knifepoint and my money was stolen twenty minutes ago. I told that to this man before he offered me a ride to the police station and now he's trying to fucking blackmail me on top of it!"

In the middle of this screaming match that I was a second away from turning into a physical confrontation, the girl behind the counter suddenly said, "Mr. Lanegan, if you need money to pay this man, I am authorized to provide you with a cash advance on the card that was left to pay for the rooms."

News to me, but I instantly seized on the opening.

"Oh yeah, my road manager told me that. Five hundred guilders, please."

And just like that, she began counting it out.

I couldn't believe that, just when it appeared my painful race had been run, by some totally unexpected hand of mercy, I had been given a sliver of light to grab on to. I had managed to navigate this bent and twisted, desperate maze so far, but I knew it couldn't last forever. Death was on my heels, and I felt sure Death would have my head.

After collecting my advance of five hundred guilders off Wilkins's band credit card, I asked for change of a ten guilder note. I counted out six guilders in coins, dropped it on the floor in front of this rotten cunt of a cab driver, and ran down the stairs and into another cab that drove me back to the square.

The square. Where I had painlessly scored good, powerful dope several times in the past yet in this frozen-over wasteland of a brutally cold November hell night-turned-early-morning, with me at the outermost limits of physical and psychic pain that a human body could endure, was now vacant. It had been sixteen hours, a television appearance, two rip-offs, and a couple hundred painful miles since my last tiny, do-nothing hit. I had been on the verge of an incapacitating breakdown the entire time. As the gray light of day began to slowly appear, the taxi dropped me off. I paid the driver, and as weak and sick, cold, and tired as I'd ever recalled being, I stumbled out onto the empty street at the now-empty square. I began walking at as brisk a pace as I was able, as if that would prevent or slow the nightmare that was soon to come unless I got some heroin into my bloodstream.

I walked up to the statue in the square's center, then circled it. I walked the streets on the perimeter of the square, each time around increasing my circle, finding not a single soul out on a bitterly cold and now increasingly windy morning in November. Totally, hopelessly sick at this juncture, at nearly seventeen hours since my last puny shot, I began to walk up one side and down the other of the canals running through the red-light district. I hoped to catch a girl still working or heading home after work and pay her for a fuck she'd not have to endure in exchange for a reliable hook-up. That strategy had worked famously in other countries. In Australia once, I had been in the room of a brothel with an attractive young hooker. She'd been shocked that I hadn't wanted to fuck, just pay her to go score heroin for me as I'd stayed waiting alone in her room. She ran out, got two rigs and a couple grams that we shared in her room. "Oh my God, I wish every customer was like you," she'd said, and had asked me if I wanted to get together after she was done working.

In the smoky, gunmetal light of an icy, fog-covered early Amsterdam morning, I prayed against hope into the void for a similar angel to appear out of the mist, but one would not materialize. Not one single person crossed my path. I stopped and puked. *Here it comes, motherfucker. Get ready, it's go time*, I thought. *I have given it everything I possess against impossible odds and have been found lacking. There is no shame in defeat.*

If I was honest, there was nothing but shame in the way I lived my life. I was nothing if not an abject failure, a fucking shitbag liar, a junkie loser if ever there was one. As I stood, hands hanging on to my shoulders like a human self-straightjacket as I attempted to keep my body from collapsing into a heap on the ground vomiting, I heard a strange, bird-like sound coming from out of the thick fog behind me.

I looked across the canal and saw a thin, very tall, probably six-foot-seven-inch man with straight pitch-black shoulder-length hair riding a bicycle triumphantly over the cobblestone with no hands on the handlebars. He was making loud, strange whooping sounds and turning his head from side to side like a giant wild bird of prey, riding exuberantly as if from the scene of some successfully committed bank robbery. I watched as he crossed the bridge coming toward my side of the canal, took a left, then headed directly toward me on the small, narrow street on my side of the water. As he got closer, I recognized that the noises and throwing of his head side to side was not a bird imitation at all. As I watched him twitch and turn all the way down the fifty yards in front of me with a nonstop series of verbal clicks, ticks, grunts, and expletives to go along with the bizarre *whoop-whoop* sounds invoking some huge prehistoric bird, it was a textbook display of Tourette syndrome.

When he neared, I jumped in front of him, blocking his path with arms held up, money in hand.

"Stop!"

He slammed on his brakes.

"I need some dope, man. Some *real* dope. Now! Where can I get some?" I croaked in excruciating pain before puking on the ground between my feet and the front wheel of his bike.

He quickly looked side to side with the nervous, head-spinning, wide-eyed stare of a gigantic Charlie Chaplin impersonator. Seeing no one, he looked me in the eye and spit three balloons into his fingerless-gloved hand. So great was my exhaustion and relief that I almost collapsed on the street.

"Where do you live?" he asked.

"I'm staying at the American, on Leidsekade."

"Too far. We go to my place."

He told me to get on the hard, unpadded metal book tray behind his seat and, facing backwards, we rode for about twenty minutes. My bony ass bounced painfully on the uncomfortable tray and I puked what seemed like every minute as he banged over train track after train track I never saw coming, which I absorbed with the painful compression of my already-bent spine. We finally stopped at one of the thousands of identical Dutch row houses in the city. After he locked his bike to a rack and stole another unlocked bike right in front of his apartment building, we entered the steep winding staircase. We climbed five flights of stairs to his apartment, he carrying the heavy old-school bicycle up the narrow, claustrophobic set of steps, me following behind. I was painfully out of breath, fighting the urge to void the poison in my stomach, bowels, and throat every step of the way.

Once inside, he put the bike he'd stolen on top of a big pile of other bikes. The tiny place was completely packed with them, as well as pile upon pile of bicycle parts. While I vomited uncontrollably into his shitter, he got out a clean rig from a new bag of them, grabbed a clean spoon and a glass of clean water. He pulled out a piece of a cotton ball for a small filter and, tearing open a small bag of the store-bought citric acid needed for the dope, cooked and drew me up a very large shot.

Seated now on yet another stranger's toilet with explosive sick, slick black water firing out my asshole, I shakily found a vein. Not only did the shot get me well, I actually got fully loaded for the first time in over a week.

My savior finally introduced himself as Bram.

"I'll take you to meet my connection at eight and you can get as much as you want," he said while making his whooping, clicking, clacking, grunting, and tongue-popping array of incredibly authentic birdlike sounds. With each verbal tic came a physical contraction, convulsion, herky-jerky motion, or hand gesture. I felt for this guy who was plagued with such a painful condition and who had been my unlikely hero. I thought about the lonely, solitary existence he must lead in this place, stuffed to the gills with a bicycle-and-parts hoard, cut off from society because of his affliction. I also couldn't believe that after the nightmarish events of the previous seventy-two hours, I'd finally done a proper shot, not the tiny amounts I'd been forced by circumstance to limit myself to. I closed my eyes, still not believing my incredible lucky streak. I finally, gratefully, fell into a nod.

After again riding on the back of Bram's uncomfortable bike downtown a couple of hours later and scoring at eight a.m., I took a cab back to my room at the American Hotel to catch a few hours of much-needed rest. My personal journey through Hades had taken me to the limits of what I had previously thought I could physically and mentally endure. Yet endure it I had.

I came awake with a start at four p.m. from a generic wake-up call I'd not ordered. Wilkins must have arrived with the band and our sound-man Hutch, who rode with us everywhere.

I loved Hutch. He knew, of course, as did everyone in band and crew, what terrible shape I was in. But he always went out of his way to put an arm around my shoulder, offer his love and encouragement, one of the few consistent beacons of light in what was an overwhelmingly dark thousand miles of midnight I'd forced myself to travel.

"Mark, did I ever tell you how much I love to run your sound and hear your voice every day? You are my favorite singer, brother. You can do this, you are master, don't forget that."

He went out of his way to lift me up daily. A genuine, lifesaving grace.

When I met the band in the lobby for the short walk to the Paradiso in order to set up and soundcheck, Wilkins scowled, came up next to me, and whispered in my ear.

"You've done it this time, buddy. All that money is coming out of your final pay for this tour. And I hope you're proud of yourself; James quit today. He wouldn't even come out of his room to talk to me or let me in. You scared the shit out of him, buddy. I'm ashamed of you. James is a family man with two young children."

"Then he shouldn't have gone out of his way to fuck me over and provoke me. I swear to you, Kevan, not only would he not give me my money like you said he would, he wouldn't even open his door to talk. He sat behind his locked door, taunting and threatening me, called me a dirty animal, while I was a completely respectful professional. I was a total gen-tleman, Kevan. You know me! Who are you going to believe? This prick or a guy you've known for years? We both know I have issues, but when have you ever seen me be abusive or rude to a crew member? Or anyone, ever? Besides Lee, of course . . . Fuck James, I swear he's mentally ill, and on top of it, he's a pure mean-spirited dickhead. Excuse my language, but this pisses me off. Fuck his false fucking accusations, dude. Someone should seriously report this to the merch company and get his ass fired so he doesn't rip them off or fuck them over again by being such an out-of-control prick to the next band they put him out on the road with."

"Don't worry about reporting it, buddy. The company already called today and said we are responsible for finding local vendors to sell at the rest of the shows. They weren't very happy with you."

"Weren't happy with me? Are you fucking joking? I hope to fuck you told them this was on him! I'm glad that piece of shit is gone; I would have kicked the fuck out of him if he wasn't. He should be fired. He was completely out of line and out of hand. I'll never use this fucking merch company again, sending us this fucking amateur to do a man's job."

Character assassination being a lifelong hobby of mine, I skidded wildly out of my lane while trying my damnedest to send that motherfucker James a personal love-letter of a parting gift.

—

BACK IN THE UK AT the end of the month, we were scheduled to appear on the hugely popular television program *Later . . . with Jools Holland*. When we got in the night before, I took the Tube from our hotel across town to King's Cross, found a street dealer pretty quickly, and bought everything he had. It was enough to see me through that night and would hopefully see me through the day of filming, but it wasn't enough to see me through the next night, nor would it get me all the way back to Seattle. I would have to come straight down to King's Cross after the show was finished and procure enough to get that job done.

Starting in the daytime, Jools Holland's show ran well into nighttime, with a format different than any other TV show. Five or six completely different acts all set up in a circle in the huge studio soundstage where it was filmed and then, in front of a small live audience, he went around the circle announcing the bands one by one. I was psyched because a band called Electronic was also on the show. They were a group with Bernard Sumner, guitarist of Joy Division and singer of New Order, both bands I considered to be among the greatest ever; and guitarist Johnny Marr of the Smiths, another heavy favorite of mine. I was deeply disappointed when their tunes turned out to be the weakest of tea. After a couple times around the room, each act had played two songs apiece. In between acts, Holland would also play a boogie-woogie song or two on the piano, something he'd done before his television career as an early member of the beloved British pop band Squeeze. After running through our songs and enduring the half-baked witticisms of the scripted banter between host and guests, we headed back up to our hotel. As we arrived, Josh said, "Hey, Scratch, a good friend of mine is a huge fan and wants to meet you at the after-show in our hotel bar; I told her I'd introduce you."

"I'm sorry, dude, but I've got somewhere to be. I don't have time for it."

I planned on counting out the huge collection of British coins and a few bills I'd managed to accumulate and making one last score at King's Cross to see me through the night and home.

"Just ten minutes, please. She's a cool chick and a great singer. Her name is Martina and she sings with Tricky."

Damn, I thought. I had purchased a copy of *Mojo* magazine in the airport when we'd first hit England and the free CD that came with the issue had been my only soundtrack on this exploratory trip through the hinterlands of hell and deep into its darkest corners. The track "Christiansands" by Tricky had been my favorite tune on it and I had played it obsessively, over and over again, listening to it through cheap headphones on my piece-of-shit portable Discman CD player the entire tour. It had been one of my only sources of comfort.

"I love her singing. Yeah, I'll meet her, but it's gotta be really fast."

As I sat up counting my change in my hotel room, Josh called from the bar, telling me to come down. My bag of clothes still lost courtesy of British Airways, I had poured by the handful fifty thick, heavy one-pound coins along with another ten pounds' worth of smaller-denomination coins into a doubled-up pair of sturdy, brand-new, unworn sweat socks I had recently bought and knotted up the top. I stuffed it into my coat pocket, tucked two rolled-up fifty-pound bills into my pants pocket, then left the room.

I stopped in the crowded bar as promised to meet Martina. Straight off, I found her funny, friendly, and magnetically attractive. With a slight sting of regret, I knew I had to quickly leave, though I hoped to further explore this intriguing woman's charms at some later date. After promising each other we'd do some music together someday, I headed out onto the street, toward the Tube station to King's Cross to find some dope as fast as possible. Our lobby call was early and I could not allow my search to turn into yet another infuriating all-night slog, nor could I come away empty-handed.

I got off the train and came up out of the station to an unusually empty street. It was cold but not freezing and I wondered who had hidden all the dealers in London that night. Finally, I spotted a suitably furtive-looking character across the street, hanging out on a shadowy corner. I walked up.

"What are you looking for, mate?"

"Some gear, brown," I whispered back.

"How much you want?"

"I don't know, I gotta see it first."

"Okay, follow me," and he began leading me around a corner and into a dark alley.

Not wanting a repeat act of my Amsterdam knifepoint disaster, I looked back over my shoulder a couple times to make sure we weren't being followed in by another weapon-wielding scumbag. I held in my right hand the end of the tightly knotted socks full of the seventy-plus heavy coins shoved in my coat pocket. The other hand I curled into a fist inside its pocket to keep it warm.

He stopped up ahead of me, turned around, and began fumbling in the inner pocket of his jacket as if to retrieve the dope while walking back toward me. Then he abruptly lunged forward and shoved his hand into my left pocket, thinking that was where I carried my money.

"Wrong pocket, shithead," I said.

Grabbing his wrist with my left hand and pulling the sock out of my right pocket, I viciously clubbed him with it like a truncheon in the side of his head as he fruitlessly fought to pull out of my grip.

"You stupid fuck!" I rasped as he fell straight to the ground. I leaned down to savagely pound him in the head twice more, taking out the frustration of years of affliction on this hapless dolt.

Suddenly, all the repressed anger, pain, and extreme anxiety I'd held on to throughout this entire trying ordeal, one that had carried me way over what body, mind, and soul could handle, came pouring out. As I stood over where he lay, I began kicking him with machinelike repetition and maximum velocity in the head, ribs, groin, back, and face, over and over and over again. All the grief I'd put myself through, sadistically transferred to this desperate and foolhardy character who'd simply had the extraordinary misfortune of picking the wrong target. As I continued mindlessly unloading on the guy, my attack was fury-driven not by the fact that he'd tried to burn me, but instead because he'd not had the goods I'd been promised. All that ran through my head was that I had better end this beatdown soon because it was already past midnight and I would fast have to resume my wearisome, late-night search. I absolutely had to find heroin in order to make it home on the plane scheduled to leave at nine a.m., with a lobby call of five thirty that morning.

As I persisted in the unrelenting beating, I became aware of a dull, cemetery-dead emptiness inside. I had stopped feeling anything at all. No rage, sadness, fear, nothing. I had finally crossed the line and ceased to give a damn about life, death, or any other meaningless thing in between. I only stopped robotically connecting my boot with his body when forced to by sheer, broken exhaustion.

Unable to see clearly through itching, irritated eyes blinded by stinging sweat, without thinking, I rubbed at them with the socks full of coins still in my hand. I realized I had just wiped his blood onto my face when I glanced at the now scarlet-stained cloth. Under the burning, wet, bloodstained, jaundiced eyes of his torturer and would-be executioner, the unsuccessful thief slowly attempted to crawl away from his self-sought torment.

Wiping the blood off my face with the sleeve of my coat, I croaked, "You goddamn idiot. I should fucking finish you." Then I turned and walked back toward the station to seek out a real dealer. As I high-stepped it down the alley, I heard him groan in agony where he lay, inching away on the ground.

41

COTTON FEVER

NOT WANTING TO BE ALONE FOLLOWING THE DEATH OF HIS GIRL-friend Demri, Layne Staley moved into my place while I was acting the rat-on-a-wheel through a hell tour of Europe. He and my alleged-statutory-rapist, cross-dressing protégé St. Louis Simon lived in my apartment smoking and selling crack and arguing with one another over junkie etiquette while I was gone. The first thing Layne said when I walked through the door was "Whoa, man. What the hell happened to you?"

"Let's just say it was a rough fucking ride," I said and left it at that. I was relieved to have reliable sources of heroin at my disposal once more, and the three of us stayed awake for days on end, alternately hitting the pipe with Simon obsessively scanning the floor looking for what we might have dropped. Eventually he, like so many other addicts and transients who had lived with and worked for me in the past, went for a walk one day and simply never came back. Three weeks after my return from Europe, I got buzzed from the front door late one night and when I went downstairs and looked out, there was my traveling bag, sitting on the front steps to my building, courtesy of British Airways.

Layne spent a few more months in squalor with me in my small one-bedroom apartment. He never stopped grieving Demri's death. After a while, his father Phil, also an addict, took up Simon's dubious duties as our runner, which made for a weird dynamic. Layne would often nod standing up, bent over at what appeared to be a painful angle with his head almost to the floor. Nonetheless, he became angry whenever Phil quietly caught a nod sitting on the couch. He would videotape his father, then force him to look at it, cruelly ridiculing his own dad for doing the same thing we all did every day. He obviously carried some resentment of Phil, a man I'd found to be just as sweet, funny, and smart as his son, as well as his physical mirror image. Finally, after almost four months, Layne began to crave isolation and moved back into the impenetrable penthouse condo in the University District he had bought and I was again by myself. As I'd come home with next to no money from my painful, fruitless tour, my phone and electricity were soon shut off. Before long I was cooking up my daily batches of crack to sell on a small old Coleman propane camping stove and shooting dope by candlelight at night.

I still had a pager. One day, I received a page from Layne. I walked across Ninth Avenue to Harborview hospital, to the grimy, germ-covered pay phone at the bus stop I always used but hated to touch. I wiped off the receiver with the sleeve of my shirt and called him collect.

"Hey, man, I heard from somebody that the cops are looking for you. Something about stolen property. Keep your head down."

I asked him where he had heard it and his answer was a bit vague but the story nonetheless gave me pause.

After Layne's warning, I stayed in my bathroom all day and night, waiting for customers. I had turned the buzzer off long before because not only did those street people I'd foolishly given my apartment number to harass me around the clock, I had run into Christian so often while meeting some shabby crackhead at the front door that it was way too obvious. Now I told them not to shout up at me anymore but to throw a small piece of gravel up to get my attention. Then I would quietly creep down the back stairs and do the deal at the door into the alley behind the building. I kept all the drugs on me so I could flush them down the toilet if indeed the cops did burst through the door someday.

After a week or so had passed, I started feeling like the coast was clear. I got some dough together to pay the power bill, eased up, and allowed myself to live in the rest of the apartment again. I started letting a young homeless dealer named Cyril I'd met on the corner of Third and Pine in downtown Seattle sleep on the mattress in my dining room in exchange for a few balloons of heroin a day. It was a boon for me. Unlike many of the homeless addicts who had shared my place in the past, Cyril didn't aggravate me and kept quiet whenever he was around.

Rather than having to hit the streets to hustle, Cyril did all that for me. Thanks to his efforts, I could stay home and focus on making and selling crack and staving off the dopesickness that constantly hounded me.

Early one morning, I was nodding on the couch when there was a knock on my door.

"Seattle Police Department! Open up!"

"One minute," I said, thinking, *Goddamnit, you idiot! He told you they were coming!*

I scrambled to get up and flush what I had. Halfway through the bedroom, I tripped on a chair and ate shit, hitting the floor with a huge resounding thud that reverberated throughout the place, badly fucking up my knee. After flushing all the drugs I was holding, I limped back to the door. With the chain still hitched, I opened the door an inch or so.

"Mark Lanegan?"

"Yes, that's me."

"My name is Officer Davis. I'm coming in to have a chat with you."

"What about?" As if I didn't know.

"Listen, pal," he growled through the crack in the door, "if you know what's good for you, you'll shut the fuck up and let me in."

After several long moments of hesitation, I unchained the door. One solitary uniformed officer strode in, straight past me. He peered at the crack pipes and spoons on the table I hadn't had time to clean up and the mound of used syringes on the floor in the corner, probably two feet high.

"Sit down," he said. "I'm gonna take a quick look around."

Officer Davis stuck his head into the other room where Cyril was out cold, facedown on the bare mattress. A dirty mason jar half-filled with bright red balloons of heroin sat in a large flowerpot alongside a huge rotting cactus near his head. The cop looked back over his shoulder.

"Is he dead?"

"No, sir, just asleep."

He pulled up a chair and sat across from me at the coffee table.

"I'm not here to bust you for whatever you guys are doing up in this place. I'm here to talk to you about a stolen laptop you pawned a couple weeks ago. I just need to get a statement from you about it."

My mind quickly went back to the computer I'd gotten for a ten-dollar piece of rock from my former street colleague turned nemesis—the reckless, car-prowling Eritrean crackhead named Dawitt—and sold at the pawnshop for seventy-five bucks. I thought, *You finally got me, motherfucker.* Without intending to, he'd finally succeeded in bringing me to my knees.

"Because Rob Chandler is a friend of yours, I'm not gonna hang you up on this. Instead, I'm gonna give you two options. Either go to rehab and get yourself cleaned up, or leave town. If I find out you're still here or out on the street, I'm going to make what happened in San Francisco seem like Disneyland."

Rob Chandler was a longtime friend, the owner of Capital Loan, the pawnshop where I sold stuff, borrowed money, and used the phone daily. The cop was referring to my arrest in San Francisco a few months earlier for possession of crack cocaine and paraphernalia. I'd gotten popped early one morning in the sketchy, drug-ridden Tenderloin district while the Trees were in the Bay Area playing some shows. I spent a dopesick day in jail and the arrest was reported on MTV News and in the local Seattle newspapers. It had been a small nightmare, both immediate and sustained. But since an acquaintance of our tech Danny Baird was childhood friends with the prosecuting attorney, he'd simply dropped the charges and I'd walked away scot-free.

The cop stuck a piece of paper in front of me.

"I want you to sign this statement. Then I'm giving you a week to get lost. Either rehab or leave town, I don't care which."

I sat there listening in silence. Without reading it, I signed the piece of paper he'd put in front of me. Without another word, he stood up and walked out.

After the visit from the cops, things went downhill pretty quickly. I felt eyes on me everywhere. Unable to deal crack and not wanting to leave town, I attempted to go to rehab. With my health insurance from the musicians' union, I checked myself into a grim detox facility in the Ballard neighborhood, northwest of the city. After filling out some forms, a gray-haired nurse led me to an uninviting ice-cold room. Without giving me meds of any kind, she handed me a hospital gown and told me to get in bed . . . at eleven o'clock in the morning. I undressed and put on the uncomfortable gown, then lay there under a threadbare blanket watching the incessant rain beat down on the cement sidewalk outside the window. After about thirty minutes, I knew I wasn't going to stay. I said "Fuck this" out loud to nobody, put on my clothes, and slipped out a back door. I collect-called Danny Baird, who was functioning as my manager by that time. He came and got me in his old Ford pickup truck and drove me back up to First Hill.

The first of the month was coming. I didn't have rent and was plagued by a rotten wisdom tooth and an infuriating infestation of lice. I shoplifted tube after tube of Orajel and was continuously squirting it into the hole in the back of my mouth where the remaining jagged piece of bone made my jaw throb with pain. Still, my head pounded round the clock, making it hard to focus on anything, and I was constantly trying to brush off the vermin that I could feel crawling on my neck night and day. I stayed until the eviction notice was put on my door. Then I left with just the clothes on my back. Everything of value had already been sold or traded for drugs.

I spent some nights on a couch in a house occupied by some impressionable young guys from my hometown of Ellensburg. Other nights, I crawled under a dingy blue tarp I had fished out of a dumpster and slept in an overgrown, bushy area next to the freeway populated by homeless people and addicts known as "the Jungle." I sold heroin on the street for my former all-night connection, the agoraphobic black dude named Val. He had been my go-to 24/7 dealer for years, the guy I could score from day or night, although I mostly tried to avoid him when possible. He was a wannabe rock star who took perverse delight in the fact that I had made records as a rock singer. He forever grilled me with questions about the "music biz" and forced me to listen to him play his knock-off Fender Strat, something akin to unpleasant cock-and-ball torture. With his throwback processed hair and old-school-style nylon shirts and flared trousers, he looked like a parody of a seventies blaxploitation pimp. He lived in the Yesler Terrace projects nearby on First Hill and rarely if ever left his pad. Every morning, after my seven a.m. soup-and-sandwiches in the mission at Broadway and Jefferson, I would get five dollars from Val, go buy his coffee and donuts from a shop down the way, and bring it back to his apartment.

I had been a singer and a dealer who used to have guys doing this for me, but now I was the gofer, the runner, the shitboy. It didn't sit well with me. It started to wear on my mind like a foul, vicious thug. I began planning a way out.

After my wake-up shot in Val's bathroom, I would head off the hill with some heroin to sell downtown. Every day, after I sold out of product I would stop at Nordstrom's department store and steal a bag of tube socks. I would tear the tops off to use as bandages for the huge, gaping, self-inflicted wounds on my forearms, and would use the bottom part as intended: a covering for my filthy, aching, open-blistered feet. After that, I'd stop at a drugstore and fill my coat pockets with double-A, triple-A, and nine-volt batteries, which I also peddled on the street. Cyril had hipped me to that hustle. It was amazing how many people would buy batteries, almost as many as would buy dope.

Once, while standing on a street corner with my mouth full of balloons, I heard someone say my name from inside a passing car. I had told myself no one would ever recognize me in my current state: skeleton-thin with huge beard, long dreaded hair, and greasy, unwashed clothes, still sporting the leather pants I'd bought in Europe, the only pair I owned. But someone had.

I was wary of cops in the best of times but was now hypervigilant in case Officer Davis might make good on his promise to catch me out. I wore a dark gray hoodie even on the rare days of good weather and always kept my head down, looking the other way whenever I saw a police car.

I stopped into the pawnshop one afternoon to hit Rob Chandler up for some dough. He had actually taken the filthy pants in exchange for a loan and found a pair of jeans in the back for me to wear. Then he had dropped it on me.

"Davis knows you're still here, still using. He said to tell you it's on."

I was tired of the grind of working for Val and formulated a plan to rip him off. The chances of him actually leaving his place to come find me were needle-slim. He was so afraid of people that I had never once even seen him outside of his apartment. After delivering him his coffee one day, I took the balloons he gave me and just never went back. Instead of selling them, I did all of the dope myself over the next few days.

I kept boosting and moving batteries and started getting my dope from a huge forty-something ex-con, a New Yorker named Donny who lived directly across the street from my old place. He'd gotten convicted on an armed robbery charge and spent his ten years in a New York state prison writing poetry. Donny often lamented the fact that nobody in penitentiary knew how to read or write, and he liked to show me his folder of writings. Sometimes he read me his poems aloud in a booming voice with a heavy East Coast accent. He nicknamed me "Red." I enjoyed hanging out with him, primarily because he would always share his Marlboros with me. They were a thousand times better than the rollies I smoked, always made out of butts I collected off the sidewalk.

Donny usually held court while lying on a bed with his edema-swollen feet and legs elevated, but sometimes he'd get up and we'd go out and do what he called "the creep." The two of us would take the city bus up Broadway to Capitol Hill, where I would go into random stores and stroll through the place looking furtive. With my dirty clothes, long unkempt hair and beard, wild-staring Charles Manson–esque eyes, pronounced limp, and herky-jerky way of walking around, I cut a crazy-street-person, wraith-like figure and any employee in the shop immediately locked down on me with a suspicious gaze. While all eyes were on me, Donny would go in through the door at the other side of the shop and walk straight into the back room, where he would search until he hit the petty cash box. More often than not, he would come straight out again with a coat pocket full of stolen bones. I would shortly thereafter wander out, talking to myself, still drawing attention. It was an incredibly successful routine. Soft, mushy legs but balls of cold blue steel, that Donny.

Late one rainy night, I was camped out in the Jungle when I was roused by Donny's unmistakable voice.

"Red! Red! Where are ya, Red?"

"Shut the fuck up, man." Another resident of the Jungle.

"You telling me to shut up? I'll break your fucking neck, mister."

I quickly got up and followed the sounds of the commotion. The situation was immediately defused when Donny saw me.

"Hey, Red!" he boomed with a big smile. "I got a job for ya." A deadly serious look quickly replaced his smile.

An hour earlier, Donny had just re-upped and was walking down the street with a small canvas bank bag full of heroin in his pocket when he noticed a police car slowly following him. He'd cut behind a fenced-in building site and, out of their view for an instant, tossed the bag over the tall chain link and barbed wire. Seconds later, they turned the corner, hit the lights, and got out of the car to shake him down. Not finding anything, the cops had to let him go. Now he needed me to climb over and retrieve the dope.

We walked the quarter mile or so back to the unfinished building in the dark. After a couple tries, he managed to throw his long black duster over the wire, then hoisted me up onto the twelve-foot-high fence. I almost got hung up and sat shakily straddling the top for a minute, temporarily unable to get my leg to the other side.

"For fuck's sake, Red, get on with it."

I swung over and climbed down a couple feet. Then my cold fingers lost their grip on the rain-wet chain link and I fell eight feet the rest of the way down. I picked myself up off the muddy ground and quickly located the bag behind a large pile of two-by-fours. Easy money.

The instant I picked up the bag, a bright white motion-sensor floodlight came on. With a howl that sounded like it came from the depths of hell, a huge Rottweiler came galloping out of the shadows. I tried to sprint for the fence, bit ass on the slippery ground, and fell backwards in the mud. Here was not death, but deformity: this dog would chew my face off. At the last possible second, the Rott snapped back on a heavy chain attached to its collar, snarling and snapping at the air, its jaws clicking like a dry-firing pistol, just inches from my face.

"Jesus Christ. Throw me the bag!" Donny hissed.

I ignored him, stuffing it down the front of my pants instead. I'd be damned if he split before I got out and was paid in dope for performing this wretched task. I picked up a wooden pallet, leaned it against the fence, and used it as a stepladder to launch myself back up to the top and over. We left his coat hanging on the barbed wire and took off across the lot to the street and back up the hill, the Rottweiler barking at the top of its lungs and throwing itself against its chain in a frenzy all the while.

—

I WAS ON THE PAY phone in my old First Hill neighborhood hitting up Laurie, the Screaming Trees' accountant, for nonexistent royalties when a rental car pulled up. The window rolled down and a man stuck his head out.

"Hello, Mark."

My father? He hadn't left his home in Alaska in a couple years, not since our depressing Christmas vacation together.

"Hey, son, I thought I'd come stay with you for a couple weeks. If that's okay."

"Dad, I'm sorry, I can't have visitors right now." I didn't have it in me to tell him I no longer had an apartment. "My place is a total wreck right now." Not so far from the truth.

I told him to take the ferry across to Bainbridge Island where my sister Trina lived with her kids and husband, that I would visit him there in a couple days.

"Um. Okay, Mark. That's fine." After giving me twenty bucks, he took off.

I had the distinct feeling he knew I was full of shit. The look in his eyes as he drove off hurt me a little, but I had the business of survival to attend to and quickly put it out of my head.

I had been estranged from my mother ever since I'd threatened to kill her in her truck. The last time I had seen her in Seattle had been before that, while she was in town visiting my younger stepbrother. Brendan had lived only four blocks from me on First Hill for years but I rarely visited him. While in my active addiction, I was persona non grata there.

I had knocked on the door and Brendan answered. I had asked for my mother.

"Wait a second," he said, not inviting me in. He shut the door and a few moments later my mother had emerged. After one quick glance at her twenty-eight-year-old junkie son, she gave me a disdainful look.

"What do you want, Mark?"

It had literally been decades since she had given me money for anything, but I thought, *What the hell, give it a shot.*

"Hey, Mom, good to see you. Is there any way I can borrow twenty dollars?"

"I'm not giving you any money for drugs," she flatly said.

No shock there.

"Okay, but can you give me a ride to the other side of the Hill? Five-minutes' drive, that's all."

To my surprise, she agreed. But the minute her car started moving, I was suddenly stricken with cotton fever, a muscle-tightening, jaw-cramping, debilitating malady that caused uncontrollable shaking. Cotton fever happened when, to get one last shot, a junkie squirted some water on the old cottons or cigarette filters used to strain the heroin while drawing it up from the spoon and then, with the pusher end of the rig, squeezed out what dope he could. Sometimes it released microscopic, sickness-causing bacteria in the cotton that were then injected into the vein. Fifteen minutes later, you were having a major fucking drag. For years at that point, my first shot of the day always came from pounding out the previous days' cottons. On the few occasions the fever hit me, it was a crippling nightmare, complete with crushing headache and a severe clenching, cramping of the jaw that made it nearly impossible to speak.

"What in the hell is wrong with you? Are you having an overdose?" she yelled.

"No, Mom, just keep driving," I stammered.

With some difficulty, I was able to convey that I needed her to roll up the windows and crank the heat, which she begrudgingly did. It helped mitigate my unhinged shaking until we arrived at a dope house where I hoped to get something fronted to me. She stopped the car and stared icily straight ahead. With some difficulty I managed to sit up straight and then crawled out without so much as a "See you later" from her.

The very next day after my sad encounter with my father, I was walking down an empty street when I glanced up and saw a middle-aged couple shuffling tentatively in my direction. As they got closer, I was stunned to discover it was my mother and stepfather coming toward me. Both parents in two days—it felt like a cruel joke. In the couple of years since I'd last seen her, we had both aged what looked to be twenty. As we met on the sidewalk, she stuck out a trembling hand with a piece of paper she wanted me to take. I grabbed it without a word and she stumbled and collapsed into her husband's arms as I kept walking. It was a pamphlet for a rehab facility in eastern Washington. I immediately crushed it in my hand and dropped it into the gutter.

42

LAST RUNGS

AFTER WORKING FOR DONNY FOR A WHILE, I GAINED HIS TRUST. I became his confidant, friend even, and began selling on the street for him. It was the same as I had done for Val: getting a couple handfuls of balloons in the morning, selling them downtown, and bringing him back the proceeds in the afternoon. At one point, when his legs were too fucked up to walk on, Donny sent me out to meet his Mexican connection Julio to re-up for him. I was waiting on a corner with five hundred bucks in my pocket when an old primer-gray Plymouth Duster pulled up.

"Red?"

"Yeah, that's me."

"Well, get in, homie. Ain't got all day."

I handed him the dough and he gave me back three times its street value in tar. Before getting out, I asked him for his number, looking forward to a time when I could go back into business for myself, and he gave it.

"Thanks, man," I said. "Let's keep this to ourselves, okay?"

"No problem, man, see you around."

After a couple weeks of meeting with Julio on Donny's behalf, I began skimming some of the dope off the top and keeping it for myself. Just a gram or so, not so much that he'd notice. But in time, I became more brazen. One day, after I brought the package back to Donny, he looked at it hard, then at me.

"This is light, Red. Are you ripping me off?"

"No way, Donny."

"You'd better hope not, pal."

"This is what he gave me."

"If you're lying to me, I'm gonna fuck you up. Empty your pockets, motherfucker."

I could feel beads of sweat forming on my face as I turned my pockets inside out. All I had in them was some change, a used outfit, a Reese's peanut butter cup, a packet of Zig-Zag papers, and a couple cigarette butts. Luckily, I had stashed the dope inside a small open seam in the waistband of my jeans where I always hid shit. Donny calmed down and then started cooking up a couple shots for us, to my profound relief.

But suddenly there was a different dynamic at play. Donny made little attempt to disguise his newfound suspicion of me. His edema was blowing up and caused him excruciating pain. Leaving the bed was torture for him. His condition reminded me of the kid Tim the day before he died, unable to get up off the ground, his legs swollen to twice their normal size. Donny no longer trusted me with his livelihood . . . but I was his only option to pick up the shit from Julio. I saw the writing on the wall and knew my days were numbered.

The next time Donny sent me out to re-up, I made a desperate, foolhardy decision. I met Julio on the corner with the grand Donny had given me, got the dope, and instead of returning to Donny's, hopped on a city bus headed to the far side of Capitol Hill. I holed up in the house of some using acquaintances for a few days, sharing some dope with them in exchange for a bed.

After a week or so, I ran into Patrick Conner, the younger brother of my Screaming Trees bandmates Van and Lee. Pat invited me to stay at the large house in the Central District he shared with some other kids from Ellensburg, a house I'd crashed in before. It was a huge, comfortable, three-story house. I slept on a couch in a closed-in balcony on the top floor with my old piss-yellow corduroy stadium coat I still had from 1993 as a blanket, my only worldly possession left from my thirty-three years on earth.

Early one morning, I was awakened by a loud disturbance.

"I know he's in there, you pissants! Get the fuck out of my way!"

I got up in a hurry, recognizing Donny's robust, angry voice from the street below.

"I don't know what you're talking about," said Pat's roommate Adrian. "He's not here, mister. Get off my property or I'm calling the cops."

Then all four of the kids who lived there started yelling.

"Yeah, man! Get lost! The cops are on the way! Get outta here, mister!"

How had he found me? I'd been careful to never tell him about the place. Well, find me he had, and now I was deep in the shit. His big, booming voice tore through the crisp, still morning air.

"You fucked the wrong guy, Mark," he was now shouting at the top of his lungs, using my real name for the first time ever. "You fucked the wrong guy! I see you, motherfucker! I know you! You're dead, Red! You're fucking dead!"

I descended after I was sure he'd left. The guys were visibly shaken. Turns out they had stood together in a line to prevent him from getting into the house. I was heartened, proud of the balls my young eastern Washington homeboys had shown. But I'd put them in danger, and now I'd have to leave. If we'd won the battle, we would lose the war. Donny was not someone to be fucked with. I'd once seen him mercilessly beat down a large, tough-looking homeless guy who had spit at him. And though it was illegal for a felon, he kept a pistol under his mattress.

At long last, I was face-to-face with the dilemma I'd been desperately avoiding forever. I was thirty-three but looked twice as old. I weighed a skeletal one hundred sixty-five pounds with huge open wounds on my arms. I had no money, no safe place to stay. I had burned every bridge from both ends and every church from floorboard to ceiling. I was the ghost that wouldn't die. When I first hit the city, I would have climbed Mount Everest for a shot of heroin. Now I barely had the strength to climb a single flight of stairs. With trouble in every direction—the cops, Donny, Val, countless other friends and foes I'd ripped off and fucked over—there was no possible way I could remain on First Hill. But the ten-block radius around it was the only home I'd known for years. But for those years, my existence had been brutally, dysfunctionally hopeless. It reminded me of a cartoon I'd seen in *Cracked* magazine as a kid: my life there was like standing in front of a shit-throwing machine in a white suit 24/7, continuously pushing the button with my own shaking hand. With an unfamiliar sadness, I admitted to myself I had to get the fuck out of Dodge. It was time to disappear.

As I stood shivering, dopesick, on a corner, waiting for the inevitable hammer to fall, my mind went back to something that had happened months earlier. During my daily trip to Capital Loan to use the phone and pawn something, Rob had asked me to come into the back room.

"Hey, Mark, a weird thing happened yesterday. Courtney Love came into the shop and asked if I knew how to get a hold of you. She gave me some literature from a program in California that helps musicians with drug problems, puts them through rehab."

"Fuck that shit. You can tell her to shove her rehab."

Rob was a good guy, a family man with wife and kids, a successful businessman who owned two pawnshops. He had a soft spot for me, always taking the dirty stuff I brought in, believing or at least pretending to believe my bullshit excuses for where I had gotten it. He had also, on occasion, offered to take me to a twelve-step meeting. I always declined. After knowing him for years, I easily owed him upward of twenty grand. At different times, besides all the stolen shit I sold, I had handed over my 1996 Harley-Davidson Fat Boy, reels of unreleased Screaming Trees tapes, boxes of rare silver dollars, and a Fender Jaguar Kurt Cobain had given me to attempt to pay off my debt. Now, with nowhere else to turn, I remembered Rob and what Courtney had offered. A way out.

I trudged the long mile down to the shop, eaten up with worry I might run into Donny or Val or Officer Davis now, in the eleventh hour, but I got there without incident.

"Hey, Rob," I called out to him the instant I made it through the door, "what was that thing Courtney left here for me?"

He gave a little smile and reached under the counter and retrieved a thick folder full of information about the Musicians' Assistance Program, MAP as it was commonly referred to.

"I've been hoping for a long time that you'd ask about this," he said.

I spent less than a minute looking it over.

"Will they take me somewhere warm out of town?" I asked, the only thing I cared about.

"Let me get in touch with them and see what the deal is," he said.

In less than ten minutes, Rob had me booked on a flight to Los Angeles the very next day where the MAP people had a bed in a rehab for me.

"Thanks, Rob. I appreciate it, man." We shook hands and I left.

I had no intention of going to a rehab or anywhere else these people might want to take me. My plan was to get off the plane and hit the streets. Yes, I was sick, and yes, I needed help, but the only kind of help I wanted was help getting out of town and then getting loaded.

The next day, Rob met me on an agreed-upon street corner to pick me up. I convinced him to put one last loan on my tab and drive me to a dope house where I cooked up four shots and put the full rigs in my socks. I had him pull over on the way to Sea-Tac airport and let me smoke a couple hits of crack in his truck, then he dropped me off at the check-in counter. I hit the bathroom twice during the three-hour flight, doing two full shots both times.

I hadn't planned on getting so loaded, but I was suddenly overcome by exhaustion from all the previous years of running and gunning that by the time we landed, I was so high and worn out I had trouble walking. I also hadn't planned on the huge security guy waiting to pick me up. Unable to get free, I unhappily followed him to his SUV, got in, and immediately passed out.

"Hey, pal, time to get up, let's go."

I groggily rubbed my eyes and got out of the truck onto the sidewalk outside what looked to be a nondescript office building in Hollywood, not the rehab facility I had anticipated.

"Buddy wants to see you before we send you to the hospital."

"Who's Buddy?"

"Buddy Arnold, man!" The driver laughed. "The guy who brought you here!"

We went upstairs where a friendly woman smiled at me.

"Hello, Mark, we've been expecting you. Please take a seat."

About fifteen minutes later, a thin gray-haired dude in his early seventies bounded through the door.

"Jesus Christ," he said with a big grin. "Look at you, man! We got you just in time! You are definitely in the right place."

He took me back into his office and told me a little bit about himself. He had been a professional jazz saxophone player who had played with Buddy Rich, Tommy Dorsey, and the Stan Kenton Orchestra, among others. His career had been derailed several times due to his heroin addiction and he had been in and out of the penitentiary for years. After getting clean during his last stint in prison, he and his wife had started the Musicians' Assistance Program and had helped many musicians and other music-business people get free of their addictions. He pointed to a large, almost unrecognizable photo of himself on the wall. Shirtless and emaciated with eyes closed and long greasy hair, he had obviously been deep in his crippling dependency.

"I keep that to remind me of where I've been. And where I never want to go again. I'm gonna take a Polaroid of you. Hang on to it so you never forget this day."

He gave me a hug and then sent me back to the muscular dude who drove me out to what was, unbeknownst to me, the Pasadena psychiatric hospital where I was to be evaluated and detoxed.

It was late November and cold in California. I sat shivering in my thin, long-sleeved shirt and filth-encrusted coat near a fountain outside the intake office of Las Encinas Hospital for what seemed like hours, waiting to be admitted. To kill time, I started talking to an elderly lady who sat near me on the bench, chain-smoking cigarettes. She seemed perfectly comfortable, dressed in an ancient, ragged bathrobe.

"Excuse me, ma'am, but could I please have one of your cigarettes?"

"You have one on your head, young man," she said.

I put a hand to my head and did indeed find a partially smoked butt stuck up in my disgusting, never-washed hair. I must have traveled all the way from Seattle with it there. I asked her what she was doing here.

"I just finished electroshock treatment. I have been suicidal all my life and I'm trying to get better. It feels good out here; my room depresses me."

Electroshock? What kind of fucking place was this? Jesus, had they sent me to a goddamn psych ward? Still, as the hours dragged on and the dope wore off, I was too weak and exhausted by years of ritualistically nailing myself to get up and leave.

It was nighttime before they finally ushered me down to the small substance abuse unit on the hospital grounds. The doctor on duty took one look at my arms and wanted to immediately send me to an actual medical hospital but I was able to talk him out of it. After being given a mercifully heavy dose of phenobarbital, I was led to a bungalow room with a single bed. I climbed in and fell into a bottomless well of sleep.

43

PSYCHIC STORMS, EPIPHANY, AND REBIRTH

THE NEXT FEW DAYS WERE LOST IN A HAZY CLOUD OF PHENOBARB-
induced dreamscape horizons. I was aware of crashing wind and rain,
a huge, ceaseless storm outside shaking and pounding the bungalow I
occupied. I kept having the same dream over and over. Sitting in a chair
in this same room where I slept through my kick, it would burst into
flames—the walls, ceiling, and floor all at once—engulfing everything
in fire, myself included. I woke only to get another dose of meds and go
back under. I would come to from time to time and see a plate of food on
a stand next to the bed but would instantly roll over and pass out again.
At some point, a nurse made me get up out of bed and get undressed.
She put me on a stool in a shower where I sat dry heaving under the hot
water for twenty minutes, so weak I was barely able to stay on the chair.
Later, I became conscious of someone cutting my hair but it seemed
more like an imaginary midnight-movie scene as I was sitting in a lawn
chair, unable to lift my head off my chest.

Late morning on the fifth day, I lay in bed in total darkness, slightly
uncomfortable and unable to sleep all day now that I was being slowly
weaned off the meds. There came a light knocking on my door.

"Go away," I said.

Now a louder knock.

"Go away, I'm sleeping!"

The door opened a crack and a guy stuck his large round head in.

"Hey, man, how you doing? The nurses told me your story and it
sounds a lot like mine. I'm Keni."

I raised up in bed about to go off on this fucking jerk when I saw his profile in the light. He looked familiar, but in a way I couldn't place.

"I know you."

"Well . . . yeah, man, I'm a musician, too. I was in a band called Autograph."

That band name instantly cast my mind back to my high school days. I'd skip sixth period every day to go drink beer and smoke weed at Matt Varnum's house, getting him to listen to cassette tapes of my punk rock records and watching MTV with the sound off. Of all the terrible hair-metal videos they aired, the one that particularly drew my ire was "Turn Up the Radio" by Autograph. I hated it so much that one day it had come on and I'd thrown a full can of beer at my friend's mother's TV set. I especially detested the horrible hammy mugging by the camera-hogging drummer. Now, during arguably the worst stretch of my life, that same dude was actually in my sickroom. My mind was blown, the irony too cruel for my brain to process. I begged him to leave and he finally relented, only to return a week or so later, the beginning of an unlikely friendship between this still over-the-top character and myself. His name was Keni Richards.

After the storm subsided, I was finally able to shake off the imaginary steel band that had been threatening to make my skull implode. The beautiful California sun had emerged from behind the storm clouds and an orderly had set me up in a lawn chair out on the impeccably groomed, endless expanse of gorgeous green lawn on the hospital grounds. I sat there alone, basking in the not-too-hot, not-too-cool air.

My hair was short and clean, as were my clothes. I had awakened one day to find my room filled with several bags of brand-new clothes that Courtney had sent over. I felt more aware and alive then I could ever remember, although my arms looked as though I'd tried to kill myself, white bandages from wrist to elbow. I was no longer imprisoned by any drug, did not have to hit the streets and hustle. For the first time in years, I had nowhere to be at all. It was an exceptionally peaceful moment. I marveled at my incredible good fortune. I smiled, then began to laugh, then laughed maniacally. I had escaped. I had survived. They had failed to destroy me and I had woken up here in this paradise.

"I'm still here, motherfuckers! You can't kill me!" I howled hysterically at the sky.

Before my sick crowing had even receded, an unwelcome truth lodged itself in my head: *Anything that happens next can only be worse than what came before.* That degree of suffering was beyond my imagination.

My manic laughter turned instantly into uncontrollable sobbing. I hadn't cried in a long time. It felt as though the tears were being ripped from inside whatever I had that passed for a soul, clawed out from that lifelong aching place. I moaned and gasped, unable to catch my breath.

Suddenly, spontaneously, out of a moment of abject despair, I said out loud, "God, change me."

I had never believed in a traditional Christian God or in any supreme being. I had hated sitting through midnight mass, Catholic weddings, Catholic funerals, and especially those torturous Wednesday morning masses at the mission I was forced to endure before getting in line for soup and sandwiches. I didn't know who I was calling out to . . . but the second I cried out for mercy, I was nailed by some invisible but over-whelming force, as powerful and sudden as a shotgun blast. A surreal, instantaneous, sixteen-hits-of-acid epiphany, as though I had pissed on an incredibly powerful electric fence.

I was knocked from my chair and my life flashed before my eyes: my wasted childhood, my arrogant youth, my anger and obsessions, crime, delusions, self-loathing, paranoia, hopelessness, fury, and sad junkie downward spiral. I'd heard that cliché a million times—my life flashed before my eyes—but I finally understood what that meant. In that single instant, it had been powerfully, intensely true, the most authentic experience of my entire life in one second on the lawn of a Los Angeles psychiatric hospital.

Lying there, sobbing in the grass for the first time ever, I stared directly and honestly into the mirror of my life. In an instant, I saw that my entire life's way of thinking and behaving was the corrupted opposite of what it should be. My morbid thought process was the wrong side of right. I had grown up believing you took whatever you could from whoever you could and always looked out for number one, screwing anyone and everyone in the process. From my earliest childhood memories, I had been a thief and a flagrant, transparent, nonstop liar and cheat. Music, which I had loved, which I had lived for, which I credited with giving me a life, had long ago become just a means to an end: sex, money, drugs, a place to crash, a bargaining chip, a free ride, whatever I could milk from it. I had been a rank nihilist who lived each day with an obsessive, burning need to pay back twice as hard anybody who fucked me, and spent hours in my mind digging the graves of my enemies, real and imagined. My extreme, retrograde sickness had cut me open and left me eviscerated. I had asked to be changed and now, in a second, I was changed. Maybe not by anybody else's God but by some very real force that intervened in the life of one sad piece of human roadkill the moment it was asked to.

In order to survive, in order to move forward, I would have to change every single fucking sorry thing about myself. I would have to start over again clean.

Epilogue

THE WOLF IN SEAL'S CLOTHING

AFTER ALMOST A YEAR AT LIVE-IN TREATMENT FACILITIES AND halfway houses in California, much of it funded through the continued kindness and generosity of Courtney Love, I was tracked down by detectives from the criminal branch of the IRS. Still newly clean, it was a shock to find out that I was facing significant prison time for tax evasion. The back taxes on those Mad Season royalty checks I had hidden from my accountants years before had ballooned, with penalties and interest accrued, to almost a half million bucks. A tax attorney got them to drop it to fifty grand cash and I was given a month to come up with the payment. I might as well have tried to swim underwater from Japan to Australia holding my breath as to get that much dough together. At zero hour, my producer friend from Houston, Randall Jamail, stepped in. His publishing company offered me a songwriting deal for that exact amount and the check went directly to the government.

Several days before I was to be kicked out of the treatment house where I had been living, I came home from my job doing demolition on old buildings in East Los Angeles to find someone waiting for me on the porch. It was a fellow musician from Seattle I'd never met. He'd heard of my situation and, acting on impulse, had come looking for me. Before long I was functioning as caretaker of Guns N' Roses bass player Duff McKagan's homes.

Still unwelcome in the houses of most people who had known me before, I was befriended by Duff, who took me under his wing like a guardian angel. I had been sleeping under an uncomfortable thin wool blanket on a bare canvas army cot in Keni Richards's fume-filled art studio when Duff asked me to stay at his home to keep an eye on things. When his family was in Los Angeles, I'd live in and watch his house in Seattle. When they'd come back, I would go to Los Angeles and do the same thing there. I was with him at the Seattle house when he married his kind and beautiful girlfriend, Susan Holmes. I didn't have any suitable clothes to wear to the ceremony, so Duff dug out a garbage bag full of clothes that the singer Seal had left at his house, stashed in the basement. From it, he selected a sweater for me to wear.

In Los Angeles, my young friend Josh Homme who I'd bonded so tightly with and who had made my final days in the Trees bearable had started his own band, Queens of the Stone Age. Heading toward great success, he asked me to come along for the ride. By giving me another shot at music, he handed me a new lease on creative life.

Some of the ghosts of my old life still haunted me. Nearly two years clean, I stopped at a Starbucks in Seattle to grab a coffee one day. While I waited in line to make my order, I looked down at the local paper. Its huge headline read "Joe DiMaggio Dies." I glanced at the other of the two local newspapers, stacked side by side. Its headline read "They Were Victims of a Serial Killer." There, in the middle of three mugshot photos of the African American women who had been murdered, was the face of my girl Shadow. Now I finally knew where she had disappeared to. Her body and two others, found in the Jungle.

A few years later, I was recording in Houston with Randall Jamail, fulfilling my end of the bargain that had kept me out of tax debtor's prison. One night in my room at the Holiday Inn, I got a phone call from Laurie Davis, my huge-hearted, long-suffering accountant, the only person from my time in the Trees who continued to care enough to work with me.

"Mark, please sit down. I'm so sorry but I have some terrible news and it's going to hurt. I'm so, so sorry."

"Layne?" I asked.

"Yes, honey. He's gone."

It was a call I had expected for years but it destroyed me nonetheless. His loss left a void I've felt every day since. I expect I always will.

ACKNOWLEDGMENTS

Shelley Brien

Mishka Shubaly

Ben Schafer

Byrd Leavell

Anna Hrnjak

Dylan Carlson

Ben Shepherd

Jonathan Poneman

Roger Trust

Jerry Cantrell

Jeff Barrett

Dan Peters

Rich Machin

Gus Brandt

Dean Karr

John Powers

Dean Duzenski

Billy Walsh

Paul Bearer

Calvin Johnson

Joshua Homme

Duff McKagan

Susan Holmes-McKagan

Tom Hansen

Alain Johannes

Steve Gullick

Kevin Gasser

Charles Peterson

Greg Dulli

Mike Inez

Acknowledgments

Trina Lanegan

Jack Endino

Courtney Love Cobain

Sietse van Gorkom

Roberto Bentivegna

Selene Vigil

Paolo Bicchieri

Randall Jamail

David Coppin-Lanegan

Peter Mensch

Steven "Thee Slayer Hippy" Hanford

Clay Decker

Phil Staley

Robert Chandler

George Drakoulias

Cliff Burnstein

Kevan Wilkins

Sue Tropio

Brian Benjamin

Bob Pfeifer

Teo Bicchieri

Rosemary Carroll

Jason Reynolds

Michael Goldstone

Laurie Davis

Donal Logue

Susan Silver

Greg Werckman

Van Conner

Mike McCready

Eric Erlandson

Michael Jobson

Brother Aldo Struyf

John Agnello

Mike Johnson

Joe Cardamone

Hans Antonides

Nick Marson

Mark Pickerel

Dean Overton

Hutch

Danny Baird

Donna Dresch

Martin Feveyear

Barrett Martin

Travis Keller

Terry Date

Steve Fisk

Acknowledgments

Sam Albright

Matt Varnum

Cleon Peterson

Gary Conner Sr.

David Catching

Rob Marshall

Patrick Conner

Adrian Makins

Gary Lee Conner

Special thanks to D. W. Lanegan